Texas Longhorn COOKBOOK
and Campfire Tales

TEXAS LONGHORN
Breeders Association of America

Additional copies may be obtained by writing:
Texas Longhorn Cookbook and Campfire Tales
Texas Longhorn Breeders Association of America
P.O. Box 4430
Fort Worth, Texas 76164

First Printing, November, 1998
Second Printing, May, 2000
Third Printing, June, 2001
Fourth Printing, September, 2002
Fifth Printing, October 2002

ISBN: 0-9677932-3-8 Hard Cover
ISBN: 1-931294-38-0 Paper Cover

Front Cover Photo: Jim Curry, Poolville, Texas
Back Cover Photo: Gordon Laiz, Fort Lauderdale, Florida
Cover Design: Spray Gleaves, Fort Worth, Texas

Published and Manufactured in the
United States of America by

Cookbook Resources, LLC
541 Doubletree Drive
Highland Village, Texas 75077
972-317-0245
www.cookbookresources.com

cookbook
resources LLC

BREEDERS
ASSOCIATION *of* **AMERICA**
P.O.Box 4430   Fort Worth, Texas 76164
(817) 625-6241   Fax (817) 625-1388

Texas Longhorn cattle are the most wonderful breed in the world!
The living symbol of the Old West, their historical significance is
well known. However, to today's breeders, they are more than a
symbol. To some, the cattle are their livelihood; others use the
personable animals as their "relaxation therapy"; and all consider
them as part of their family. From the many colorful comments in
this book, I believe you will see the pride our members have in
their cattle.

During the past centuries, the Texas Longhorns traveled many trails.
From Mexico, they walked to the eastern and southern states, to the
north and west. Today there are Longhorn cattle in all the mainland
states as well as Canada, Australia, New Zealand, and several
European countries. The roads our cattle traveled are represented in
the recipes collected from Texas Longhorn breeders across the
country so you will have the opportunity to sample some delicious,
unique dishes. In addition, you will be able to learn more about
the majestic Texas Longhorn breed and its impact on our heritage
and future.

It is with great pride that the Texas Longhorn Breeders
Association of America presents this Texas Longhorn Cook Book
and Campfire Tales.

Sincerely,

Don L. King
Executive Director

"When I look at one of these Texas Longhorn cows, it honestly brings tears to my eyes. They are so beautiful and so perfect."

—*Linda Moore, Gainesville, Texas*

Linda surveying her herd

Dedicated to Linda Moore, an enthusiastic TLBAA Texas Longhorn breeder. Her vision, direction, and persistence made this cook book a reality.

Thanks to TLBAA President Tim Miller, Executive Director Don L. King, Membership Services' Larry Barker, and the Board of Directors who wholeheartedly supported this project.

A special thanks goes to SuzAnn Spindor of the TLBAA who coordinated the production of this book and to member Linda Sims, who helped organize the contents. To the TLBAA Trails' staff Carolyn Hunter and Jim Curry, who gathered Texas Longhorn material and photographs—to graphic artists Spray Gleaves and Marina Whigham—to the TLBAA office staff who willingly sampled as many recipes as they could—to Marsha Proctor and Sherri Spindor who typed the recipes and resisted the urge to get in the kitchen to try them.

The biggest thanks of all goes to those TLBAA Texas Longhorn breeders who shared their favorite family recipes with us—and to God who created the Texas Longhorn for us to enjoy.

Table of Contents

The Texas Longhorn
Symbol of Survival

Forged by Nature

Evolution is a strange and wondrous process that has been responsible for the creation of a multitude of forms and shapes in the kingdom of nature—forms and shapes that are unique to their time and totally adaptable to the environment in which they evolved. The Texas Longhorn is such an animal.

Its origin began centuries ago in Africa. From there it traveled with the Moors to Spain and then with Columbus to the New World in 1493. Taken by Gregorio de Villalobos to Mexico in 1521, the breed eventually worked its way up to Texas and the Southwest with explorers, settlers and expeditions to establish missions. These cattle propagated as they escaped, were scattered by Indians or abandoned when missions failed.

Neglected by man and left to drift on their own, the cattle developed the survival instinct that only nature can create. They developed horns for protection, allowing the dominant males to propagate the breed, and strengthened their feet and legs by walking many miles for water, food, and procreation. Only the strong survived. These were the ones which developed resistance to disease, learned to forage on whatever nature provided, and still thrive.

Thus was created the Texas Longhorn, defined and refined by nature, tested by the crucible of time, and found not wanting.

On The Trail

Left on their own, the sturdy Texas Longhorn multiplied. Early settlers in the Southwest began to gather these cattle and send them to northern markets. A trickle of the flood that was to follow began in 1846 when the first documented drive to Missouri occurred. These cattle were held in Ohio that winter and sent to eastern markets in 1847.

> *By 1860, the census recorded 4,000,000 head of cattle and only 600,000 people in Texas.*

During the 1850s, sporadic drives of probably less than 1,000 cattle each were moved north. These drives were handled by small groups of men. A herd of 500 head might have three men and another might have eight men.

Then came the Civil War. With the northern markets closed, the trail drives were turned to the east and Texas beef began to supply the Confederacy. The eastern drives had many new and different obstacles. The rivers, swamps, and vast timbered areas were extremely difficult to negotiate, and the herds were consequently smaller than those that were driven north over the open prairies. A majority of the herds swam the mighty Mississippi at Vicksburg on their way to a final destination, which in some instances, was as far east as Mobile, Alabama.

By 1860, the census recorded 4,000,000 head of cattle and only 600,000 people in Texas. The number of inhabitants diminished as men went to join the war, but the Texas Longhorn, left on its own again, continued to multiply. When the soldiers returned home after the Civil War, they found the only thing of value left were the vast herds of longhorned cattle running loose.

Industrious men began once again to gather the cattle and move them north where the demand for beef had driven the price of sirloin steak in New York to the exorbitant price of 25 cents to 35 cents a pound. In 1866, some 260,000 head were moved up the trail to Kansas and Missouri, but less than half reached their destination. The herds were driven by cowboys, many of whom were in their teens. They faced constant hazards from storms, floods, Indians and those who would steal their herds.

The trickle that had begun in 1846 became a flood and some 10,000,000 cattle were sent over the northern trails before they were closed. More than 700,000 Texas Longhorns were driven north in 1871, the year of maximum effort.

The Texas Longhorn, which actually could gain weight on the trail, was responsible for the start of the economic recovery of Texas. The net profits of $8 to $20 per head, when returned to Texas enabled the owner to invest in vast tracts of land, often at 50 cents per acre. Thus, one Texas Longhorn was worth 15 to 40 acres of land. Thus began the great ranches of the Southwest.

The Vanishing Herd

The Trail drive era ended with the advent of barbed wire and the railroads. The supremacy of the Texas Longhorn in the beef industry diminished as consumers demanded "fatter" beef. Cattlemen began to "improve" these fine cattle with the importation of bulls from England and Europe. In the space of only four generations, the Texas Longhorn declined into obscurity.

---❖---

"The Texas Longhorn was responsible for the start of the post-Civil War economic recovery in Texas. Profits from one Texas Longhorn were worth 15-40 acres of land. Thus began the great ranches of the Southwest."

---❖---

The Texas Longhorn was nearer extinction than the buffalo or the whooping crane, when in 1927, the federal government appropriated $3,000 for the requisition and preservation of a herd of Texas Longhorns. Forest Service employees found it necessary to travel almost 5,000 miles through South Texas and Mexico to discover and acquire 20 cows, four calves, and three bulls with which to develop a herd that was the remains of some 4,000,000 cattle in Texas only 60 years before.

This small herd of cattle was placed on a federal reserve, now named the Wichita Mountains National Wildlife Refuge, at Cache, Oklahoma. Fearful of an outbreak of disease, some were eventually moved to establish a second herd at Fort Niobrara National Wildlife Refuge at

Valentine, Nebraska. The descendants of that original herd still graze the pastures of the Refuges.

From Extinction to Distinction

In addition to the government endeavor, some ranchers retained a few Texas Longhorns in their own herds. Through their efforts, the number of Texas Longhorns increased until it was estimated that there were about 2,500 in the United States. In 1964, concerned cattlemen organized the Texas Longhorn Breeders Association of America (TLBAA) to preserve and promote the breed.

The first president of the fledgling association was Charlie Schreiner III of the Y.O. Ranch at Mountain Home, Texas. Mr. Schreiner set up an office in San Antonio. As the presidency changed hands, records were often kept in the home or office of the present president. Eventually as the number of members and cattle increased, it was necessary to find a permanent home for the registry. It is appropriate that the TLBAA offices are now located in the historic stockyards area of Fort Worth, Texas, a city in which Texas Longhorns played a large role.

Today, there are over 4,000 TLBAA members and more than a quarter million head of Texas Longhorns in the registry. Through the efforts of these dedicated breeders, the future of this magnificent breed of cattle is secure.

Texas Longhorn breeders always enjoy good company and good food – especially beef! (L-R) Founder and First President of the TLBAA, Charlie Schreiner III, Y.O. Ranch, Mountain Home, Texas; Norma Schreiner; C.Q. Davis, Brownwood, Texas; Thirteenth TLBAA President John Baker, Sunrise Ranch, Liberty Hill, Texas; Joan Carter; H.C. Carter, Austin, Texas; and Betty Baker, enjoy a meal together in the mid '70's. (From the archives of the Texas Longhorn Breeders Association of America.)

Why Texas Longhorns?

Nothing is more western than Texas Longhorn cattle, windmills and mesquite. (Photo by Greg Briney)

✦ **Calving Ease**
Texas Longhorn cows with their larger pelvic opening give birth easily. The bulls produce low birthweight calves, allowing cattle of all breeds to produce live calves.

✦ **Longevity**
Texas Longhorns produce well into their late teens and early twenties—several years longer than most other breeds of cattle.

✦ **Fertility**
The breed is well known for its reproductive efficiency, producing and maintaining a live calf each year and sometimes even two in a year.

✦ **Disease & Parasite Resistance**
An ability developed through the years and an asset to today's cattle-man.

✦ **Browse Utilization**
The Texas Longhorn is not a "picky" eater. It will forage on most beneficial plants—a result of the survival instinct.

✦ **Hardiness**
A trait directly connected to "survival of the fittest".

✦ **Adaptability**
The breed is able to easily adapt to various climates and tem-peratures.

✦ **Low Maintenance**
With its inherent attributes, the Texas Longhorn requires less man-agement time and less health expenses than other breeds.

✦ **Lean Beef**
Studies have proven that Texas Longhorn beef is lower in saturated fats and cholesterol than other beef.

Texas Longhorn Terminology

Around the Curve — A horn measurement ascertained by measuring down the horn, across the head and up the other horn.

Babysitter — The cow who remains watching over the calves while the other cows graze or travel to water.

Bull — The male of the species. Has a thicker horn base than the cow's.

Cow — The female of the species. Her horns have a smaller base than the bull's, but are usually longer. Some measure over 60".

Grandma — The oldest cow in the herd.

Heifer — A young female which has not had her first calf.

Herd Sire — A rancher's best bull which he uses to produce improved calf crops.

Mossy headed or mossy horned — Refers to age and temperament. Usually old steers which have become so tricky that they are rarely seen and even more rarely captured.

Texas Longhorns are a curious and loving breed. Vicky King of Arlington, Texas enjoys an affectionate kiss. (Photo by Richard King)

Roper — A steer or heifer used for recreational rodeo events, such as team roping and calf roping. The #1 ropers have horns which extend at least 1" past the ears.

Steer — Neutered male. Has a thick horn base and grows the longest horns. Many measure well over 7-8 ft, at maturity and are called trophy steers.

Texas Twist — A form of horn development, basically going out and then twisting over towards the tips.

Tip-to-Tip — A horn measurement meaning straight across from one tip to the other.

Yearling — A male or female which is a year old.

The Stonewall Jacksons. Don, Velma, Donna and Donny Jackson, with "Koolaid", "Talk of Texas", and "Captain Twiggs". Stonewall Valley Ranch, Texas

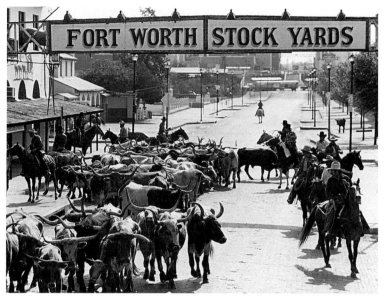

Texas Longhorns played an important part in the history of Fort Worth, Texas, the city know as "Cowtown". (1982 photo courtesy of the Texas Department of Commerce.)

Cattle Brands

For almost 4,000 years, branding has been the most effective and economical means of identifying livestock. The use of branding for identification of cattle can be traced to the ancient Egyptians. The practice was brought to the New World by Hernando Cortez in 1521. With the establishment of Spanish missions throughout the present southwestern United States, a cattle industry took root. Along with the cattle came a practice of branding to establish ownership. Records indicate a system for the filing of brands was started in California where the Spaniards were grazing thousands of head of cattle. To record a brand, the owner had to provide a section of hide carrying the brand or a piece of leather with an imprint of the brand.

Following the Civil War, there were thousands of unbranded cattle roaming the southern United States. As these cattle were gathered and branded a way of life gave rise to a thriving cattle industry. The need to brand cattle and record brands became increasingly important. State governments and cattlemen realized the necessity of brand records to prove ownership and to protect against theft.

Texas Longhorn breeders must register their "holding brand" (ownership brand) with the Texas Longhorn Breeders Association of

America. Members must also state the location of the brand (right hip, left shoulder, etc.) as well as a private herd number. These branded numbers are the rancher's filing system, and may indicate month and year of birth, and sex. Many ranches are referred to, not by the name, but by the brand of the owner.

Commonly used symbols for brands are letters, numbers and their variations, geometric symbols and picture symbols. Brand are read top to bottom, left to right, and from the outside in. Selection of the brand is very important. Consideration must be given to the angles, etc. so that the brand is one that is easily applied to an animal's hide. A complicated, intricate brand is difficult to apply and is often illegible.

——————————————— ❖ ———————————————

For almost 4,000 years, branding has been the most effective and economical means of identifying livestock. The use of branding for identification of cattle can be traced to the ancient Egyptians.

——————————————— ❖ ———————————————

Brands are created in a number of ways. It may come from the names or initials of family members, perhaps a landmark on the ranch, or even an historical event. Following are the histories of some of the brands owned by contributors to this cookbook:

Lazy 5B — Stan & Priscilla Briney, Bowie, Texas.

The L5B or "Lazy 5B" was designed to represent the five Brineys— Stan and Priscilla and their three children (Jeff, Kristi, and Greg), none of which are lazy. Jeff is a regional manager for Hagen Dazs Ice Cream. Kristi is a juvenile probation officer, and Greg is the Longhorn cattle manager at El Coyote Ranch.

6+6 — Norman & Myrna Carpenter, Stephenville, Texas.

In the early 1900s, Henry Clark of Stephenville, Texas, Erath County, owned a large ranch east of Stephenville. Mr. Clark called his ranch the 6+6, named for his balanced cattle feed. He owned and operated a feed store in Stephenville, using his own brand of feed. 6+6 it was called. Some burlap bags can still be found today with the 6+6 on them.

Henry Clark served as the mayor of Stephenville for 16 years in different terms, starting in 1928 and ending in 1954. A cousin worked for Mr. Clark from time to time on the ranch. His name was E.R. Tog Carpenter. When Henry Clark became ill, he gave Mr. Carpenter the 6+6 branding iron. It lay dormant for 40 years and then Mr. Carpenter handed down the branding iron to his eldest son, Norman, and he registered the brand and is now the owner of the 6+6 Registered Texas Longhorn Ranch.

IIE — Kenneth & Windelyn Tharp, Caldwell, Texas.

While writing a history of our farm this year (1997-98), we found this brand that was registered to my great grandfather, Rudolph Duewall, It was registered in Burleson County on June 1, 1883. We re-registered it on March 20, 1998. The Duewall Farm has been in our family since 1881.

O-S-O — Jeff Miller & Carol Erikson, Wellington, Colorado.

In the mid 1860's, my great grandfather J.D. Miller moved west from Ohio to the Gunnison country. JD developed several ranches, owned a bank and a slaughter house before the turn of the century. The O-S-O was used on cattle starting around 1875. Although we are not sure what those cattle were, we do know that he was running up towards a 1,000 head. The state of Colorado did not develop a brand board until 1899, at which time the O-S-O was registered, making it one of the older brands in this state.

❖

*Many ranches are referred to,
not by the name,
but the brand of the owner.*

❖

My grandfather Jacob Alonzo inherited the brand and kept it in Gunnison until right after the depression. Apparently that was all that was left of the magnificent operation that was lost due to those hard times. Upon returning home from the war in 1945, my father, Charles Miller, began using the brand on his horses and cattle in and around Fort Collins, Colorado. Dad has been the consummate cowman all his life. He worked many ranches in his younger days before finally settling down north of Fort Collins in an area called "Buckeye".

In 1952, the reverse O-S-O was recorded. It is a mirror image to Dad's brand. It gives brand inspectors fits. They are never really sure for the first time which one they are reading. This brand belonged to my mother. When she passed away in 1961, the brand was not used again until Carol and I began acquiring Longhorns in 1991. Today both brands are found on our ranch—Sunnybrook Cattle Co.

 Rockin' H — Dale Hunt, Gene Autry, Oklahoma.

The Rockin' H with two rockers came about from a conversation with my blind grandfather. He asked what we were going to call our ranch. When we advised him, the Rockin' H with one rocker, he said, "That's silly. Have you ever seen a rocking chair with one rocker?" Now you know how the Rockin' H came about to have both rockers.

MF — Randi & Mary Ellen Maddox, Frisco, Texas.

Our brand stands for two great ranching families in Clay County, Texas. The M represents Maddox. Randi's grandfather, J.W. Maddox, was orphaned at age 15 in Arkansas. He rode his horse to Texas, working on different cattle ranches until he bought 10,000 acres in Clay County.

The F represents Fenoglio. My father was a farmer and rancher in the Stanfield Community of Clay County. He passed away at the early age of 56, leaving my mother a widow at 52. She never re-married, but continued farming and ranching until she was 81 years of age.

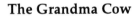

The Grandma Cow

"How honorable are the Texas Longhorn cattle? For many years, she stood proud on the hillsides, delivering me a calf every year. She had earned total respect from the whole herd through her keen wisdom and leadership. Nearing 20 years old, she lay down on the creekside where it made a horseshoe shape, and the trees broke the cold February wind from her. Checking the cattle daily, I found her, unable to get up. I carried grain and water to her for three days. On the third day, she gave me a look before taking her grain, as if to say, "So Long!" The next morning I came to find an amazing sight!! Diamond W Cherry had passed on that night, and the WHOLE HERD lay circled around her. All with their heads facing outside as if to say there will be no varmints taking our friend. It was a keen sight to see 50 Longhorn cows circled around the Grandma cow. "

—Dale Hunt, Rockin' H Ranch, Gene Autry, Oklahoma

Wet Your Whistle

Campfire Coffee

Now here is the recipe, time-tried and true,
For chuck wagon coffee, the buckaroo's brew:
Use Arbuckle's Roasted, in case you can get it;
Pour in enough water to just sort of wet it.
Boil hard for an hour, then into it toss
The well rusted shoe off a clubfooted hoss;
Gaze into the pot for a few minutes steady—
If the hoss shoe is floatin', your coffee is ready!

❖

Campfire Coffee

Use a large old-fashioned granite coffee pot. Allow 1 tablespoon of coffee for each person, and then 1 extra tablespoon for the coffee pot. Then into pot, measure 1 cup of water for each person and allow 1 extra for the pot. Put over low heat and let steep slowly. Add more coals to fire and bring coffee to a boil when ready to serve. Remove from fire and throw in a scant cup of cold water to clear the coffee. Serve.

❖

"Follow the Leader"

"The Longhorns show many traits that differ from the beef breeds. When being driven, they string out and walk exceptionally fast instead of bunching up as domestic cattle do. In handling them, it is well to have riders in front of them as well as behind them in order to keep them from running. When Longhorns are being moved with a rider in the lead, one steer often falls in behind the horse and the other steers will 'follow the leader'."

Mother's Punch

1	(6 ounce) can frozen lemonade (made according to directions)	1	(46 ounce) can unsweetened pineapple juice
		3	(12 ounce each) cans Sprite

Mix all ingredients.

Makes 3¹/2 quarts.

What do you do when you see an endangered animal that eats only endangered plants?

Norma Holmes
H and H Longhorns
Robstown, TX

Granny's Russian Tea

This was my grandmother's recipe for curing a cold, healing a broken heart or just sharing a memory with a special friend.

1	juicy orange	1	teaspoon allspice
1	lemon	1	teaspoon whole cloves
1	cup sugar	1	teaspoon ground cinnamon

Slice orange and lemon in half. Squeeze juice into medium sauce pan (spoon out seeds). Grate the peels of the orange and lemon, being careful not to get down in the bitter white part of the skin. Add sugar and spices. Stir to dissolve sugar. Heat at medium heat, stirring often, for about 10-15 minutes. Mixture will be thin, but thickens somewhat after cooling. Pour into glass container with lid. When ready for some consolation, add one to two teaspoons of this mixture into a cup of hot tea. Russian Tea stays good in the refrigerator for two months.

Carolyn Hunter
Texas Longhorn Trails
Fort Worth , TX

"Wet your Whistle" Lemonade

1½ cups water
1½ cups sugar

1   tablespoon finely grated
    lemon peel
1½ cups lemon juice
    (6-8 lemons)

In medium sauce pan, heat water until almost boiling. Remove from heat. Add sugar and lemon peel. Stir until sugar is dissolved. Stir in lemon juice. Pour into jar and chill in refrigerator.

To Serve: Combine 2 ounces of lemonade syrup and 5 ounces Sprite in glass with ice.

Great refreshing drink, can also be colored for Party Punch.

Beverly Sorem
Flying S Cattle
Nevada, IA

Frosty Fruit Cup

1   (15 ounce) can pineapple
    chunks
1   (16 ounce) bottle low-
    calorie lemon-lime
    carbonated beverage

Few drops green food coloring
2   tablespoons lime juice
1   cup seedless green grapes
2   cups cantaloupe balls

Drain pineapple, reserving juice. Combine reserved juice, carbonated beverage, lime juice, and food coloring; stir. Pour into 3-cups refrigerator tray; freeze just to a mush, about 2-2½ hours. Combine fruits. Break frozen mixture apart with fork, if necessary. Spoon into 8 sherbet glasses; top with fruits. Trim with mint sprigs, if desired.

Velma Slater
Slater Longhorns
Mexia, TX

---------- ❖ ----------

"It's said that one reason Texas Longhorn breeders live longer is that they always want to see what color the next calf is. No two calves are the same color so finding a new calf is like going Easter Egg hunting."

Strawberry Punch

1	(10 ounce) package frozen strawberries	1	(8 ounce) can crushed pineapple
1	(6 ounce) can frozen lemonade	3	quarts Ginger Ale

Put all ingredients in a blender except for the Ginger Ale. Pour into a punch bowl. Add Ginger Ale just before serving.

Makes 1 gallon.

Bonnie Damrow
Roca, NE

Chocolate Martini

3	ounces Ketel	1/2	ounce Cream de Cacao
1	ounce Vodka		

Mix all ingredients. Coat rim of martini glass with cocoa powder.

Laney Weise
Lazy LYZ Ranch
Voca, TX

Hot Chocolate

4	squares (1 ounce each) semisweet chocolate, grated	1/4	teaspoon ground cinnamon
1/2	cup baking cocoa	1/2	cup powered sugar
			dash of salt

In a bowl combine all ingredients.

To serve: add 2 teaspoons mix to $3/4$ cup hot milk.

Makes 1½ cups dry mix.

Bonnie Damrow
Roca, NE

Schnapps

4	cups sugar	1	ounce Peppermint extract or
10	cups water		any other flavoring
1	pint Everclear		

Bring sugar and water to a rolling boil. Add other ingredients. Cool.

J-J *Jody Nelson*
J Bar J Longhorns
Salix, IA

Chilled Chocolate Cow

chocolate milk
chocolate ice cream
cold soda water

serving glass with a long
handled spoon

Fill glass half full with chocolate milk. Add a scoop of chocolate ice cream. Fill rest of the glass with soda water. Watch it fizz!!

Chelsey Damrow
Roca, NE

Cappuccino Mix

1	cup instant coffee crystals	1/4	teaspoon ground nutmeg
1	cup instant chocolate	1/2	cup sugar
	drink mix	1/2	teaspoon ground cinnamon
2/3	cup instant coffee		

Combine all ingredients; mix well. Store in an air tight container.

To serve: add 3 teaspoons mix to 6 ounces hot water. Stir well.

Makes 3 cups dry mix.

 *Jolene Allen*
Lincoln, NE

Grandma Burton's Homemade Wine

2	gallons dewberries or grapes	1/2	yeast cake
2	gallons boiling water	3	lbs sugar

This wine must be made in a 5 gallon stone or pottery crock and should be kept on the kitchen table in good light where it can be stirred several times a day. Cover top with cheese cloth and place a tin cover or plate on top of the cheese cloth. Wash berries, drain in colander and place in crock. Bring water to boil, then pour immediately on berries in crock. Add sugar and stir for 15 minutes. In 25 hours, add 1/2 yeast cake. Stir well, and taste. If sweet, as very sweet lemonade, it does not require more sugar for the present. Taste every day and add 1 cup sugar. On the tenth day, mash berries through colander, then strain through cheese cloth. On the twelfth day, stir mixture and mash berries twice.

Wash crock and return to it the strained liquid. Allow to stand for nine days more, but taste every day to make sure that the wine is no less sweeter than it was in the beginning. Siphon off or dip off the sediments and put in large bottles. Once every 2 weeks, pour into other clean bottles, leaving the sediments. Be sure to keep sweet and in 6 months you will have a most delicious wine of high alcoholic content. Don't cork too tightly until the wine is mature or it will blow the cork out.

This recipe comes from my grandmother. Our family was one of the early settlers of Navarro County near the tiny town of Richland, TX. She lived through the hard times of growing up in the early 1900's and living off the land. Vanna Burton was a good Baptist and a teetotaler, but she could surely make some tasty wine. I remember that she made one last batch before she had to go into the hospital. Carolyn and I had to carry the crock home and keep it stirred. Every time we visited her, she asked whether we were stirring the wine.

Dan Hunter
DH Cattle Company
Sunset, TX

Dried Beef Dip

2 small jars dried beef (Armor)
16 ounces sour cream
1 large green or red bell pepper

1 (8 ounce) package cream cheese
1 tablespoon garlic powder

Chop pepper, cut beef into small pieces. Mix all ingredients, place in baking dish. Bake at 350 degrees for 30-45 minutes. Best when served warm, but can also be served cold. Serve with large fruits or crackers.

Rick and Joyce Grundon
Painted Prairie Farm
Baldwin City, KS

Mexican Layer Dip

2 cups bean dip
2 cups mashed avocado

1 pkg taco seasoning mixed with 8 ounces sour cream
tomatoes, chopped
cheddar cheese, grated
green onion tops, chopped
chopped black olives

In a large pie plate, spread each ingredient layer by layer. Serve with tortilla chips.

Rick and Joyce Grundon
Painted Prairie Farm
Baldwin City, KS

❖

"When a flash flood filled our creek, the cows started trying to get to the other side, taking their calves with them. I was worried that the calves weren't strong enough to make it, but the mothers swam on the down stream side of their calves, helping them along. Everybody made it just fine."

—Linda Sims, Sims Ranch, Weston, Texas

Longhorn Bill's Avocado Espana

high dollar olive oil
chili oil
onions, chopped
mushrooms, sliced
garlic clove, chopped

brandy
sherry
avocado
freshly ground pepper
sour cream

Cover skillet with olive oil and add chili oil to taste. Sauté onions, add mushrooms and garlic. Cook 5 minutes, add brandy and flame. Add sherry, cook 5 minutes and add chunks of avocado. Stir in sour cream, cover, cook over medium to low heat '"until looks good" 3-5 minutes max.

Serve with sourdough bread or a good dry French bread and it is great with Merlot.

Makes a great meal - Cook one avocado per person.

Bill Jowell
Rafter L Longhorns
Midkiff, TX

Guacamole

2   (8 ounce each) ripe
    avocados
2   tablespoons fresh
    lime juice
2   fresh, hot chili peppers,
    stemmed, seeded and
    chopped

6   green onions, chopped
1   tablespoon fresh cilantro,
    chopped

Half avocados, remove pits. With a spoon, scoop out the flesh into bowl. Mash with fork and sprinkle with lime juice. Quickly mix chili, green onions, cilantro into avocados. Serve immediately.

Sarah Branyon

Guacamole

2	soft avocados	a few drops hot sauce	
1	teaspoon olive oil	a few drops lemon juice	
1	tablespoon minced onion	salt to taste	

Mash avocado with a fork until creamy. Add rest of ingredients and mix well. A truly Mexican salad.

Bonnie Damrow
Roca, NE

No Smashing the Avocados Guacamole Dip or Bill's Favorite Snack

1	tablespoon oil	1	(4 ounce) can chopped green chilies and liquid
2	tablespoons vinegar - *I prefer balsamic vinegar*	2-3	tomatoes, finely chopped
1	teaspoon salt	4-5	green onions, finely chopped
1	teaspoon garlic salt		
1/4	teaspoon pepper	2	ripe avocados, chopped
1	(4 ounce) can chopped black olives and liquid		

Combine all ingredients in a bowl. Serve with tortilla chips. To prepare ahead of time, combine all ingredients except the avocados and refrigerate. Chop and add to mix just before serving.

Leslie Moseley
The Woodlands, TX

Longhorn Cheese Dip

1	lb Longhorn ground beef	2	(10 ounce each) cans Rotel tomatoes
2	lbs Velveeta cheese	2	teaspoons corn starch

Brown ground beef, drain well. Set aside. Melt cheese with tomatoes. Add ground beef. Mix cornstarch with a little water, add to thicken.

Vonda Burden
Town Creek, AL

Cheese Dip

2	cups grated cheese	2	tablespoons prepared
			mustard
1/4	cup mayonnaise	3-4	tablespoons milk
2	tablespoons blue cheese		

Blend ingredients together. Add enough milk to make it the right consistency. Makes 1 1/2 cups dip.

Judy Walton
Wellfleet, NE

Shepherd's Dip

2	pkgs wafer meat (beef)	2	tablespoons parsley
2	cups sour cream	2	teaspoons Beau Monde
			spice
1	cup mayonnaise		garlic powder

Cut wafer meat into small pieces. Mix all ingredients together the day before serving and refrigerate. Fill hollowed out bread with dip just before serving. Use the bread taken out to dip in the mixture and as you eat the dip, use the sides as well.

Crawfish Dip

1	medium onion, chopped	1	(10 3/4 ounce) can cream of
1	green pepper, chopped		mushroom soup
3-4	ribs celery, chopped	2	lbs crawfish tails, peeled
3-4	green onions, chopped		salt and pepper
1	stick butter		cayenne pepper
3/4	cup flour		

Sauté vegetables in butter. Stir in flour, the mushroom soup (at this point make sure there are no lumps of flour in mixture). Add crawfish tails, salt, pepper and cayenne pepper to taste. Serve warm with your favorite chips or crackers.

Chili Con Queso

2	cups finely chopped onions	1¼	lbs Kraft American cheese (in the blue box), grated
1	small clove garlic, chopped	2	lbs Velveeta, grated
1	stick of butter	½	teaspoon black pepper
1	tablespoon Worcestershire sauce		Dash cayenne pepper
3	(10 ounce each) cans Rotel tomatoes, chopped tomatoes	1	(14 ounce) can chopped

Sauté onions and garlic in butter. Add Worcestershire sauce and tomatoes to onions and cook until thickened. Add cheeses and stir until melted. Pour into containers. Store in refrigerator. Serve hot or cold with chips, crackers or fried tortillas.

Kim and Robert Richey
R3 *Triple R Ranch*
San Angelo, TX

Meat-Cheese Dip

1	lb ground beef	2	lbs Velveeta, grated
1	lb sausage	1	(10¾) can cream of mushroom soup
1	onion, chopped		
1	(10 ounce) can Rotel tomatoes		

Brown the ground beef, sausage, and onions. Add the cheese, soup, and Rotel. Pour in a crockpot to keep dip warm.

Sue Muennink
Hondo, TX

Mexican Spinach Dip

1	(8 ounce) cream cheese, softened
2	cups Monterey Jack cheese
1/2	cup finely chopped onion
1	tablespoon finely chopped jalapeño
1	(10 ounce) package frozen chopped spinach, thawed and drained

Heat in microwave on medium heat until smooth. Serve warm with your favorite corn chips.

Priscilla Briney
Briney's Lazy 5B Ranch
Bowie, TX

Spinach Dip

1	(8 ounce) package cream cheese, softened
1/4	cup milk
1	(10 ounce) package frozen chopped spinach, thawed and drained
1	(8 ounce) can water chestnuts, drained and chopped
1/2	cup chopped red pepper
1/2	teaspoon garlic salt
1/8	teaspoon hot pepper sauce

Mix cream cheese and milk with electric mixer on medium speed until smooth. Blend in remaining ingredients. Refrigerate. Serve with assorted cut-up vegetables or chips. Makes 3 cups.

Cathy Zapalac

Martillo Chile/Cheese Dip

2	lbs Velveeta
1	(40 ounce) can of Wolf Brand Chili without beans
1	(16 ounce) jar of medium Pace Picante Sauce

Cut cheese into small pieces. Melt cheese, add chili and picante sauce. Heat. Serve with chips.

Evelyn Rasmussen
Rolling Hills Ranch
Houston, TX

Stonewall Jackson's Spicy Spinach Dip or Side Dish

1   lb chopped spinach, cooked, drained, and patted dry
1/4 cup water
1   (2 ounce) package cream cheese, softened
1/8 cup half-and-half

1/2 tablespoon minced garlic
1-2 tablespoon pickled serrano peppers or chopped green chilies
Pinch of salt
1-2 tablespoon coarse ground black pepper

Place spinach and 1/4 cup water in a large sauce pan over high heat. Cover and cook until spinach is tender. Drain and set aside. In a mixing bowl, combine cream cheese, half-and-half, garlic, serranos or chilies, salt and pepper. Stir until well-blended. Add the warm, dry spinach to the cream cheese mixture and stir to incorporate.

Makes 2 cups.

   The Stonewall Jacksons
Stonewall Valley Ranch
Austin, TX

Reuben Dip

3   (4 ounce each) package corned beef
8   slices American cheese, divided

1   (8 ounce) package shredded Swiss cheese
1   (16 ounce) can sauerkraut, drained
1   cup mayonnaise

Dice 6 slices of cheese. Mix with all other ingredients except the remaining cheese. Place in a 2 quarts rectangular baking dish. Slice the remaining 2 slices of cheese and put on top. Bake at 325 degrees for 30 minutes or until cheese melts. Serve with party rye slices. If you like reuben sandwiches, you will really like this recipe. Given to me by Juanita Nieporte, Cincinnati, OH

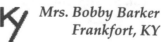   *Mrs. Bobby Barker*
Frankfort, KY

Cheese Dip

12	ounces bacon, crisped and crumbled	2	cups mayonnaise
1	lb sharp Cheddar, grated	4	green onions, chopped
			cayenne pepper

Mix and refrigerate. Serve with chips.

Theresa Lavender
Lake Charles, LA

Chicken Dip

1/2	cup boiled, chopped chicken or 4 small cans chicken	1	cup mayonnaise
			salt and pepper
1	(10³/4 ounce) can cream of mushroom soup	1/2	cup finely chopped onion
		1	jalapeño pepper, finely chopped

Mix all ingredients and chill. Serve with chips, snack crackers, etc. I also add black olives and green onions.

Roop Ranch
Keatchie, LA

Fruit Dip

1	carton strawberry cream cheese	1	(7 ounce) jar marshmallow creme

Mix ingredients. Chill and enjoy with sliced fruits. You can also use pineapple cream cheese.

Roop Ranch
Keatchie, LA

Pecos Red Meatball Appetizers

MEATBALL MIXTURE:

1	lb ground beef	1/4	teaspoon pepper
1/4	cup breadcrumbs	2	garlic cloves, crushed
1/2	teaspoon salt	1/2	cup chopped onion

Mix all ingredients and shape into balls. Bake at 350 degrees for 20 minutes.

SAUCE MIXTURE:

1	cup ketchup	2	teaspoons chili powder
1	cup water	1/2	teaspoon salt
1/4	cup sugar	1/4	teaspoon pepper
1	teaspoon dry mustard	1/2	cup of prepared salsa or
2	teaspoons Worcestershire sauce		picante sauce

Mix all ingredients in saucepan, bring to a boil, add meatballs, reduce heat and simmer 15 minutes.

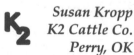

Susan Kropp
K2 Cattle Co.
Perry, OK

Jalapeño Fudge

4	eggs, beaten	1	lb grated cheddar,
2	heaping tablespoons chopped jalapeños		longhorn, or Mexican mix cheese

Butter a 9"×9"×2" pan. Beat eggs, add jalapeños. Add mixture to cheese. Bake at 350 for 20-30 minutes. Cut in 1" cubes.

Delicious for barbecues and get togethers of any kind.

Joyce Smith
What We Wanted Farmstead
Poolville, TX

Hot and Happy Hour Cheese Roll

1 lb Velveeta, softened
1 (8 ounce) package cream cheese, softened
1 (4 ounce) can chopped green chilies
1 (2 ounce) jar diced pimientos, drained
3 green onions, chopped
1/2 cup chopped pecans
3-4 pickled jalapeños, seeded

Carefully roll Velveeta between two pieces of 11"×17" waxed paper; remove top layer of waxed paper. Beat cream cheese until the proper consistency to spread. Spread cream cheese evenly on top of Velveeta like a frosting. Sprinkle green chilies, pimientos, green onions, jalapeños and pecans evenly on top of cream cheese. Roll jelly roll style, removing wax paper with each 1/4 turn until mixture forms a roll. Place seam side down and refrigerate until ready to serve.

Norma Holmes
H and H Longhorns
Robstown, TX

Cocktail Meatballs

MEATBALLS:

1 lb ground beef
1/2 cup dried bread crumbs
1/2 cup minced onion
1/4 cup milk
1 egg
1 tablespoon parsley
1 teaspoon salt
1/8 teaspoon pepper
1/2 teaspoon Worcestershire sauce

Mix all ingredients. Shape in 1" balls. Brown in skillet or in oven. Drain fat and add chili sauce and jelly. Serve hot. Makes 5 doz.

CHILI SAUCE:

1 (12 ounce) bottle chili sauce
1 (10 ounce) jar grape jelly

Mix chili sauce and jelly and heat until the jelly is melted. Add meatballs. Serve hot.

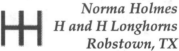

Jan and Howard Sears
J H Ranch
Leon, IA

Tortilla Roll Appetizer

1   (8 ounce) package cream
     cheese
8   oz sour cream
1   (4 ounce) can chopped
     green chilies
1   cup grated Cheddar cheese
1   package large soft
     flour tortillas
1   jar jalapeño salsa dip

green onions, diced
jalapeño peppers, diced
black olives, chopped
garlic salt to taste
seasoned salt to taste

Blend cream cheese and sour cream until smooth. Add remaining ingredients, except salsa. Spread on tortillas and roll up. Cover tightly. Refrigerate for at least 4 hours. (Can be made a day ahead.) Cut roll into slices, about 1/2 inch thick. Serve with salsa dip.

Harley and Linda Krukow
4 K Longhorns
Hampton, IA

Pinwheel Appetizers

1   (8 ounce) package cream
     cheese, softened
1   tablespoon prepared
     horseradish

1   tablespoon chopped chives
10   slices thinly sliced ham
10   slices of thin cheese

In small mixer bowl, beat cream cheese until smooth; stir in horseradish and chives. Spread each meat slice with 1 tablespoon of cheese mixture. Top with cheese slice and spread another tablespoon of cheese mixture. Roll up. Chill for several hours. Before serving, slice each roll into five pieces. Serve with toothpicks in each piece if desired. Refrigerate leftovers.

"Always do right. This will gratify some people and astonish the rest."

—Mark Twain

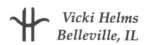

Vicki Helms
Belleville, IL

Cowboy Caviar

1	(15 ounce) can black beans, rinsed and drained	¹/₄	teaspoon salt
		¹/₄	teaspoon ground cumin
1	(4 ounce) can chopped ripe olives, drained	¹/₈	teaspoon black pepper
		1	(8 ounce) package cream cheese, softened
¹/₄	cup finely chopped onion		
1	clove garlic, finely chopped	1	medium red pepper, chopped
2	tablespoons vegetable oil		
2	tablespoons lime juice	1	green onion with top, sliced

In a medium bowl, combine the beans, olives, onion, garlic, oil, lime juice, salt, cumin and black pepper. Cover and refrigerate at least 2 hours. Spread cream cheese on serving plate. Spoon bean mixture evenly over cream cheese. Arrange chopped pepper on bean mixture around the edge of plate. Sprinkle with green onion. Chill and serve with tortilla chips.

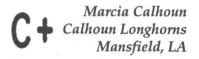

Marcia Calhoun
Calhoun Longhorns
Mansfield, LA

❖

"I got home one day from work, and my husband Frank had left me a note that one of our Longhorn heifers had just had her first calf, a bull. Well, I went out to see the new baby, and discovered it was a heifer calf. When Frank got back, he went to check and came back and said, "no, it was definitely a bull calf." The next time I looked, it was most certainly a heifer. This went on a few days with us arguing, until I got to watching the new mother. She would nurse her baby, always watching nervously back towards the other end of the pasture. As soon as that calf had sucked, she tore back off, so I followed her. You guessed it. She had twins—a heifer and a bull—and was doing the best she could to take care of both of them until they were strong enough to get together."

—Sue Bowdoin, Crawford, Texas

❖

Grandmother's Cheese Straws

3/4 cup butter	1/2 lb finely grated sharp
1/2 teaspoon cayenne pepper	Cheddar cheese
	2 cups flour

Mix butter, pepper and cheese together. Add flour. Squeeze through a cookie press into bars. Bake at 400 degrees for 10 minutes. These are great snacks and go well with everything. We like to make them extra spicy. Perfect with a beer.

Robert and Kim Richey
R3 *Triple R Ranch*
San Angelo, TX

Deviled Eggs

12 hard cooked, peeled eggs	1 1/2 teaspoons mustard
1 teaspoon Worcestershire	4 teaspoons vinegar
sauce	6 tablespoons mayonnaise
salt to taste	2 teaspoons sugar

Slice eggs in half. Remove yolks and mash. Mix with all other ingredients. Put mixture back in egg whites.

Options: Add chopped black or green olives.

Jody Nelson
J-J *J Bar J Longhorns*
Salix, IA

Puppy Chow

1 (6 ounce) package	1 cup peanut butter
chocolate chips	1 (16 ounce) box Crispix
1/2 cup butter or margarine	cereal
2 cups powdered sugar	

Melt chocolate chips and butter; add peanut butter. Microwave until softened. Pour Crispix in large mixing bowl; add the melted ingredients and toss. Pour powdered sugar into paper bag; add cereal mixture and toss. Pour out on a cookie sheet to cool.

Allison Damrow
Roca, NE

Nuts on a Hot Tin Roof

1¹/₂	tablespoons butter	¹/₂	teaspoon ground cumin
2	cups salted pecans or cashews	¹/₂	teaspoon ground coriander
¹/₄	cup chopped cayenne peppers		

Melt butter in sauce pan. Add nuts and sauté 3 minutes. Drain on paper towels. Combine nuts, peppers, cumin and coriander. Stir well. Store in airtight container.

Sarah Branyon

Sugar Coated Pecans

2	egg whites	6	cups pecans
1	cup sugar	1	stick of butter or margarine
dash of salt			

Beat egg whites until stiff. Gradually beat in the sugar and salt. Fold in nuts until they are well coated with sugar and egg mixture. Melt the butter or margarine in large shallow pan. Put the nuts in pan with butter and stir gently. Spread out in the pan and bake in a 325 degree oven for 45 minutes. Stir every 15 minutes. These are delicious.

Mrs. Bobby Barker
Frankfort, KY

———— ❖ ————

"Every now and then our bull will get into a pasture that he's not supposed to be in. All my husband, Bob, has to do is walk over to him, slap him on the butt, and tell him, "Get back home, you old SOB", and he'll amble on back home.

—Linda Moore, Gainesville, Texas

———— ❖ ————

Easy Butter Dips

1/3 cup butter	3 1/2 teaspoons baking powder
2 1/4 cups flour	1 1/2 teaspoons salt
1 tablespoon sugar	1 cup milk

Heat oven to 450 degrees. Melt butter in oven in a 13"×9"×2" glass baking pan. Remove pan as soon as butter is melted. Mix dry ingredients, add milk. Stir slowly with fork until dough clings together. Turn onto well-floured board, roll over to coat with flour. Knead lightly about 10 times. Roll out 1/2" thick into rectangle about 12"× 8". With floured knife cut dough in half lengthwise then crosswise into 16 strips. Dip each strip on both sides in butter and lay close together in two rows in pan. Bake 15-20 minutes till golden brown. Serve hot!

VARIATIONS: Add 1/2 cup grated cheese; or add 1/2 clove garlic to butter; or sprinkle garlic salt, onion salt, paprika, celery seeds, poppy seeds over tops before baking; or add 1/4 cup minced chives, onion or parsley; or sprinkle 2 tablespoons sugar and 1/2 teaspoon cinnamon over before baking.

Marilyn Wood
WildWood Ranch
Lindale, TX

❖

"Our herd sire, Vegas, is very gentle, but he's also very independent. When we go to move the bulls, Vegas will just keep grazing. Even with six cowboys, two trucks and three dogs, he won't move. The only way we can get him going is for my husband Harvey to tell him to "come on", and Vegas will follow him. Consequently Harvey has to do a lot of walking to get Vegas from one pasture to another. It's also the only way we can get Vegas in a trailer."

—Evelyn Rasmussen
Rolling Hills Ranch, Houston, Texas

❖

Trimmings

I'll Be In It To The End

An old cowboy — the other day
Was just sittin' down by the barn.
As I rode by, he said to me
"Stop, let's spin a yarn."

He spoke of the good ol' days,
Bad broncs and wild cows,
And how folks thought he was gettin" old
and should cowboy from the house.

Then he spoke of doctors tellin' him
Time had come to slow it down.
And how he'd be much better off
Just to quit and move to town.

That cowboy life was much too hard
And he must try something new.
There are young ones still out there,
For that cowboy work to do.

And he told me
"I've got horses to ride.
Strays that like to hide.
Teachin' young ones with desire
How to drag calves to the fire
In the saddle my time I'll spend
And I'll be in it to the end."

I could tell as I listened
He was a cowboy to the bone.
He'd be that way until they
Lay him 'neath the cold cold stone.

And now when frustrated and
Think I've got it rough,
I think of that man, neared
Twice my age, who still hasn't had enough.

And I tell myself
"I've got horses yet to ride,
Strays that like to hide,
Teachin' young ones with desire
How to drag calves to the fire.
In the saddle my time I'll spend
And I'll be in it to the end."

—Mel Raley, Kingsville, Texas

Grilled Chicken Salad

boneless, skinless chicken
    breasts
1   cup lemon juice

¹/₂ cup soy sauce
1   tablespoon minced garlic
1   teaspoon black pepper

Mix ingredients and marinate chicken breasts for at least 2 hours. The longer they marinate, the more flavorful and tender the chicken. Grill or broil the chicken until done, about 20 minutes. Slice thinly and place chicken strips on mixed greens. Sprinkle with your favorite salad topping and dressing.

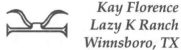

Kay Florence
Lazy K Ranch
Winnsboro, TX

Black Bean and Corn Salad

¹/₃ cup vegetable oil
1   tablespoon red wine
    vinegar
1   teaspoon cider vinegar
1   clove garlic, minced
¹/₂ teaspoon ground cumin
¹/₂ teaspoon dried oregano
¹/₂ teaspoon salt
¹/₄ teaspoon sugar

¹/₈ teaspoon red or cayenne
    ground pepper
2   (15 ounce each) cans
    black beans, drained
1   (15 ounce) can whole
    kernel corn, drained
³/₄ cup chopped onion
¹/₂ cup chopped red or green
    bell pepper

In a bowl, whisk together the first 9 ingredients. Add the beans, corn, onion, bell pepper and toss. Cover and chill for at least 8 hours to blend flavors. Serves 12.

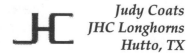

Judy Coats
JHC Longhorns
Hutto, TX

Shrimp and Broccoli Salad

4   cups cooked, peeled   salt and pepper
      shrimp cut bite size   paprika
lemon juice   2   teaspoons finely chopped
2   cups fresh broccoli   capers
1¹/2-2 cups chopped celery   Hellman's Mayonnaise
¹/2   cup finely chopped red   lettuce leaves
      Bermuda onion

Sprinkle shrimp liberally with lemon juice. Cut broccoli into bite size flowerets. Peel broccoli stems as you would a carrot, and slice into small thin pieces. Combine shrimp and broccoli in a large bowl. Toss celery and onion with salt, pepper and paprika. Add capers and mayonnaise. Chill well. Check seasonings. Add more mayonnaise if needed. Serve on lettuce.

Suggestions for a complete luncheon or hot weather supper: Serve with cherry or quartered tomatoes, hard boiled eggs, avocado slices, green pepper strips (if not added to salad), artichoke hearts, crackers, garlic toast or your favorite rolls.

OPTIONAL VARIATIONS- add snipped fresh parsley and/or ¹/2 cup chopped fresh bell pepper

Mary Elizabeth Scott
Copa de Vino Ranch
Goliad, TX

Cornbread Salad

2   (6 ounce each) pkgs   1   onion, finely chopped
      cornbread mix   1   green pepper, chopped
12   slices bacon, fried and   2   large tomatoes, chopped
      crumbled   1¹/2 cups mayonnaise

Prepare cornbread as directed on package. Cool and crumble, add bacon and vegetables. Stir in mayonnaise. Chill until served. It gets better each day. Serves 10.

Lorene Graves & SuzAnne Graves Hickman
Dayton, TX

Black Bean Salad

DRESSING:

2	tablespoons extra virgin olive oil	3-4	tablespoons fresh lime juice
1	tablespoon red wine vinegar	1	teaspoon salt
		1/2	teaspoon freshly ground pepper

Whisk olive oil, vinegar, lime juice, salt and pepper until blended. Set aside.

2	(15 ounce each) cans black beans, drained and rinsed	1	avocado, pitted, peeled, and chopped
1	(10 ounce) pkg frozen corn, cooked and drained	2	large tomatoes, peeled, seeded, and chopped
1/4	cup chopped fresh cilantro	2	fresh jalapeños, seeded and minced
1	small red onion, chopped		

Combine black beans, corn, cilantro, onion, avocado, tomatoes and jalapeños in large serving bowl. Toss salad gently to mix. Pour dressing over salad and toss gently to coat.

Evelyn Rasmussen
Rolling Hills Ranch
Houston, TX

Sauerkraut Salad

1	cup chopped celery	1 1/2	cups sugar
1	cup chopped onions	1/2	cup water
1	jar pimientos	3/4	cup oil
1	can sauerkraut, drained	1/2	cup vinegar

Mix all ingredients together and put in covered dish overnight.

Do hungry cows have ravenous appetites?

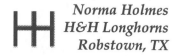
Norma Holmes
H&H Longhorns
Robstown, TX

Blue Cheese Dressing

64	ounces yogurt	2	teaspoons granulated garlic
1	cup mayonnaise	1	teaspoon lemon juice
4	ounces blue cheese, crumbled	2	dashes Tabasco sauce

Drain yogurt overnight. Mix mayonnaise, blue cheese, garlic, lemon juice and Tabasco. Add drained yogurt and mix well. Let stand overnight to let flavors blend. Makes 1 quart.

Note: A very robust and healthy dressing that also works well with hot wings.

Jeff Miller & Carol Erickson
Sunnybrook Cattle Company
Wellington, CO

Best Ever German Potato Salad

1/3	cup bacon, diced	1/4	teaspoons pepper
2	tablespoons flour	3/4	cup vinegar
1/4	teaspoon dry mustard	1/2	cup water
1/4	cup sugar	3	cups cooked diced potatoes
2	teaspoons salt	1	onion, chopped

Fry bacon. Mix next 5 ingredients and add to bacon in skillet. Add vinegar and water and stir until thick. Add potatoes and onions and mix well.

Priscilla Briney
Briney's Lazy 5B Ranch
Bowie, TX

"A Longhorn cow will stand over her calf to protect it from a hail storm."

—*Fayette Yates, Tuscola, Texas*

Marinated Carrots

1	lb carrots, thinly sliced	3	tablespoons vegetable oil
1/3	cup chopped onion	1/3	cup sugar
1/3	cup chopped green pepper	1/4	teaspoon prepared mustard
1/3	cup vinegar	1	teaspoon Worcestershire sauce

Cook carrots in a small amount of boiling water for 5 minutes or until crisp and tender. Drain. Combine carrots, onions and green peppers. Set aside. Combine vinegar, oil, sugar, mustard and Worcestershire sauce in jar. Cover and shake. Pour over vegetables and toss lightly with fork. Refrigerate overnight.

Kathy King
DK Ranch
Fort Worth, TX

Evan's Salad Dressing

1	cup oil	1	teaspoon celery salt
1/2	cup vinegar	1	teaspoon salt
1	teaspoon garlic salt	1/2	teaspoon black pepper

Combine all ingredients in a covered jar. Shake well and serve.

Marian Stancliff Evans

Blue Cheese Salad Dressing

2	cups sour cream	1	teaspoon garlic salt
1	cup mayonnaise	4	ounces crumbled blue cheese
1	tablespoon lemon juice		

Mix together and refrigerate.

Evelyn S. Rasmussen
Rolling Hills Ranch
Houston, TX

Cranberry Salad

1	(3 ounce) pkg raspberry Jell-O	1	(16 ounce) can whole cranberry sauce
3/4	cup boiling water	1	tablespoon lemon juice
3/4	cup sour cream.	1/4	cup chopped walnuts

Add raspberry Jell-O to boiling water and stir until dissolved. Remove from heat. Add sour cream. Mix until smooth with egg beater. Stir in cranberry sauce, lemon juice and walnuts. Chill just until mixture begins to thicken. Spoon into 1qt salad mold. Chill until firm. Unmold. Serves 4-6.

Note: *Recipe may be doubled if desired.*

Barb Overturf
Parkman, WY

Marinated Vegetable Salad

2	(16 ounce each) cans French style green beans, drained	1	can sliced water chestnuts, drained
		2	cups cauliflower
1	can bean sprouts, drained	1	onion, sliced
1	can diced carrots or 1 can sliced mushrooms, drained	2	cups sliced celery
		1	green pepper, cored, seeded and chopped

DRESSING:

1 1/4	cups apple cider vinegar	1/2	cup salad oil
1	teaspoon pepper	1 1/4	teaspoons canning salt
1	teaspoon seasoning salt		

Stir dressing and pour over vegetables.

Note: *Lasts a long time.*

Jan Barnard
Barnard Longhorns
Herman, NE

Overnight Alfalfa Celery Salad

1/2 cup alfalfa sprouts	2 teaspoons sugar
1 1/2 cups chopped green onion	1/2 teaspoon salt
2 cups chopped celery	1/2 teaspoon pepper
1 (8 ounce) can sliced water chestnuts	1 cup shredded Mozzarella cheese
1 (10 ounce) pkg frozen peas, thawed	1/2 cup shredded Parmesan cheese
2 cups mayonnaise	

Layer alfalfa sprouts, green onions, celery, water chestnuts and peas in a 4 quarts bowl. Combine mayonnaise, sugar, salt and pepper. Mix well. Spread over top sealing to edges. Combine cheeses and sprinkle over top. Cover and chill for 24 hours. Toss before serving.

Jan and Howard Sears
J H Ranch
Leon, IA

Feta Cheese Salad

1 head leaf lettuce	1 cup crumbled feta cheese
1 head red leaf lettuce	1/2 lb bacon, cooked and crumbled
1 lb fresh spinach	
2 cups mandarin oranges	1 red onion, sliced

DRESSING:

1/4 cup sugar	1/2 cup olive oil
1 teaspoon onion powder	poppyseeds
1 teaspoon dry mustard	sesame seeds
1/4 cup vinegar	

Layer vegetables in order. Toss with dressing. Sprinkle top with poppyseeds and sesame seeds.

D-S *Carol Sward*
D-S Ranch
Mountain Home, AR

Cabbage Crunch Salad

1/2-3/4 head cabbage, finely
    chopped
4   green onions, chopped
1   pkg chicken ramen noodles

2   tablespoons sesame seeds
1/2   cup silvered almonds,
    toasted

Combine and toss lightly.

DRESSING:

2   tablespoons sugar
1/2   cup oil
1   teaspoon salt

3   tablespoons vinegar
1/2   flavor packet from noodles

Mix all together and add dressing 15 minutes before serving.

Cindy Long
Nebraska

Layered Salad

1   head lettuce, chopped
1   cup sliced onions
1   cup sliced celery
1   (6 ounce) can sliced
    water chestnuts
1   (10 ounce) pkg frozen
    English peas
2   cups mayonnaise

2   teaspoons sugar
1   teaspoon salt
pepper
1   cup shredded mozzarella
    cheese
1/2   cup Parmesan cheese
bacon bits
sliced tomatoes

Layer first 5 ingredients in order. Mix mayonnaise, sugar, salt and pepper. Spread over the vegetables. Add cheeses. Cover and refrigerate overnight. Just before serving sprinkle bacon bits and top with sliced tomatoes.

Velma Slater
Slater Longhorns
Mexia, TX

Granny's Secret Cranberry Salad

2	pkgs fresh cranberries	3/4	of the small pkg of-
4	large delicious apples, cored		miniature marshmallows
		1	pound pecans, chopped
1½	cups sugar	1	cup whipped cream

Put cranberries and apples through a medium course grinder. Add sugar, marshmallows and nuts. Let set overnight in refrigerator. Add whipped cream. Eat.

Note: Walk 2 miles a day for the next month to return to previous weight, unless you ate the whole thing without help, in which case you might have to get off that three-wheeler and round up cattle on foot.

Barbie Moore
Houston, TX

Lime Jell-O Salad

1	large lime Jell-O	1	large can fruit cocktail, drained
1	large carton small curd cottage cheese, drained	1	cup or more small marshmallows
1	large can crushed pineapple, drained	1	cup pecans, crushed
		1	large carton Cool Whip

Sprinkle Jell-O over cottage cheese, add fruit, mix well and fold in Cool Whip.

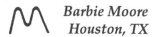

Carla Jo Payne
CP Longhorns and Quarter Horses
Katy, TX

Confetti Slaw

1 small head cabbage, cored and chopped	1 large yellow bell pepper, cored, seeded and chopped
3/4 cup celery	1 small cucumber, peeled and chopped
1 large bell pepper, cored, seeded and chopped	1 large onion, chopped
1 large red bell pepper, cored, seeded and chopped	2 bunches green onions, chopped

Toss cabbage, celery, bell peppers, cucumber and onion in a serving bowl. Set aside.

DRESSING:

1 cup plus 2 tablespoons white vinegar	1 teaspoon salt
1/3 cup vegetable oil	1/4 teaspoon freshly ground pepper
3/4 cup sugar	

Whisk vinegar, oil, sugar, salt and pepper until blended. Pour dressing over vegetables and toss evenly. Cover and refrigerate. When ready to serve, drain excess dressing and toss.

Evelyn S. Rasmussen
Rolling Hills Ranch
Houston, TX

❖

"One of my special Longhorns was the one, which at age 10, had given birth to ten calves (no twins). She was born January 15, 1984, and had her first calf (her one and only bull calf) one week shy of her second birthday. On April 27, 1994, she delivered her tenth calf."

—*Ed Coale, Taylor, Texas*

❖

Marinated Asparagus

1	cup extra virgin olive oil	2	tablespoon chopped pimento
1/3	cup red wine vinegar		
1	tablespoon salt	2	tablespoon chopped green onion
1	teaspoon sugar		
1/4	cup chopped green bell pepper	1	lb thin, fresh asparagus, trimmed and blanched
1	tablespoon chopped fresh parsley		

Combine oil, vinegar, salt, sugar, bell pepper, parsley, pimento and green onion in a shallow, non-metallic bowl. Add asparagus, tossing to coat. Cover and marinate several hours in the refrigerator. Serve chilled or room temperature.

Evelyn S. Rasmussen
Rolling Hills Ranch
Houston, Texas

Golden Parmesan Potatoes

6	medium potatoes		flour
1/2	cup butter or margarine	1/4	cup Parmesan cheese
3/4	teaspoon salt		

Peel and quarter potatoes. Melt butter in pan. Place salt, flour and Parmesan in a plastic bag and shake to coat. Place potatoes in butter and bake 1 hour at 350 degrees. Turn once during baking. Sprinkle additional cheese over potatoes if desired.

❖

"I learned real early when milking a Longhorn cow to keep my nails real short so when I got home, I had more milk than manure in my bucket."

—*Graves Peeler, pioneer Texas Longhorn breeder*

Delicious Frozen Corn

4	quarts corn, cut from the cob	1	cup sugar
1	quart water	4	heaping teaspoons salt

Combine corn, water, sugar and salt. Boil lightly for 10 minutes. Cool and pack in containers and freeze. Don't drain any of liquid off.

Sheryl Johnson
J5 Longhorns
Molalla, OR

Pinto Beans

2	cups pinto beans, sort and discard any spoiled-looking or split beans	1	small or ¹/₂ medium onion, cut in 6-9 pieces
3-4	cloves garlic, peeled, whole or sliced	1-2	slices bacon, cut into about 1" pieces
		1¹/₂	teaspoon salt
		¹/₂	cup tomato sauce

Bring 3 quarts of water to boiling over high heat. Rinse beans well in a colander. Add beans and return to boiling. Add all ingredients except tomato sauce. When boiling again, reduce heat to continue cooking at a slow boil. Stir periodically during the next 1¹/₂-2 hours to be sure beans do not stick to bottom of pot. There should always be a lot of liquid. If juices seem to be thickening, add more very hot water. After 2 hours, add tomato sauce and simmer 30 minutes longer. Check for seasoning. Add pepper and salt to taste. Check beans to see if tender*. If still very firm, cook longer.

Serve in a cup or bowl to enjoy the "soup" as the savory juices are called. Delicious to "dunk" your cornbread in.

NOTES: *Cooking times are approximate as beans vary widely from season to season, where they were grown and how long they have been stored. Dropping beans into boiling water and adding only very hot water eliminates the need to soak before cooking. Beans will thicken upon standing - especially after cooling. Before reheating cold beans, add a little cold water and stir well to restore liquid.

Mary Elizabeth Scott
Copa de Vino Ranch
Goliad, TX

Old Settler's Baked Beans

1/2	lb ground beef
1/2	lb bacon
1	medium onion, chopped
1/3	cup sugar
1/3	cup packed brown sugar
1/4	cup ketchup
1/4	cup BBQ sauce
1	tablespoon prepared mustard

1/2	teaspoon pepper
1/2	teaspoon chili powder
1	(16 ounce) can pork and beans
1	(16 ounce) can kidney beans, rinsed and drained
1	(16 ounce) can great northern beans, rinsed and drained

In a large skillet, cook beef, bacon, and onion until meat is done and onion is tender. Drain any fat. Combine all remaining ingredients except beans. Add to meat mixture, and mix well. Stir in beans. Place in a greased 2 1/2 quarts casserole. Bake covered at 350 degrees for 1 hour or until heated through. Serves 8-10.

Ellen Goodnight
Married to a relative of Col. Charles Goodnight
Meade, KS

Crazy Beans

1 1/2	lbs hamburger, cooked and drained
1/2	cup brown sugar
1/2	lb bacon, fried crisp and chopped
1	tablespoon dry mustard
1	large onion, chopped and sautéed

2	tablespoons Worcestershire sauce
1	(15 1/2 ounce each) can each: Pinto beans, red beans, lima beans, northern beans, and kidney beans
2	teaspoons vinegar
1/2	cup ketchup

Drain juice from beans. Mix ingredients; season to taste. Simmer 2 hours.

J-J *Jody Nelson*
J Bar J Longhorns
Salix, IA

Bourbon Baked Beans

2	(1 lb 15 ounce each) cans pork and beans	1/2	cup ketchup
1	large onion, chopped	1/2	cup Worcestershire sauce
1/2	cup chopped green bell pepper	1	cup brown sugar
1/2	cup chopped celery	1/2	cup bourbon whiskey
			bacon strips

Preheat oven to 350 degrees. In a large bowl, combine all ingredients and mix thoroughly. Place beans in 13"×9"×2" casserole. Cover with bacon strips. Bake for 1 hour and 45 minutes.

Different, and very good.

Lorene Graves
Dayton, TX

Oven Beans

1 pkg any size pinto beans	seasoning to taste
sliced onion	ham hock

Wash beans. Place in big, oven-proof pan. Put in onions, seasoning, ham hock and water close to top of pan. Cook at 325 degrees oven overnight.

A sure crowd pleaser that is easy on the cook.

Barbara Flynn
Double Bar A Ranch
Evant, TX

Cabbage with Sausage

8 sausage links	salt and pepper
1 1/2 quart minced cabbage	

Fry sausage until brown. Remove sausage and pour off all but 4 tablespoons of fat. Put cabbage in pan and cook about 5 minutes. Arrange cabbage on hot dish, and garnish with sausage.

Lorene Graves
Dayton, TX

Louisiana Cabbage Rolls

30	large cabbage leaves	3	stalks green onions, sliced
3	lbs Texas Longhorn ground beef	1	(8 ounce) can tomato sauce
1	onion, chopped	2	cups chopped cabbage
1	small green bell pepper, chopped	1½	cups cooked rice
3	garlic cloves, chopped	1	jar tomato gravy
		salt	and pepper

Place cabbage leaves in boiling water long enough to soften them slightly and let cool. Brown ground beef, bell pepper, garlic and onions together in large pot. Add chopped cabbage, tomato sauce, rice, salt and pepper. Cook mixture until cabbage is soft and tender. Place a generous amount of mixture in the center of each cabbage leaf. Roll and fold sides to form a tight pouch. Hold ends together with toothpicks. Place cabbage rolls in baking dish in one layer. Use additional dish if necessary. Pour tomato gravy over cabbage rolls. Bake about 45 minutes at 350 degrees. Serve hot as a main dish or side dish.

Ed Durr, Jr.
Heaven View Farm
Amite, LA

Fried Sweet Corn

1	dozen ears of corn	1	tablespoon sugar, optional
½	stick margarine or butter		salt and pepper
1⅓	cups water		

Shuck and wash corn. Cut the kernels off the cob off into a large bowl. Be sure not to cut into the cob. After cutting off the tips, take knife and scrape the milk from the cob into the bowl. Put all ingredients in a large skillet. Cook on high until it comes to a boil. Turn heat to medium and continue to cook down. Corn should be creamy. Takes about 25-30 minutes. If the corn is real sweet, it might not need the sugar. Stir occasionally as it begins to thicken.

Mrs. Bobby Barker
Frankfort, KY

Scalloped Corn

1	(17 ounce) can creamed corn	3	eggs, beaten
1	(17 ounce) can corn, drained	12	ounces sour cream
1	stick margarine	1	(8½ ounce) pkg Jiffy cornbread mix
		1	cup Cheddar cheese, grated

Mix together all ingredients, except cheese. Put in a greased 13"×9"×2" pan and bake at 350 degrees for 35-40 minutes. Sprinkle grated cheese on corn and return to oven until the cheese is melted.

S/K
Karen King
S/K Ranch
Granbury, TX

Mexican Corn

2	(10 ounce each) pkg frozen corn	2-3	tablespoon butter
1	(12 ounce) pkg cream cheese	1	small jar chopped green chilies and pimentos

Put all ingredients in a crockpot and melt. Ready in 1 hour.

S/K
Karen King
S/K Ranch
Granbury, TX

Herbed Corn

½	cup butter, softened	1	teaspoon dried thyme
2	tablespoons minced parsley	½	teaspoon salt
2	tablespoons minced chives	¼	teaspoon cayenne pepper
		8	ears sweet corn, husked

In a small bowl, combine first six ingredients. Spread 1 tablespoon of the butter mixture over each ear of corn. Wrap corn individually in heavy duty foil. Grill, covered, over medium coals for 10-15 minutes, turning frequently, or until corn is tender. Serves 8.

Louisiana Stuffed Peppers

2-3	lbs Texas Longhorn ground beef	3	garlic cloves, chopped salt and pepper
1	small to medium onion, chopped	2	cups seasoned bread crumbs
1	small bell pepper, finely chopped	5	medium to large bell peppers, cored and seeded
3	stalks green onions, chopped	2	cups boiling water
		3	beef bouillon cubes

In a large pot, brown ground beef and chopped vegetables until vegetables are tender. Add salt and pepper to taste. Cook mixture for about 15-20 minutes covered. Remove from heat and add bread crumbs. If mixture appears to be dry, add a little water. Stuff peppers as desired, but try to pack lightly. In boiling water, dissolve bouillon cubes. Place peppers in baking dish large enough for all peppers. Pour bouillon liquid over peppers and cover. Bake at 350 degrees for about 1 hour or until peppers are tender. Baste with syringe type baster a few times during baking time. Serve as a main dish with salad and rolls.

Ed Durr, Jr.
Heaven View Farm
Amite, LA

Fried Green Tomatoes

4-5	medium green tomatoes	pepper
1/3	cup flour	shortening
3/4	teaspoon salt	

Wash tomatoes and remove stem ends. Cut crosswise into 1/2" slices. Blend flour, salt and pepper. Dip tomatoes into mixture. Brown quickly on one side in shortening. Turn and reduce heat. Cook until soft in center. Remove and drain.

Jackie Craver
Cedar Rose Ranch
Timmonsville, SC

Green Rice

1	cup sliced green onions	1/3	cup minced parsley
2	tablespoon oil	3	cups chicken stock
1½	cups rice	1	teaspoon pepper
2/3	cup chopped green bell pepper		

Sauté green onions in oil. Mix all ingredients well and place in a casserole. Cover with foil or lid. Bake at 350 degrees for 45 minutes.

Great with BBQ.

2h   *Marcie Wirick*
Dayton, TX

Cheesy Mexi Rice

3/4	cup water	3/4	cup thick 'n' chunky salsa
1	cup (4½ ounce) can chopped green chilies	8	ounces cubed pasteurized process cheese spread
1	cup uncooked instant rice		

In medium saucepan, bring water to a boil. Stir in chilies, rice and salsa. Add cheese; stir to blend slightly. Reduce heat, cover and simmer 5 minutes. Stir; let stand 5 minutes before serving. Serves 6.

Patty Dudley

Potato Pancakes

2	large potatoes, grated	1/2	teaspoon baking powder
2	eggs	1/2	cup flour
salt		fat	

Combine potatoes and eggs. Salt to taste, add baking powder and flour. Mix well and fry in hot fat.

Cheesy Potatoes

6	teaspoon melted butter	1	teaspoon salt
1	(2 lbs) bag frozen hash brown potatoes, thawed	1/4	teaspoon pepper
8	ounces sour cream	1¾	cups cream of mushroom soup
1	cup shredded Cheddar cheese		dried onions, if desired

Combine all ingredients and bake in 13"x9"x2" pan at 350 degrees for 50-60 minutes.

Beverly Sorem
Flying S Cattle
Nevada, IA

Hash Brown Potato Pie

5	large eggs or 1¼ cup egg substitute	1/2	teaspoon salt
1/2	cup milk	¼	teaspoon hot pepper sauce
3	cups frozen hash brown potatoes, thawed	1½	cups sharp Cheddar cheese, shredded, divided
1/3	cup thinly sliced green onions	4	slices bacon, cooked crisp and crumbled or 1/3 cup real bacon bits, divided

In a medium bowl, beat eggs and milk; stir in hash browns, green onions, salt and pepper sauce. Stir in 1 cup cheese and half the bacon. Pour into a greased 9" pie plate or quiche dish. Bake at 350 degrees for 25-30 minutes or until center is set. Sprinkle with remaining bacon and cheese. Bake 3-4 minutes longer or until cheese is melted. Serves 6.

J-J

Jody Nelson
J Bar J Longhorns
Salix, IA

Potato Puffs

2	cups leftover mashed potatoes	1	cup sifted flour
2	eggs, well beaten	2	teaspoon baking powder
4	slices crumbled crisp-fried bacon, optional	1	teaspoon salt
			oil

Mix all ingredients and drop by teaspoons into deep, hot oil. Fry 3-5 minutes until brown. Drain on paper towels. Serves 6.

"Happiness makes up in height for what it lacks in length." — Robert Frost

Vicki Helms
Belleville, IL
Heartland Texas Longhorn Breeders Association

Best Ever Potatoes

6	medium-sized new red potatoes.	1/4	lb margarine
1	small green bell pepper, chopped	1	(10³/4 ounce) can mushroom soup
1	small onion, chopped	1	small can Pet milk
3	ribs celery, sliced	1	small jar pimentos, diced
		1/2	lb Velveeta cheese

Cook potatoes. Cut into chunks and put into a baking dish and set aside. Sauté bell pepper, onion and celery in margarine until tender. Add soup, milk, pimentos and cheese. Stir until cheese melts. Pour over potatoes and bake at 350 degrees until bubbly hot.

(If you prepare too much sauce, it will freeze well for later use.)

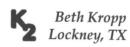

Beth Kropp
Lockney, TX

Spinach Madeline

2	(10 ounce each) pkg frozen spinach	1/2	cup evaporated milk
4	tablespoons butter	1/2	cup chopped celery
2	tablespoons flour		salt to taste
1/2	reserved spinach liquid	6	ounces roll jalapeño cheese, cut into small pieces
2	tablespoons chopped onion	1	teaspoon Worcestershire sauce
1	teaspoon minced garlic		red pepper to taste

Cook spinach according to directions on package. Drain and reserve 1/2 cup liquid. Melt butter in pan, add flour and cook until blended but not brown. Add spinach liquid slowly. Cook on low heat, stirring constantly until it makes a smooth sauce. Add onion, garlic, milk, cheese, Worcestershire sauce and red pepper. Stir until the cheese is melted. Add spinach. Mix well and pour into a casserole dish and bake. The flavor is improved if you put the casserole into the refrigerator and bake it the next day. Bread crumbs may be put on top just before baking if desired.

Oven-Fried Eggplant

1/2	cup mayonnaise	1/3	cup grated Parmesan cheese
1	tablespoon minced onion		
12	(1/2" thick each) slices unpeeled eggplant	1/2	teaspoon dried Italian seasoning
1/3	cup fine dry breadcrumbs		Vegetable cooking spray

Combine first 2 ingredients; stir well. Spread evenly over both sides of eggplant slices. Combine bread crumbs, cheese and Italian seasoning in a shallow bowl; dredge eggplant in bread crumb mixture. Place eggplant on a baking sheet coated with cooking spray. Bake at 425 degrees for 12 minutes. Turn eggplant over, and bake 12 minutes or until golden brown. Serves 4.

"Ridin' the Bog"

"The early day ranchmen did not feed them in winter, but let them rustle their own living. Some got very poor and weak and when they went to some muddy waterhole to drink, they would get stuck in the mud; and then too exhausted to pull themselves out or struggle more, they would lie down. Cowboys made practice of riding these waterholes, a custom known as "ridin' the bog". When an animal was found, the rider would toss a loop over its horns, take a turn around the saddle horn and haul the Longhorn from the mud on its side. Then he'd get off his horse, take the rope from the horns, and grab the animal by the tail and lift up to help it to its feet. Almost always, the Longhorn would try to turn around and would chase the man if it could stand on its feet at all. If the Longhorn did not fall down again, it was up to the man to beat the animal to his horse. Sometimes the horse also would become frightened and run off. On these occasions, the man had to outrun the Longhorn, get to a tree or ditch, or as a last resort fall flat on the ground. Riders who'd worked with these cattle learned that a Longhorn would jump over the body of a man who was flat and motionless on the ground, but it was not a good plan to get up too soon, otherwise the animal would turn around, come back, and chase him some more."

—Forest Ranger Earl Drummond
Wichita Mountains National Wildlife Refuge
Cache, Oklahoma (1939)

One Pot Meals

"The Chuck Wagon"

Charles Goodnight, a Texas cattleman, is credited with having invented the first authentic chuck wagon in 1866. The chuck box that Goodnight built fit into the tail end of a ranch wagon bed. It was about four feet high and contained shelves and compartments for storing food supplies and cooking and eating utensils. Its hinged lid was designed to drop down and stand level with the aid of a scantling or pole; this served as the work surface. A water barrel (which often contained stale water, wiggling with wildlife) rode on one side of the wagon. Another box was often attached on the other side to carry odds and ends of tools such as pot hooks, branding irons, a shovel, a pick and an ax.

The wagon bed itself held the main food supplies and the top food staple was beef. A cattle drive outfit with little beef was considered to be very stingy. During warm weather a wet tarpaulin was often wrapped around fresh beef to slow down the spoiling process. If it spoiled severely, it was "doctored" up with chilies, spices and tomatoes and became Texas chili.

Surrounded by a few thousand head of cattle every day, you would automatically think that the cowboy would eat beef steak three times a day. That's not the way it really was, although the cowboy would have preferred it (and still does). But the cook did the best he knew how from pan-fried beef steaks to son-of-a-gun stew.

Beef not only served as a favored food by the cowhand, but also as bargaining power for the trail boss. Many cattle drives were allowed to pass peacefully through Indian territory after a few head of cattle or "wohaw" changed possession.

Other staple food supplies were beans, dry salt pork, bacon, flour, coffee, cornmeal, molasses, vinegar, salt and sourdough starter. To supplement these staples, dried fruit, onions, potatoes, canned milk, canned tomatoes and spices might be included.

The cowhand considered canned tomatoes a real treat and when possible used them to quench the thirst they would get from riding the hot dusty cow trails and drinking too much alkaline and "not so pure" water. Many Texas cooks liked to make a sweet pudding treat using leftover bread, molasses or sugar and canned tomatoes.

Chow from the chuck wagon varied from region to region and from season to season, but three cowboy dishes that rarely ever changed were—beef, beans and bread. About a 30 day supply could be carried in the chuck wagon. It was guarded by the cowboys as if it contained gold, and it went first on the trail.

The well equipped chuck wagon carried a very large coffee pot and a rod for hanging it, various sizes of kettles and skillets and several Dutch ovens. Other cooking aids were extra tripods for holding pots and pans above the fire and coals, spoons for stirring, knives for cutting, and of course, a dish pan and flour sacks for a little cleaning.

—*Campfire Cooking* by **Jalynn Burkett**
Texas Longhorn breeder and County Extension Agent, Fort Worth, TX

Oyster-Artichoke Casserole

4 dozen oysters	1/4 cup chopped green onions
1 (7 ounce) pkg Pepperidge Farms bread cubes chicken broth	3/4 stick butter
	2 cans artichoke hearts quartered and drained
1/2 cup chopped onions	1/2 teaspoon thyme
1/2 cup chopped celery	salt and pepper
2 cloves garlic, minced, optional	1/2 cup parsley
	2 tablespoons Absinthe liqueur

Drain oysters and reserve liquid. Soak bread cubes in oyster liquid and chicken broth. (This mixture should be very moist.) Warm oysters until they curl. Reserve. Sauté onions, celery, garlic and green onions in butter. Add oysters, artichokes, bread cubes, thyme, salt, pepper and parsley. Cook 10-15 minutes. Pour into 14"×10"×2" casserole. Sprinkle Absinthe liqueur and seasoned bread crumbs on top. Bake 20-30 minutes.

Make at least 2 hours ahead or day before serving.

T
Ruth Hoffman
Seven T Ranch
Metairie, LA

Crawfish Casserole

1 cup chopped onions	1 1/4 cups milk
1 cup chopped bell pepper	8 ounces jalapeno Cheese Whiz
2 tablespoons butter	1 lb peeled crawfish tails
1 (10 ounce) pkg broccoli, thawed and chopped	salt and pepper
1 (10 3/4 ounce) can cream of mushroom soup	3 cups cooked rice

Sauté chopped onions and bell pepper in butter until clear and tender. Add broccoli and cook until tender. Add all other ingredients (except cooked rice). Cook 15-20 minutes on medium heat. When crawfish are cooked, add cooked rice and mix well. Serves 4-6.

Helen Dardeau

Nacho Cheese Chicken Casserole

1 medium bag Nacho Cheese Doritos
1 (10 ounce) can white chunk chicken, drained
1 (10³/4 ounce) can cream of mushroom soup
1 (10¹/2 ounce) can cream of celery soup
1 (10³/4 ounce) can cream of chicken soup
1 (4 ounce) can chopped green chilies
8 ounces sour cream
1-2 cups shredded Cheddar cheese

Crush chips and place in bottom of baking dish. Mix all other ingredients, except cheese in large bowl and pour over chips. Sprinkle cheese on top and bake 25-30 minutes at 350 degrees until cheese melts and other ingredients are bubbly. Serve with salad, refried beans, and tortillas. For added flavor add Tabasco or Cholula Sauce to recipe.

Marilyn Wood
Wild Wood Ranch
Lindale, TX

Chicken Pie Casserole

1 chicken, cut in pieces
3 cups chicken broth
1 cup cream of chicken soup
1 cup cream of celery soup
salt and pepper
butter
2 cups Bisquick
1¹/2 cups milk

Cook chicken, then debone and place in casserole dish. Mix broth, soups, salt and pepper and pour over chicken mixture, dot with butter. Mix Bisquick and milk and put on top. Bake at 350 degrees for about 30 minutes or until bread is done.

Cathy Parker
Mid-Atlantic Texas Longhorn Association
Lincolnton, NC

Mexican Chicken Casserole

1	chicken (about 4 lbs) or 3 whole breasts	1	(10½ ounce) can Rotel tomatoes
2	teaspoons salt	½	cup chicken stock
1	teaspoon pepper		additional salt and pepper
1	bay leaf	12	tortillas, torn in small pieces
1	(10¾ ounce) can cream of chicken soup	2	onions, finely chopped
1	(10¾ ounce) can cream of mushroom soup	3	cups grated sharp cheese

Cook chicken in water to which has been added salt, pepper and bay leaf. Remove cooked chicken; reserve ¹/₂ cup chicken stock. Cut chicken into large, bite-size pieces, set aside. Combine soups, Rotel, chicken stock and salt and pepper to taste. Mix well. In a 3 quarts casserole, make three layers in the following order: corn tortillas, chicken, tomato mixture, chopped onions and grated cheese. Use all ingredients in the three layers, being sure that cheese is on top. Bake at 350 degrees for about 45 minutes. Can be prepared a day ahead of serving and can also be frozen. Serves 6-8.

Velma Slater
Slater Longhorns
Mexia, TX

Chow Mein Bake

1	lb Longhorn ground beef	1	(10¾ ounce) can mushroom soup
1	large onion, chopped		
1	cup chopped celery	2	cups water
3	tablespoons soy sauce	½	cup uncooked rice
1½	tablespoons Worcestershire sauce	1	can chow mein noodles

Brown beef, onion and celery. Mix with all other ingredients. Bake 1 hour at 350 degrees. Sprinkle with noodles and bake 20 more minutes.

Nancy Meade
Windmill Ranch
Milo, IA

Fancy Ham Casserole

³/₄	lb cooked spiral macaroni	1	tablespoon lemon juice
1¹/₂	quarts cubed ham	1¹/₂	tablespoons grated onion
2	cups cooked asparagus	1	tablespoon dry mustard
¹/₂	cup butter	1	tablespoon parsley
¹/₂	cup flour	1	teaspoon salt
4¹/₂	cups milk	½	tsp rosemary
¹/₄	cup chicken broth	¹/₂	teaspoon pepper
1	cup grated Colby cheese	1	cup Miracle Whip
¹/₂	cup Parmesan cheese	butter	

In 13"×9"×2" pan, layer macaroni, ham and asparagus. Make a sauce of the rest of the ingredients and pour over the layers. Top with butter and refrigerate overnight. Bake at 350 degrees for 1 hour.

Jan and Howard Sears
J H Ranch
Leon, IA

Casserole

1	(7¹/₄ ounce) box macaroni and cheese	1	(4 ounce) can chopped green chilies
1	cup milk	1	can chopped mushrooms
1	(10³/₄ ounce) can mushroom soup	1	can chopped pimentos (optional)
1	(10³/₄ ounce) can cream of chicken soup	3	chopped (cooked) ham or chicken
grated cheese			

Cook macaroni as directed on box, but add 1 c more of milk. Add the rest of the ingredients. Mix and bake at 350 degrees for 30 minutes, until bubbly. Sprinkle with grated cheese and bake another 5 minutes. Serves 12.

COOK

Georgia M. Cook
Cook Longhorn Ranch
Ree Heights, SD

Cabbage Casserole

1	medium cabbage	1	cup raw rice
1	lb Jimmy Dean Pork Sausage		onions, bell pepper, celery and garlic, optional
1	lb ground meat		salt and pepper
1	(10 ounce) can Rotel tomatoes		

Cut cabbage in small pieces. Reserve. Brown sausage and drain. Add ground meat and brown. Add seasonings and sauté. Next add Rotel, 1/4 cup water, and raw rice and cook 5 minutes. Add cabbage and cook 10 minutes. Put into covered casserole. Pour sauce over top and bake 1 1/2 hours at 350 degrees.

SAUCE:

1	cup milk	6-8	slices American cheese
1	tablespoon flour		(*I use sharp Cheddar*
1/2	stick margarine		*cheese, grated*)

Melt margarine. Add flour and blend a few minutes. Add milk and cheese. Melt until smooth.

T   *Ruth Hoffman*
Seven T Ranch
Metairie, LA

❖

"We got started in the Longhorn business in 1979. The cattle have been interesting over the years, but the best thing has been all the people we have met and the friendships we now have from being in the Longhorn cattle industry."

—*Nancy & Pat Meade*
Windmill Ranch, Milo, Iowa

Coffee Can Casserole

This is called Coffee Can Casserole because if you are out camping, you can make it in a 1 lb coffee can, covered with foil, and buried in campfire coals. Takes a little longer to cook that way, but if you're out working cows, it will be ready when you get back.

1 lb Longhorn ground beef	5-6 medium carrots, peeled and sliced
salt and pepper	
2-3 medium potatoes, peeled and sliced	1 medium onion, sliced

Cover bottom of 2 quarts round casserole dish with ground beef and season with salt and pepper. Add layer of potatoes, then layer carrots and layer of sliced onions. Start layering again with potatoes, carrots, and onions. Cover and bake in 350 degree oven for about 1 hour.

Carolyn Hunter
Texas Longhorn Trails
Fort Worth, TX

Wrangler Beef Casserole

2 lbs ground Longhorn beef	1 (28 ounce) can tomatoes
1 medium onion, chopped	1 (8 ounce) pkg shell macaroni
1 tablespoon salt	
pepper	

Break meat into chunks, and lightly brown meat and onions in frying pan, stirring as necessary. Stir in salt, pepper and tomatoes. Cook macaroni as directed on package. Lightly stir into meat mixture. Turn into 2 1/2 quarts casserole. Cover and bake in 350 degree oven for 45 minutes.

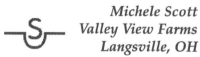

Michele Scott
Valley View Farms
Langsville, OH

Cowboy Dinner

4	potatoes, divided	1	lb Longhorn hamburger, divided
	salt and pepper		
1	onion, diced, divided	1	(10½ ounce) can tomato soup, divided

Slice 2 potatoes in the bottom of well greased casserole dish. Salt and pepper. Add ½ onion. Break ½ of the hamburger into small pieces. Add ½ of the soup. Repeat the process. Bake at 400 degrees for 1 hour, then 375 degrees for ½ hour.

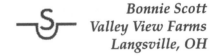

Bonnie Scott
Valley View Farms
Langsville, OH

Beef and Eggplant Casserole

1	lb lean ground beef	1	large onion, sliced and quartered
1	clove garlic, chopped		
1	medium eggplant, cut in ½" cubes	1	teaspoon salt
		1	teaspoon basil
2	green peppers, cut in ½" cubes	½	teaspoon oregano
			pepper
1	(16 ounce) can tomatoes	2	medium-sized potatoes
2	medium-sized potatoes		

Brown beef and garlic and drain. Add eggplant and cook over low heat for 10 minutes. Add peppers, tomatoes, onion and seasonings. Cook over low heat until well blended. Meanwhile boil potatoes. Peel, slice, and place in bottom of buttered casserole dish. Turn meat mixture into dish over potatoes. Bake at 350 degrees until bubbly.

Mrs. Leonard Stiles
King Ranch
Kingsville, TX

Kristi's Superb Mexican Casserole

6	corn tortillas		sliced cheese (any kind you want, including Velveeta) to layer over beans
1	lb Longhorn lean hamburger		
1	chopped onion	1	(10 ounce) can Rotel Tomatoes
1	(16 ounce) can Ranch style beans	1	($10^3/4$ ounce) can cream of chicken soup (or cream of mushroom)

Grease pan. Layer first 5 ingredients in the order listed. Mix the Rotel and soup and pour over the top. Bake at 350 degrees until bubbly.

Priscilla Briney
Briney's Lazy 5 B Ranch
Bowie, TX

Ruby's Surprise

Ruby is our butcher. She shared this recipe and it is the kids' favorite.

Brown 2 lbs hamburger with chopped onion. Add 1 packet Taco Seasoning, and lightly dust with chili powder. Drain. In a deep Pyrex dish layer from bottom in order, hamburger meat, 1 can Ranch style beans, 6-8 corn tortillas shredded, 1 can Rotel, 1/2 cup shredded Mozzarella, 1/2 cup shredded Cheddar and 1 can cream of mushroom soup. Bake at 350 degrees for 30 minutes.

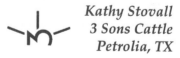

Kathy Stovall
3 Sons Cattle
Petrolia, TX

Casserole

corn tortillas
1   lb browned ground meat
1   (16 ounce) can undrained
    Ranch style beans

1   cup mushroom soup
1   (10 ounce) can Rotel
    chopped tomatoes
Cover with cheese - any kind

Mix all ingredients. Cook at 350 degrees until bubbly. Serve with chips and hot sauce and salad.

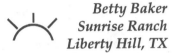

Betty Baker
Sunrise Ranch
Liberty Hill, TX

Lorene Casserole

1   lb ground chuck
1   clove garlic, pressed
salt and pepper
1   (12 ounce) can V-8 juice
1   (5 ounce) package egg
    noodles, cooked
2   bunch green onions,
    chopped

1½ cups sour cream
1   (8 ounce) pkg cream
    cheese, softened
    and cubed
2   cups grated Cheddar
    cheese

Brown meat, drain and stir in garlic, salt, pepper and juice. Simmer 30 minutes. Combine noodles, onion, sour cream and cream cheese, mixing well. Spread noodle mixture in a greased 2 quarts casserole. Spread with cheese mixture and top with meat mixture. Sprinkle with cheese. Bake at 350 degrees for about 20 minutes. Freezes well. Serves 6.

Lorene Graves
Dayton, TX

Husband's Delight

8	ounces wide noodles	1/8	teaspoon pepper
1 1/2	lbs lean ground beef	1	cup cottage cheese
1/4	cup chopped green pepper	1	(8 ounce) pkg cream
1	clove garlic, minced		cheese, softened
3	(8 ounce each) cans	1/4	cup sour cream
	tomato sauce	3-4	green onions, chopped
1	tablespoon sugar		shredded Cheddar cheese
1/8	teaspoon salt		

Cook noodles according to package directions. Cook ground beef, green pepper and garlic until beef is brown. Drain any fat. Add tomato sauce, sugar, salt and pepper. Stir in noodles. Combine cottage cheese and cream cheese. Add sour cream and green onion. Layer half of the ground beef mixture and half of the noodle mixture into a greased 13"×9"×2" baking dish. Top this layer with the cottage cheese mixture and the remaining beef and noodle mixtures. Sprinkle with Cheddar cheese. Bake uncovered at 350 degrees for 30 minutes or until hot and bubbly. Serves 8.

Loretta Miller
Tim Miller Ranch
Great Bend, KS

Squash Casserole

2	cups chopped onions	1/3	cups cracker crumbs
2	cups chopped squash	1/4	cups grated cheese
margarine		3	eggs, beaten
1	(10 3/4 ounce) can cream		salt and pepper
	of mushroom soup		

Cook onions and squash together, drain and mash. Combine all ingredients and bake at 350 degrees until brown on top and done in center.

Velma Slater
Slater Longhorns
Mexia, TX

Longhorn Bean Casserole

1	lbs Longhorn ground beef	3/4	cup brown sugar
1/4	lb bacon (may use bacon bits)		salt and pepper
1/2	cup chopped onion	1	(16 ounce) can kidney beans
1/2	cup ketchup	1	(16 ounce) can green lima beans
1	tablespoon prepared mustard	1	(16 ounce) can pork and beans
2	tablespoons vinegar		

Combine ground beef, bacon, and onion and cook. Drain. Combine with all other ingredients. Cook in crock pot on low for 4-5 hours, or bake in 350 degree oven for 1-1 1/2 hours.

Vonda Burden
Town Creek, AL

Broccoli Chicken Casserole

2	(10 ounce each) pkg chopped broccoli, cooked and well drained	Steam 1 or 2 fryers until tender, skin and debone
		Sharp cheese, grated

SAUCE:

3/4	can cream of celery soup	juice of 1/2 lemon
3/4	can cream of chicken soup	1 1/2 teaspoons curry powder
1	cup mayonnaise	

Layer broccoli, chicken and cheese. Cover with sauce. Bake at 350 degrees about 30 minutes or until bubbly.

Velma Slater
Slater Longhorns
Mexia, TX

Broccoli and Rice Casserole

2   (10 ounce each) packages frozen broccoli
1   small onion, chopped
2   tablespoons butter or margarine
1   (10¾ ounce) can cream of chicken soup
1   (10¾ ounce) can cream of mushroom soup
½   cup milk
1   (8 ounce) pkg Velveeta cheese
3   cups cooked rice

Cook broccoli, drain and set aside. Sauté onions in butter. Heat soup, milk, and cheese until cheese melts. Mix all ingredients together and pour into a 2 quarts greased casserole dish. Bake at 350 degrees for 30 minutes.

Kelly Patterson

Oriental Rice Casserole

1   cup chopped onion
1   cup chopped celery
1   (6 ounce) package Uncle Ben's long grain and wild rice
2   tablespoons soy sauce
1   (3 ounce) can broiled, sliced mushrooms, drained
1   (5 ounce) can sliced water chestnuts, drained
⅓   cup slivered almonds, optional

Sauté onion and celery in butter until tender. Add to rice mix and prepare according to pkg directions. Mix all ingredients. Bake in 2 quarts casserole at 350 degrees for 20 minutes.

Great with a steak instead of potatoes.

Marilyn Wood
Wild Wood Ranch
Lindale, TX

Christmas Casserole

2	(16 ounce each) cans asparagus spears, drained	1	(10³/4) can cream of mushroom soup
1	(16 ounce) can LeSeur peas, drained	4	slices bread cubed
		1	cup grated Cheddar cheese

butter

Layer asparagus in bottom of casserole pan. Pour peas over asparagus. Spread soup over mixture. Brown bread cubes in butter, scatter over top of casserole, then top that with the grated cheese. Pepper top. Bake in 350 degree oven for 30 minutes, or until browned on top.

We always have this at Christmas with our turkey and dressing. Very simple and quick to make.

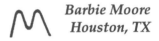

Barbie Moore
Houston, TX

Corn Casserole

2	(16¹/2 ounce each) cans creamed corn	3/4	cup corn meal
			pepper
4	eggs, beaten	2	teaspoons salt
1/2	teaspoon baking powder	1	cup shredded mild Cheddar cheese
oil			

Preheat oven to 350 degrees. Mix corn, eggs, baking powder, oil, corn meal, pepper and salt. Stir in cheese, and pour into greased casserole. Bake at 350 for 45 minutes.

Lorene Graves
Dayton, TX

Green Bean Casserole

2	lbs string beans, fresh or frozen, divided	2	(10¾ ounce each) cans cream of mushroom soup, divided
1	can sliced water chestnuts, drained, divided	2	ounces grated Cheddar or Parmesan cheese, divided
1	can bamboo shoots, drained, divided		salt and pepper
1	can French fried onion rings.		

Layer 1/2 of first 5 ingredients except onion rings in buttered casserole. Salt and pepper. Repeat. Bake 25 minutes at 400 degrees. Remove and sprinkle onion rings over top. Put back in oven for 5 minutes. Serves 8.

Mrs. James B. Rogers (Astrea)
Daughter-in-law to Will Rogers
Dog Iron Ranch
Oologah, OK

Longhorn Bill's Pazole

2	(15 ounce) cans of Pazole (hominy)	2	tablespoons butter, divided
1	(4 ounce) can chopped green chilies, divided		salt and pepper
1/4	cup milk	1/2	cup shredded cheese (Monterey Jack and/or Colby)
1/2	cup sour cream, divided		

Layer 1 can of hominy and 1/2 of chilies in greased 11/2 quarts casserole. Dot with 1/4 cup sour cream and 1 tablespoon butter. Sprinkle lightly with salt and pepper. Repeat with remaining ingredients. Sprinkle with cheese and pour milk over the casserole. Bake uncovered at 350 degrees for 30 minutes. Serves 6.

Great with Longhorn beef or any Mexican dish.

Bill Jowell
Rafter L Longhorns
MidKiff, TX

Spinach Casserole

3	(10 ounce each) pkg chopped frozen spinach.	1	small onion, chopped
1/2	lb sharp cheese, shredded	8	ounces sour cream
1/2	lb Velveeta cheese, shredded		Croutons, optional
			Parmesan cheese, optional

Cook spinach and drain for 1 hour. Mix cheeses, onion and sour cream and then mix with drained spinach. Pour into buttered casserole and top with plain or seasoned croutons and Parmesan cheese. It is good without the topping of cheese and croutons, also. Bake at 350 degrees, covered, for 30 minutes or until heated through.

Spinach haters love this one!

Priscilla Briney
Briney's Lazy 5 B Ranch
Bowie, TX

Sweet Potato Casserole

MIX:

3	cups mashed sweet potatoes	1	teaspoon vanilla
1	cup sugar	1/2	cup melted butter
2	beaten eggs	1/3	cup evaporated milk

TOPPING:

1	cup brown sugar	1	cup chopped pecans
1/2	cup crushed corn flakes	1/3	butter

Bake at 350 degrees for 30 minutes.

Susan Kropp
K 2 Cattle Company
Perry, OK

Sweet Potato Casserole

3	cups cooked, mashed sweet potatoes, canned are okay	1	teaspoon vanilla
		1/2	cup milk
		1/4	cup butter, melted
1	cup sugar	2	eggs, beaten

Combine and mix well. Spoon into greased 2 quarts casserole dish.

TOPPING:

1	cup corn flakes cereal	1/3	cup flour
1	cup flaked coconut	1/3-2/3	cup melted butter
1	cup brown sugar	1	cup pecans

Mix and sprinkle on top. Bake at 375 degrees for approximately 45 minutes or until golden brown on top. Serves 6-8.

Laney Weise
Lazy LYZ Ranch
Voca, TX

Squash Casserole

4	cups cooked, mashed yellow squash	2	eggs
		1	small onion, chopped
1	cup mayonnaise	1	cup grated cheddar cheese
1/2	cup milk	1	cup bread crumbs

Mix squash, mayonnaise, milk, eggs, and onion. Pour into greased casserole dish. Sprinkle cheese and bread crumbs on top. Bake at 350 degrees for 20 minutes. Serve immediately.

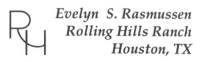

Evelyn S. Rasmussen
Rolling Hills Ranch
Houston, TX

Holiday Sweet Potato Casserole

3	cups sweet potatoes	2	eggs, beaten
1/2	cup sugar	1	teaspoon vanilla
1/2	cup butter	1/3	cup milk

TOPPING:

1/3	cup melted butter	1/2	cup flour
1	cup light brown sugar	1	cup chopped pecans

Mash potatoes. (I use Trappey's Yams - drained). Mix in sugar, butter, eggs, vanilla and milk. Put in 9" baking dish. Mix all topping ingredients. Sprinkle on top of potato mixture. Bake 25 minutes at 350 degrees. Serves 10-12.

A favorite at Thanksgiving and Christmas and delicious with baked ham anytime!

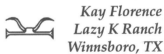

Kay Florence
Lazy K Ranch
Winnsboro, TX

Summer Squash Casserole

3	tablespoons margarine	3	cups cooked squash, mashed
1	minced onion		
1	minced clove garlic	1-2	cups cracker crumbs
1	small green pepper, chopped	1	egg, beaten
4	medium tomatoes, peeled and cut up	1	cup American cheese, grated
			oregano
			salt and pepper

Sauté in margarine the onion, garlic, green pepper, and tomatoes. Mix with squash, cracker crumbs, egg, cheese and seasonings. Bake at 350 degrees for about 30 minutes or until set. A little milk can be added to mixture if it is not moist enough.

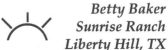

Betty Baker
Sunrise Ranch
Liberty Hill, TX

Longhorn Love

Looking at the Longhorn is a great pastime for me.
There is some of us in all of them or the way we used to be.
The unconditional love displayed in caring for their own.
A love not seen in us much more—something we failed to pass on.
Either for, or against the Longhorn seems to be.
No boggled minds with shades of gray
Like confuses you and me.
Good or bad — black or white is all the horned cow sees.
In a herd or on their own, they'll make it or they'll die
Where today's man can't survive, but worse yet, wouldn't try.
When I look at the Longhorn
The things I guess I see
Are things I've lost in years gone by
The strength bred out of me.

—Calvin Etley
Lazy K Ranch, Winnsboro, Texas

❖

Longhorns in Summer

The land where they stand
is glowing iron bracing itself
for the raised hammer of a blacksmith.
They've stood in Texas sun since the 1700's
drying live hides on racks of great ribs,
grinding grass into cud,
cud into rich blood rising from skulls
to darken thick bases of young horns,
pushing horn tips in slow motion
and twisting them through big Texas sky
like gnarled, timeless branches of mesquite.
They stand in Texas sun
They push their horn tips
They flaunt their sunstruck hides.

—Larry D. Thomas, Houston, Texas

Here's the Beef

"Beef"

"The good taste of beef is locked inside it,
Fix it as you want—in a pan or in a pit,
Pot roast or steak; chili hot or hotter,
It's still that beef flavor that makes your mouth water."

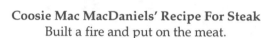

Coosie Mac MacDaniels' Recipe For Steak
Built a fire and put on the meat.

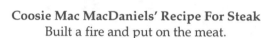

Cooking Beef

There are six basic methods for cooking beef:
1. Roasting
2. Broiling or grilling
3. pan-broiling or griddle-broiling
4. Frying (which includes pan-frying or sautéing,
   deep-fat frying an stir-frying)
5. Braising
6. Cooking in liquid

The method you use depends on the tenderness of the meat, its size and thickness, the recipe, the cooking facilities available, and sometimes on who is coming for dinner.

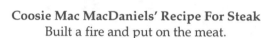

A Well-Seasoned Suggestion

Season meat, if desired, either before or after roasting. Seasoning, rubbed into the surface of a roast before cooking, adds to the aroma during cooking and to the flavor of the surface of the roast. Salt may be used before roasting because it will not penetrate the meat more than one-quarter to one-half an inch, but salt should not be used before cooking when meat is broiled, sautéed, or fried. It draws moisture and dries the meat.

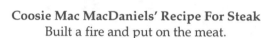

Beef Steak

Those old time Texas cowhands
Missed a heap of stomach aches,
By chompin' down on beef steaks,
Instead of fancy pies and cakes.

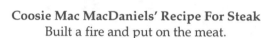

"Red meat is really a treasure trove of nutrients, including protein, iron, vitamin B12, and more. One of the healthiest red meats is Longhorn beef, which is extremely low in fat."

...Nutritionist Cliff Sheats, author of *Lean Bodies, Total Fitness.*

BBQ Brisket

Use about a 5 lb brisket. Place in a shallow baking pan. Coat well with dry seasoning mix on all sides. Let sit on cabinet about 1 hour. Preheat oven to 250-275 degrees. Bake 1 hour. Brush with mop sauce. Cover and bake 4-5 hours, brushing frequently with sauce. After enough pan juices have collected, use them rather than fresh mop sauce.

Slice, serve and enjoy!

Optional: I usually smoke the brisket for about one hour in hickory chip fire.

Dry BBQ Seasoning Mix

1/3	cup salt	1	tablespoon garlic
2	cups chili powder	2 1/2	tablespoons Accent
1 1/2	tablespoons black pepper		

Combine all ingredients and mix well. Store in covered jar.

BBQ Mop Sauce

1	(10 1/2 ounce) can beef consommé	1 1/2	teaspoons dry mustard
1 1/3	cups water	1	teaspoon garlic powder
1/3	cup cider vinegar	1	teaspoon chili powder
1/3	cup vegetable oil	1	teaspoon hot pepper sauce
3/4	cup Worcestershire sauce	1	bay leaf
1/2	teaspoon Accent	1/2	teaspoon paprika

Combine consommé and water in saucepan, bring to a boil. Add remaining ingredients. Let stand overnight at room temperature. Makes about 2 quarts.

Randi Maddox
M F Ranch
Frisco, TX

Brisket

5 lbs brisket	1 cup Worcestershire sauce
salt and pepper	1 cup ketchup
garlic salt	1 cup water
liquid smoke	dash of Tabasco sauce
2-3 large onions	

Lay meat on foil. Season with salt, pepper and garlic salt. Pat liquid smoke all over. Slice large onions on top. Then combine Worcestershire sauce, ketchup, water and Tabasco. Pour over brisket and cook on high for 40 minutes with foil open. Close foil and cook on low (about 275 degrees) until tender. Baste often.

One of the best recipes for brisket I've seen. Everyone loves it!

3h　　*Lorene Graves*
Dayton, TX

Baked Brisket

2 onions, sliced	1/2 teaspoon garlic powder
4-6 lbs boneless Longhorn brisket	1 can Coke at room temperature, use
lemon pepper	Dr. Pepper in a pinch

Place onions in the bottom of a roasting pan. Season brisket and place fat side up on the onions. Brown uncovered at 450 degrees for 30 minutes. Pour Coke over brisket, cover and reduce heat to 325 degrees. Bake 3½ hours or until tender.

Tip: Always slice meat against the grain and it will never be stringy!

This is the most tender brisket you will ever have! It sounds odd, but trust me, this is the best!!

R3　　*Kim Richey*
Triple R Ranch
San Angelo, TX

Crock Pot BBQ

4 to 6 lbs beef (chuck roast, brisket, etc.)	1 teaspoon garlic salt
1 tablespoon onion salt	1/4 cup Liquid Smoke
1 tablespoon celery salt	1/4 cup Worcestershire sauce

Place meat in crockpot. Sprinkle with dry seasonings. Pour Liquid Smoke and Worcestershire sauce over all. Cover and cook overnight on medium.

//A

Barbara Flynn
Double Bar A Ranch
Evant, TX

Pork or Beef BBQ

1   lb live weight hog per person (200 lbs hog for 200 people)

Texas Longhorn beef chuck roasts are the most flavorful cut for BBQ's. Cut roast into 1" thick steaks. Put five steaks per package.

Cut pork into approximately 8 lb packages. Slice meat into 1" wide slices wherever you can. Double wrap in aluminum foil. Add 1/2 cup BBQ sauce, 1/2 of a large onion, chopped, and sprinkle heavily with salt and black pepper.

Use 10 lbs charcoal briquettes per 50 lbs live weight of hog (200 lbs hog = 40 lbs briquettes). Use 40 lbs briquettes for 70-100 lbs of Texas Longhorn beef.

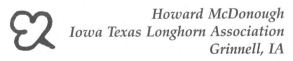

Howard McDonough
Iowa Texas Longhorn Association
Grinnell, IA

Best in the West BBQ Ribs

SPICE MIXTURE:

1/4	cup garlic salt	1/4	cup dry mustard
1	tablespoon ground white pepper	1/4	cup red wine vinegar
		1/4	cup Worcestershire sauce
1/2	cup paprika	1/2	cup beer

Combine all spice mixture ingredients in a medium bowl to form a paste (add more beer if too dry). Rub paste over all surfaces of ribs. Refrigerate until ready to cook. (Can be prepared in advance.)

COOKING LIQUID:

4	quarts beef broth	1 1/2	tablespoons garlic powder
3/4	cup red wine vinegar	1	tablespoon ground ginger
1	tablespoon paprika	1	cup tomato paste
1	tablespoon cayenne pepper	1/4	cup honey
1 1/2	tablespoons Tabasco sauce	1	tablespoon salt
1 1/2	tablespoons ground cumin	4	slabs baby-back ribs (1 1/4 lbs each)

Combine all cooking liquid ingredients in a large pot; stir well. Bring to a simmer over medium heat. Add ribs and simmer until tender, but not falling apart, about 1 hour and 45 minutes. When done, carefully transfer ribs to a cookie sheet. Reserve liquid for future use, if desired.

BARBECUE SAUCE:

1	cup chili sauce	2	tablespoons prepared horseradish
1	cup ketchup		
1/4	cup steak sauce	3	tablespoons dry mustard
1	tablespoon Worcestershire sauce	1	tablespoon Tabasco sauce
		1	tablespoon molasses
1	tablespoon finely pressed garlic	1	tablespoon jalapeño salsa
		1	tablespoon red wine vinegar

Combine BBQ sauce ingredients in a medium bowl. Whisk until well blended. Adjust seasoning to taste. Preheat oven to 400 degrees. Cover a cookie sheet with foil. Place ribs on foil and coat with 2 cups BBQ sauce. Cover entire sheet with foil and bake on center rack of oven for 10 minutes. Unwrap ribs and place on a grill (or under broiler) to char. Serve at once with the remaining BBQ sauce. Serves 4 hungry people.

Jean Smith
Fort Worth, TX

BBQ Cups

1	lb lean ground beef	1½	tablespoons brown sugar
½	cup BBQ sauce	1	can refrigerator biscuits
1	tablespoon minced onion	¾	cup shredded sharp Cheddar cheese

Brown meat. Stir in sauce, onions and brown sugar. Press biscuits into greased muffin cups. Spoon meat mixture into cups. Top with cheese. Bake at 400 degrees for 10 minutes.

R3

Kim Richey
Triple R Ranch
San Angelo, TX

BBQ Sauce

3	(8 ounce) cans tomato sauce	1	teaspoon dry mustard
1	small bottle Worcestershire sauce	2	tablespoons vinegar
		2	tablespoons lemon juice
¼	teaspoon garlic powder	⅛	teaspoon red pepper
½	lb butter	½	teaspoon salt
½	cup brown sugar	½	teaspoon seasoned pepper

Simmer all ingredients for 30 minutes.

Betty Cooper
Lady Cow Puncher Ranch
Leesville, LA

Longhorn Marinade

¾	cup Dale's Seasoning (liquid)	¼	cup meat tenderizer
		1	tablespoon Seasonall
¼	cup Liquid Smoke	⅓-½	cup Italian dressing
½	cup Worcestershire sauce		

Mix in a pint jar. Pour over meat and let marinate for one hour.

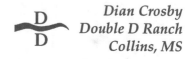

Dian Crosby
Double D Ranch
Collins, MS

Smoked Brisket

MARINADE:

1	small bottle Italian dressing	2	tablespoons Liquid Smoke Tex Joy steak sauce
5-6	shakes Worcestershire sauce		

Mix ingredients together. Pour over brisket and let marinate overnight. Put remainder of the bottle of Liquid Smoke in water pan of electric smoker. Smoke brisket for 6 hours.

Wanda Crosby

Three Day BBQ Brisket

4-7	lbs brisket	4	ounces Worcestershire sauce, divided
2-3	medium onions, chopped or sliced		salt and pepper
3	ounces Liquid Smoke, optional	1	(18 ounce) bottle BBQ sauce
		2	tablespoons flour

First day: Place brisket in large baking pan; cover with onions, Liquid Smoke and 2 ounces Worcestershire sauce. Cover and refrigerate overnight.

Second day: Add remaining Worcestershire sauce, salt and pepper. Cover and bake 5-6 hours at 250 degrees. Refrigerate overnight.

Third day: Remove brisket from pan, trim off excess fat and slice. Discard hardened grease. Combine meat drippings, BBQ sauce and flour in saucepan, and heat until thickened. Return meat to baking pan, cover with sauce and heat at 350 degrees until hot.

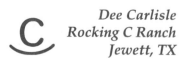

Dee Carlisle
Rocking C Ranch
Jewett, TX

BBQ Sauce

1	small onion, minced	1/2	cup vinegar
1	clove garlic, minced	1/2	cup water
1/2	cup butter	1	tablespoon sugar
1 1/2	teaspoons dry mustard	1	tablespoon Worcestershire
2	tablespoons chili powder		sauce
1	cup ketchup		

Sauté onion and garlic in butter. Add other ingredients and boil for five minutes or until thick. Use sauce for broiling or roasting meat.

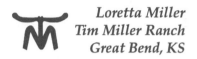

Loretta Miller
Tim Miller Ranch
Great Bend, KS

One Shot Sauce*

1	lb butter	1	tablespoon pepper
1/2	cup finely chopped onion	1 1/2	teaspoons dry mustard
2	cloves garlic, minced	1	teaspoon salt
1/2	cup whiskey	1/4	teaspoon Tabasco
1/4	cup Worcestershire sauce		

Melt butter in a saucepan; add onion and garlic. Cook slowly until onion is soft. Add remaining ingredients and beat to mix. Makes 3 cups.

Goodnight Trail Cook, TX, 1861. Charlie was a cook for the Goodnight Outfit. He was bad to drink whiskey. One day he was drinking when he saw the boss coming and he emptied a glass of whiskey into the steak sauce he was cooking. He didn't have time to make more steak sauce, so he served it with the whiskey in it. All the hands and the boss thought it was good, so he made it this way all the time.

Jean Smith
North Texas Longhorn Breeders Association
Fort Worth, TX

Chili Con Carne

1	lb ground beef	1	(10½ ounce) can tomato
3	tablespoons oil		soup
1	large onion, chopped	⅛	teaspoon black pepper
1	(16 ounce) can kidney	1½	tablespoons chili powder
	beans	1½	teaspoons salt
		⅛	teaspoon paprika

Brown the meat in the oil and sauté the onions, add the rest of the ingredients and simmer. Add water for the desired amount.

Georgia M. Cook
COOK *Cook Longhorn Ranch*
Ree Heights, SD

Chips and Chili Pie

6	cups tortilla chips, divided	1	cup chopped onion
4	cups shredded cheese	1	can (4 ounce) chopped
	(Monterey Jack and		green chiles
	Cheddar), divided		Salsa, chopped tomatoes,
8	cups chili con carne with		shredded lettuce, sour
	beans (homemade chili		cream and sliced black
	is best)		olives for garnish.

Layer 4 cups chips in a 13"×9"×2" pan. Sprinkle with half the cheese and then top with all the chili. Top with onion and chiles. Add a layer of remaining chips and cheese. Bake at 350 degrees for 25-30 minutes or until bubbly. Let stand 5 minutes. Garnish and serve.

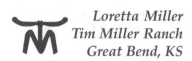

Loretta Miller
Tim Miller Ranch
Great Bend, KS

Miller's Texas-Style Chili

3¹/₂- 4	lbs boneless beef chuck blade steak	1	(12 ounce) can tomato paste
¹/₄	cup salad oil	2	cups water
2	cups chopped onions, divided	¹/₃	cup chili powder
		¹/₄	cup sugar
3	medium green peppers, diced	2	tablespoons salt
		2	teaspoons oregano
4	garlic cloves, crushed	³/₄	teaspoon cracked pepper
2	(28 ounce each) cans tomatoes	¹/₂	cup shredded Monterey Jack cheese for topping

With sharp knife, cut chuck blade steak into ¹/₂" cubes. In 8 quart Dutch oven, over medium-high heat, cook ¹/₃ meat at a time in hot oil until browned on all sides. With slotted spoon, remove meat to bowl and set aside. Reserve ¹/₂ cup onions, cover and set aside. Add remaining onion, green peppers, and garlic to drippings in pan. Over medium heat, cook 10 minutes, stirring occasionally, and adding more oil if necessary. Return meat to Dutch oven. Add tomatoes and their liquid and remaining ingredients, except cheese and reserved onion. Heat to boiling over high heat. Reduce heat to low, cover and simmer 1¹/₂ hours or until meat is fork tender. Stir occasionally. Serves 12.

Spoon chili into large bowl and sprinkle shredded cheese over top. Serve with reserved onions, if you like.

Tim Miller
Miller Ranch
Great Bend, KS

"I remember one time down in the bull pasture, an old bull got down and we knew he was going to die. The other bulls came up, formed a protective circle around him, and stayed with him until he died."

—Maudeen Marks, LH7 Ranch, Barker, Texas

Homemade Chili

3	lbs ground meat	1	(8 ounce) can tomato sauce
2	onions, chopped	1	(10 ounce) can V-8 or
1	bell pepper, chopped		tomato juice
3-4	ribs celery, chopped	1	(10½ ounce) can tomato
4	tablespoons chili powder		soup
salt		1	(16 ounce) can stewed
½	cup brown sugar		tomatoes, optional
6-8	cups water	1	(10 ounce) can Rotel
1	(6 ounce) can tomato paste		tomatoes, optional

Brown meat and add seasonings. Cook 10-15 minutes. Add remaining ingredients and cook over low heat 3-4 hours.

B
C

Bubbles Choate
TLBAA Ambassador
Judsonia, AR

Smith's Wild Card Chili

1	lb chopped Longhorn beef	1	teaspoon chopped hot peppers
½	cup chopped onion	½	teaspoon salt
1	(16 ounce) can red beans	½	teaspoon garlic salt
1	(16 ounce) can refried beans	⅛	teaspoon pepper
1	(8 ounce) can tomato sauce	⅛	teaspoon cayenne
		3	tablespoons chili powder
1	cup water	1	tablespoon molasses

Brown Longhorn beef with onions in Dutch oven; pour off fat. Add remaining ingredients. Cover and simmer 1 hour, stirring occasionally. Serves 6.

J—

Jean Smith
North Texas Longhorn Breeders Association
Fort Worth, TX

White Chili

4	chicken breasts	2	(15¹/₂ ounce each) white hominy
2	(10 ounce) cans chicken broth	1	teaspoon ground cumin
1	clove garlic, minced	¹/₄	teaspoon oregano
1	cup chopped onion	¹/₄	teaspoon basil
2	(11 ounce each) cans shoepeg corn		salt and pepper
2	(4 ounce each) cans chopped green chilies		Restaurant style white corn chips
2	(15¹/₂ ounce each) cans Great Northern beans		Monterey Jack cheese, shredded
			green onions
			sour cream

Cook chicken in broth with garlic and onion until the chicken is no longer pink. Remove chicken and add next 8 ingredients to broth. Chop chicken and put back in broth. Simmer 20-30 minutes. To serve, pour into serving bowls over chips and sprinkle with cheese, green onions, and sour cream, if desired.

Marilyn Wood
WildWood Ranch
Lindale, TX

Chicken Fried Beef Heart

1	(2 lbs) beef heart sliced ¹/₂" thick	seasoned flour
		oil

Coat heart with seasoned flour. Brown in hot oil. Add small amount of hot water and cover tightly. Cook slowly about 2 hours or until tender. Add more water if needed. Serves 6.

Jackie Craver
Cedar Rose Ranch
Timmonsville, SC

Heart

Trim any excess fat and remove large veins. Slice. (It is easier to slice if it is partially frozen.) Dredge in seasoned flour. Brown using bacon grease if you have it. Reduce to a simmer. Add water or a good red wine as it cooks, so that it won't stick. It needs the moist heat. Cook covered for an hour.

 Stan and Priscilla Briney
Briney's Lazy 5B Ranch
Bowie, TX

Baked Heart with Dressing

Trim any excess fat and remove large veins. Slice. Place in bottom of pan sprayed with a non-stick spray. Cover with dressing of your choice — homemade or Stove Top. Bake covered for 1 hour at 350 degrees.

Cold Tongue for Sandwiches

Cover tongue with water. Add salt and pepper, celery, carrot, onion, garlic. Simmer for about 2 hours. Remove tongue from liquid. Let cool so that it can be handled. Skin; discard cooking liquid and skin. Chill tongue and slice and enjoy the sandwiches!

Stan and Priscilla Briney
Briney's Lazy 5B Ranch
Bowie, TX

Broiled Kidneys

6 lamb's or 4 calf's kidneys	butter
cooking oil	lemon
salt and pepper	parsley

Cut the kidneys into halves, remove the white tubes and fat and cover with cold water for 30 minutes. Drain and dry on a piece of cheese cloth. Brush with, or dip into, cooking oil. Broil slowly until brown on both sides. Remove from the broiler and put in pan, sprinkle with salt, pepper and a little melted butter. Cover the pan and set over a slow fire for a few minutes. Serve garnished with slices of lemon and sprigs of parsley.

Fanny R. Russell (Grandmother to Linda Moore)

Fresh Off the Bull Mountain Oysters

First, build a fire in the middle of the working pens. Put in two good branding irons. After the fire is hot and the castrating is done, throw the mountain oysters into the fire. When they pop, they're done. Take the branding iron and drag em' out.

Give the cowboys a break and let them serve themselves.

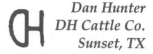

Dan Hunter
DH Cattle Co.
Sunset, TX

Sweetbreads

PREPARING SWEETBREADS:

Sweetbreads should be plunged into cold water as soon as they are received, and soaked for 1 hour, then they should be parboiled in acidulated, salted water (1 teaspoon salt and 1 tablespoon vinegar to 1 quart water) for 20 minutes. After draining, they should be plunged into cold water again to make them firm. The little strings and membranes, which are easily detached after parboiling, should be removed.

Creamed Sweetbreads

2	pairs sweetbreads	2	cups milk
4	tablespoons butter or other fat	1	cup cream or evaporated milk
4	tablespoons flour	1/4	teaspoon paprika

Follow directions for preparing sweetbreads and dice. Make a white sauce with the fat, flour, and milk or cream. Add the sweetbreads and stir steadily until very hot. Season with salt and pepper and minced parsley.

Page Russell (Father to Linda Moore)

Fried Sweetbreads

2 pairs sweetbreads	bread or cracker crumbs
salt and pepper	2 tablespoons flour
1 egg, beaten	1 cup milk

Prepare as directed and cut in even-sized slices. Sprinkle with salt and pepper, dip in beaten egg and crumbs and fry in deep fat. When well browned on both sides, place them on a platter. Make a sauce with 2 tablespoons of the fat in which the sweetbreads were fried, the flour and milk and season with salt and pepper.

Fried sweetbreads are often served with green peas, placed in a mound or a little hill in the center of the platter. Macaroni may be boiled very tender and laid on the platter and the sweetbreads placed in the center, the pipes of the macaroni being laid about them in the form of a nest.

Virginia Beef Tongue

1 beef tongue, fresh	1/4 cup butter or fat
1 cup brown sugar	1 tablespoon whole cloves
1 cup stewed cranberries	1/2 lemon, sliced

Scrub the tongue and simmer it until tender, in water to cover. Remove the skin and trim the root end. Take one cup of the liquor in which the tongue was cooked, and add the brown sugar, stewed cranberries, butter or other fat, cloves, and lemon. Simmer the tongue in this mixture for 15 minutes. Place on a dish with the sauce. Garnish with slices of lemon and sprigs of parsley and serve. Tongue may be jellied and served cold.

Daddy always had a tongue and/or heart in the refrigerator. This seemed very strange to our young friends.

Page Russell (Father to Linda Moore)

Beef Tongue

1-2	(3-3¹/₂ lbs each) beef tongues	4	tablespoons oil
4	cloves garlic	1	large onion, chopped fine

Boil tongue for 10-15 minutes, skin. Cut garlic into slivers and stuff tongue by cutting small slivers in it, evenly spaced. You may want more or less garlic depending on your taste. Brown tongue all over in oil, and remove from pan. Brown onion, then place tongue in pan again and cover. Add water as needed. Cook until tender.

Jackie Craver
Cedar Rose Ranch
Timmonsville, SC

Texas Longhorn Pickled Tongue

1	cup water	1	cup vinegar
crab boil mix		1	cup sugar
1	tongue	1	sliced onion
1	cup beef juice		

Put water and crab boil in a pan, bring to a boil. When in a boil, put tongue in, boil for 45 minutes or until tender. Take out and skin. Slice across the grain and put into dish. Mix the juice, vinegar, sugar, and water in a pan and boil. With meat in dish, put onion on top and pour the juice on top. Put into refrigerator and chill.

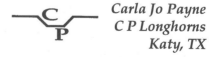

Carla Jo Payne
C P Longhorns
Katy, TX

Beef Jerky

1½ lbs brisket or flank steak
1 tsp Lawry's seasoned salt
1 teaspoon BBQ or hickory smoke salt
1 teaspoon Liquid Smoke
⅓ teaspoon garlic powder
⅓ teaspoon black pepper
1 teaspoon onion powder
¼ cup Worcestershire sauce
¼ cup soy sauce

Slice meat in strips with the grain. Combine all ingredients and marinate overnight. Hang over grills in oven. Don't let strips touch. Heat in 150 degree oven for 8-10 hours or until done. Dehydrators are good, too.

Karen King
S/K Ranch
Granbury, TX

Teri Jerky

⅓ of 1 (20 ounce) bottle Teriyaki sauce
½ of 1 (12 ounce) bottle Teriyaki glaze
4 tablespoons Worcestershire sauce
¼ cup soy sauce
3 tablespoons Liquid Smoke
4 tablespoons pepper potpourri
2 teaspoons garlic powder (fresh crushed may be used)
1 tablespoon lime juice concentrate
1 can beer

Mix all ingredients. Add any cut of beef, raw and thinly sliced. Marinate 24-48 hours. Dry as directed in your dehydrator or oven.

Duke and Linda
Flying Pig Ranch

Beef Jerky

My recipe is simple! Go to your nearest Wal-Mart and buy American Harvest Jerky Cure and Seasonings! The secret to mine, I suppose, is that I use ground round for Longhorn jerky. (My butcher winces when I order the "round" cuts of our Longhorn yearling steers made into ground round instead of roasts and steaks, but I've tried just regular ground Longhorn beef and the round suits me best for flavor and texture.) I use a jerky gun to form the strips. Dry it in the oven on cookie sheets lined with brown parchment paper on very low heat for a few hours. It then has to be refrigerated.

Rebecca Moeller
Cross M Texas Longhorns
Socorro, NM

Beef Jerky

* Cowboys on the trail drives or working large spreads usually only ate two meals a day which was breakfast and supper. They usually supplemented lunch with biscuits or corn cake that the cook had left over and the most popular was beef jerky. Here's a common method of making jerky:

Dry beef; cut in strips as long as you can. It's best to cut against the grain. Cut strips about 1" so the meat will dry quickly. Cut off as much fat as you can. Sprinkle each piece of meat with salt and pepper and a small amount of chili powder. You can hang the strips of meat in a dry place or on wire lines. It's best if you have a full sun, but a shed or smokehouse will do fine. Do not hang where the jerky has a tendency to draw dampness. Just be sure the jerky does not get wet. When the jerky looks and feels like old shoe leather, remove from its drying place and store in flour sacks or large jars. Sometimes it might have a little mold and it's just as good to eat.

*Recipe obtained from Bill, Line Shack, Montana. This recipe has been used for 150 years.

Jean Smith
North Texas Longhorn Breeders Association
Fort Worth, TX

Poor Girls Beef Jerky

Throw ground hamburger into a bowl. Marinate in $1/2$ teaspoon hot red pepper, $1/2$ of a 10 ounce bottle of soy sauce, $1/2$ bottle smoke. Soak 24 hours in refrigerator. Roll out $1/4$" thick. Put on dehydrator with a spatula. Dry.

Judy Walton
Wellfleet, NE

Homemade Summer Sausage

2	lbs extra lean ground chuck	$1/2$	tablespoon Liquid Smoke
2	tablespoons quick curing salt	$1/8$	teaspoon garlic powder
1	cup water	$1/4$	teaspoon onion powder
		$1/2$	teaspoon brown sugar
			pinch of salt

Mix all ingredients in a large bowl. Shape into three 6" log shapes. Wrap in plastic wrap and refrigerate for 24 hours. Unwrap logs and place on broiler pan. Bake at 300 degrees for $1 1/2$ hours. Be sure to turn logs over at least once during baking period to ensure thorough baking.

(This makes great sausage when ground venison is used.)

Karen King
S/K Ranch
Granbury, TX

Dick's Longhorn Meat Loaf

4	lbs Longhorn ground beef	2	tablespoons Worcestershire sauce
1	lb seasoned ground pork		
1	medium onion, diced	1	pint Bloody Mary Mix
1	pint home canned tomatoes	1	pkg (1/4 box) crackers, crushed

Mix beef and pork together well and then add the rest of the ingredients. Leave the crackers until last. (You may need to add more crackers if it is too loose to make into a loaf.) Season with salt and pepper the same as you would any meat loaf. Preferably, use a large covered glass casserole. Shape the meat into a nice loaf and leave space at the sides to remove any excess juices while it is baking. Bake at 325-350 degrees for 2½ hours. Remove cover for the last 15 or 20 minutes so that it will brown nicely.

It's Great!!!

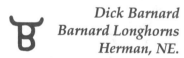

Dick Barnard
Barnard Longhorns
Herman, NE.

Easy Meat Loaf

1½	lbs ground beef	1	teaspoon salt
1/4	cup cracker crumbs	1	tablespoon Worcestershire sauce
2	eggs, beaten		
1/2	cup V-8 juice	1	teaspoon garlic salt
1/4	cup chopped onions		

Combine all ingredients. Mix well and shape into loaf in a shallow baking dish. Bake at 350 degrees for 1 hour. Serves 8.

Lorene Graves
Dayton, TX

Longhorn Meat Loaf Supreme

1½	lbs ground round Longhorn beef	¼	teaspoon basil
¾	cup Italian seasoned breadcrumbs	¼	teaspoon thyme
¼	cup ketchup	¼	teaspoon parsley flakes
1	egg, beaten	¼	teaspoon salt
2	tablespoons grated Parmesan cheese	¼	teaspoon pepper
1	teaspoon Worcestershire sauce	1	small sweet red pepper, cut into thin 2" strips
1	teaspoon dried minced garlic	1	small onion, sliced and separated into rings
		3	fresh mushrooms, sliced
		2	(6"×3") slices Swiss cheese

Combine first 12 ingredients; mix well. Shape mixture into an 18"×12" rectangle on a sheet of wax paper. Layer red pepper, onion, mushrooms, and cheese on rectangle. Leaving a 1" margin around edges. Roll meat mixture up jellyroll fashion, starting at short side and using wax paper to lift and roll. Pinch edges and ends to seal. Place loaf, seam side down, on the rack of a lightly greased broiler pan. Bake at 350 degrees for 40-45 minutes. Serves 6.

Option: Sprinkle with Mozzarella cheese before rolling up jellyroll fashion.

This can be cooked in a Dutch oven at the campfire.

J—   *Jean Smith*
            Fort Worth, TX

❖

"How spoiled can a Longhorn bull get? He would not eat his food unless I fed him in a bowl. Needless to say, the bowl got too small. He finally learned to eat from his pan."

—**Betty Cooper, Lady Cow Puncher Ranch, Leesville, Louisiana**

Meat Loaf Everybody Likes

1	egg	3	tablespoons brown sugar
1/4	cup milk	1	envelope onion soup mix or 1/2 cup chopped onion
2	slices soft bread, crumbled	1	lb Longhorn lean ground beef
1/2	cup ketchup		
2	tablespoons mustard		

Preheat oven to 350 degrees. In a large bowl, beat egg with fork. Add milk and bread crumbs. Mix well. Add all other ingredients, mixing well. Place mixture in a loaf pan. Bake for 45 minutes or until done to your liking.

Lani Fairchild
Fairchild Ranch
Stephenville, TX

Microwave Meat Loaf

1	lb ground beef	1	egg, beaten
1/2	lb lean ground pork	1	cup milk
3/4	cup finely chopped onions	3/4	teaspoon pepper
1/2	cup finely crushed corn flakes	1/8	teaspoon paprika
		2	tablespoons ketchup

Mix all ingredients except ketchup together. Spoon mixture into 9"×5"×3" loaf dish. Pat firmly to remove air. Spread 2 tablespoons ketchup evenly over top of loaf. Cover with plastic wrap, turning back one corner to vent. Microwave at medium high 29-32 minutes, rotating dish 1/4 turn after half of time. Let stand about 10 minutes to firm before serving. Serves 6.

Hint: Place another dish under the loaf dish to catch the spills.

Jan and Howard Sears
J H Ranch
Leon, IA

My Favorite Meat Loaf

2	lbs ground beef	2	teaspoons salt
1/2	cup milk	1/4	teaspoon pepper
2	eggs, beaten	1/4	cup ketchup
3/4	cup applesauce	2	tablespoons brown sugar
1	cup fine bread crumbs	1	teaspoon mustard

Combine first 7 ingredients in large bowl and mix thoroughly. Pat into 2 loaves, put in an 8"×8"×2" pan or broiler pan. Mix the rest of the ingredients and use for topping. Make several holes in top of loaves and spread topping over the meat loaves. Bake in 350 degree oven for 1½ hours.

J-J   *Jody Nelson*
J-J Longhorns
Salix, IA

Stonewall Valley Ranch Meat Loaf

3	lbs Longhorn lean ground meat	6	soda crackers, crumbled
1/2	cup chopped green onions or chives	1¼	cups milk
2	eggs	1	tablespoon soy sauce
2	tablespoons Worcestershire sauce	2	teaspoons salt
1	tablespoon horseradish		ketchup
1	teaspoon pepper	2-3	slices of bacon
1/2	cup cooked celery		green pepper slices
		10	red potatoes, cut in halves
			carrots cut in pieces

Mix first 11 ingredients together in large bowl. Form meat mixture into a loaf in a glass baking dish. Cover loaf with ketchup. Arrange bacon slices and pepper slices on top of loaf. Add potatoes and carrots along side of loaf. Cover with foil. Bake at 325 degrees for 1½-2 hours. Pour off juice after baking. Serves 8-12.

 *The Stonewall Jacksons*
Stonewall Valley Ranch
Austin, TX

Sweet and Sour Meat Loaf

1½	lbs ground beef	2	tablespoons instant
1	cup dry bread crumbs		minced onion
1	teaspoon salt	1	(15 ounce) can tomato
¼	teaspoon pepper		sauce, divided
2	eggs, beaten		

Mix all ingredients with ½ of the tomato sauce. Reserve the rest of the tomato sauce. Form into loaf in 9"×5"×3" pan. Bake 50 minutes in 350 degree oven.

TOPPING:

	reserved tomato sauce	½	cup sugar
2	tablespoons brown sugar	2	teaspoons prepared
2	tablespoons vinegar		mustard

Combine topping ingredients and bring to boil. Pour over meat loaf. Bake an additional 10 minutes.

Walter L. Bishop
Historian of the Old Trail Drivers Association
Litchfield, IL

Nacho-Rice-Meat Roll Up Loaf

4	lbs hamburger	½	can water
1	(10 ounce) can Camp-	1	cup uncooked Minute Rice
	bell's Fiesta Nacho Soup		

Roll out or press hamburger into rectangular shape. (**Hint:** Use waxed paper under hamburger for easier roll up.) Mix soup and water, then add rice. Layer soup-rice mixture evenly over meat, staying approximately 1" away from sides. Roll up and shape meat roll as needed to fit oblong pan. Bake for 1 hour at 350 degrees. Serves 8-10.

Georgia M. Cook
COOK *Cook Longhorn Ranch*
Ree Heights, SD

Santa Fe Meat Loaf

3	lbs lean ground beef	1	teaspoon curry
1/2	cup chopped green onion	1/2	cup chopped green chiles
1/4	cup dried minced onion	1/2	cup celery
1	egg, beaten	3/4	cup chopped mushrooms
2	tablespoons garlic	1	cup crushed saltines
1/3	cup Worcestershire sauce		

Mix together with your hands and make into loaf. Bake at 350 degrees for an hour.

R3
Kim Richey
Triple R Ranch
San Angelo, TX

Southwestern Meat Loaf

1	envelope Lipton Recipe Secrets Onion Soup Mix	1	small green pepper, chopped
2	lbs ground beef	2	eggs, beaten
2	cups crushed tortilla chips	3/4	cup water
1½	cups thawed or drained whole kernel corn	1/2	cup ketchup

Preheat oven to 350 degrees. In a large bowl, combine all ingredients. In 13"×9"×2" baking or roasting pan, shape into loaf. Bake 1 hour or until done. Let stand 10 minutes before serving. Serve with salsa and guacamole, if desired.

Linda Moore
North Texas Longhorn Breeders Association
Gainesville, TX

Upside-Down Meat Loaf

1/2	cup brown sugar	1 1/2	teaspoons salt
1/2	cup ketchup	1/4	teaspoon pepper
1 1/2	lbs ground beef	1	large onion, chopped
3/4	cup milk	1/4	teaspoon ginger
2	eggs, beaten	1	cup crushed cracker crumbs

Butter 9"×5"×3 loaf pan well. Press in brown sugar, then pour on ketchup. Mix remaining ingredients. Shape into loaf and place on top of ketchup. Bake 1 hour. Cool slightly and place platter over meat loaf. Flip over so sauce will run down side of meat loaf.

(It takes a little longer, but is well worth it.)

3h   *Lorene Graves*
Dayton, TX

Longhorn Lean Love Pie

This is called "Love Pie" because we write LOVE in the pie crust and take it to people we want to send "love" to. It's a quick and tasty dish for company or to take to another person's home when they are sick, have a new baby, or for a special occasion.

2	lbs Longhorn lean ground beef	2	(10 3/4 ounce each) cans cream of mushroom soup
1	(20 ounce) pkg frozen mixed vegetables	1	medium onion, chopped
		1	prepared pie crust

Brown ground beef in skillet. Drain meat drippings and pat dry with paper towels. In a large bowl, fold together frozen mixed vegetables, mushroom soup, onion, and beef. Pour into a large glass casserole dish. Top with pie crust and flute as desired. Using a thin, sharp knife, white LOVE in the middle of the pie crust. Bake at 350 degrees until pie crust is golden brown on top. Serves 8.

Donna Jackson
Stonewall Valley Ranch
Austin, TX

Longhorn Bread

1 lb of Longhorn ground meat	1 pkg French loaf frozen bread dough
salt and pepper	your favorite shredded cheese
	sliced canned jalapeño peppers

Brown meat in skillet. Season to taste with salt and pepper. Unroll bread dough flat on cookie sheet. Place ground meat in center of dough length-wise. Sprinkle cheeses onto meat, then jalapeños onto cheese. Pull sides of dough to the center to cover ingredients and turn seam to bottom. Bake at 350 degrees until dough is light brown. Remove from oven and allow to cool. Cut into $1\frac{1}{2}$-2" slices.

Allow enough time after eating to go to pasture and select next steer for more ground meat!

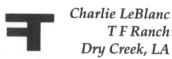

Charlie LeBlanc
T F Ranch
Dry Creek, LA

Meat and Potato Pie

$1\frac{1}{2}$ lbs lean minced pork	1 teaspoon thyme
1 lb minced beef	$\frac{1}{2}$ teaspoon mustard
1 onion, minced	$\frac{1}{2}$ cup water
1 clove garlic, minced	$\frac{1}{2}$ cup beef stock or red wine
1 teaspoon salt	1 9" unbaked double pastry shell
1 teaspoon pepper	
$\frac{1}{2}$ teaspoon cinnamon	3 potatoes, boiled and mashed
$\frac{1}{2}$ teaspoon ground cloves	1 egg, beaten

Combine all ingredients, except the pastry, potatoes, and egg, in a heavy saucepan and cook over low heat until the meat has changed color. Cover and cook for about 45 minutes-1 hour. Stir in the mashed potatoes and allow to cool. Fill the pastry shell with the meat mixture and cover with the other crust. Prick the pastry, glaze with a beaten egg, and bake in a 400 degree oven for 40-45 minutes.

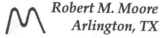

Robert M. Moore
Arlington, TX

Natchitoches Meat Pies

This recipe has been an area favorite for generations. It makes 18 but most of us double the recipe and keep a supply in the freezer for future quick and easy meals.

I usually double this part:

1/2	lb lean ground beef (preferably Longhorn)	3	tablespoons chopped parsley
1 1/2	lbs lean ground pork	6	green onions, chopped
2	large onions, chopped		salt and pepper
2	tablespoons flour		cayenne pepper

Cook meat in deep skillet until well done. Add flour and brown. Add all other ingredients except green onions and cook for 3 minutes. Add green onions and adjust seasonings. Cool to room temperature or refrigerate until you are ready to use.

PASTRY FOR TWICE THE ABOVE RECIPE:

1	cup shortening (or 1/2 cup shortening and 1/2 cup butter)	4	cups self-rising flour
		4	eggs, beaten
			Milk as needed

Cut shortening into flour. Add eggs and enough milk (approximately 3/4 cup) to make a stiff dough. Roll dough very, very thin. Cut in circles about 4" across. Place about one heaping tablespoon of cooled meat mixture on one half of pastry circle. Fold the other half over and seal the edges by brushing around the perimeter with a little milk and crimping the edge with a fork.

Meat pies are traditionally deep fried, but they are almost as good baked. Bake at 350 degrees for about 45 minutes or until golden brown.

C + *Marcia Calhoun*
Calhoun Longhorns
Mansfield, LA

Meat Pies

FILLING:

1	teaspoon shortening	1	clove garlic, minced
1	lb ground meat	1	bell pepper, chopped
1	lb ground pork		salt and pepper
1	bunch green onions, chopped		red pepper
		1	tablespoon flour

Melt shortening in heavy pot. Add meat and seasonings which have been chopped into small pieces. Stir often. When meat is done but not dry, remove from heat. Stir in 1 tablespoon flour.

CRUST:

4	cups flour	1	egg
2	teaspoons salt	½	cup shortening
1	teaspoon baking powder	1	cup milk

Sift dry ingredients together. Cut in shortening. Beat egg and add to milk. Work gradually into dry ingredients until proper consistency to roll. Break into small pieces and roll very thin. Cut into rounds using a saucer as a guide.

To assemble: Place a large tablespoon of prepared meat along the edge and halfway in the center of round dough. Fold the other half over, making edges meet. Firm edges with fork. Drop in deep fat and cook until golden brown. Drain and serve hot. Makes 18.

Gay Melder
Natchitoches, LA

———————— ❖ ————————

"Longhorns are usually gentle and easy to handle. An Oklahoma rancher had a prized red steer, a huge animal with long twisted horns, which he frequently shipped to fairs for exhibition. After the fair, the steer would be shipped back and unloaded at a station some 12 miles from the ranch. Without any driving, he'd walk straight home and the ranch hands would let him in the gate."

Spaghetti Pie

6	ounces spaghetti	1/4	cup chopped green pepper
2	tablespoons butter or margarine	1	(8 ounce) can tomatoes, cut up
1/3	cup grated Parmesan cheese	1	(6 ounce) can tomato paste
2	eggs, well beaten	1	teaspoon sugar
1	cup cottage cheese	1	teaspoon dried oregano, crushed
1	lb ground beef or bulk pork sausage	1/2	teaspoon garlic salt
1/2	cup chopped onion	2	ounces shredded Mozzarella cheese

Cook the spaghetti according to package directions; drain (should have about 3 cups spaghetti). Stir butter or margarine into hot spaghetti. Stir in Parmesan cheese and eggs. Form spaghetti mixture into a "crust" in a buttered 10" pie plate. Spread cottage cheese over bottom of spaghetti crust. In skillet, cook ground beef or pork sausage, onion, and green pepper until vegetables are tender and meat is browned. Drain off excess fat. Stir in tomatoes and their liquid, tomato paste, sugar, oregano and garlic salt; heat through. Turn meat mixture into spaghetti crust. Bake, uncovered, in 350 degree oven for 20 minutes. Sprinkle the Mozzarella cheese on top. Bake 5 minutes longer or until cheese melts. Serves 6.

Susan Kropp
K 2 Cattle Company
Perry, OK

"Old Blue"

"The late Charles H. Goodnight, noted Texas ranchman, conducted several large trail drives from his Texas ranches to Kansas shipping points. He had a blue roan steer known as "Old Blue" which would lead the herds and always keep this position at the "point" of the drive. When the steers were sold at the railhead, "Old Blue" would be turned in with the saddlehorses and go back to Texas where he would wait to lead the next herd up the trail. He made more than a half dozen trips from Texas to Kansas with the Goodnight herds."

Corn Pone Pie

1	lb lean ground beef	1	(15 ounce) can of tomatoes
1	small onion, chopped	1/2	cup water
garlic salt to taste		1	(16 ounce) can pinto beans
3	teaspoons chili powder	1/2	recipe of cornbread
1	teaspoon Worcestershire sauce		

Brown meat with onions, add seasonings. Add tomatoes and water, and simmer for 10 minutes. Add beans and heat (let it bubble a little). Pour corn bread mixture (mixed up with egg, milk, etc.) on top and bake at 400 degrees for 20-25 minutes.

I use a cast iron skillet for the whole operation. It is a good "all-in-one" meal.

R3   *Kim Richey*
Triple R Ranch
San Angelo, TX

Italian Longhorn Spaghetti Sauce

2-3	lbs Longhorn lean ground beef	1	(8 ounce) pkg fresh mushrooms, chopped
Worcestershire sauce		1	large bell pepper, chopped
oregano		1	large onion, chopped
2	bay leaves	1	(6 ounce) can tomato paste
lemon pepper		1	(8 ounce) can tomato sauce
pepper		1	(15 ounce) can diced tomatoes
salt			
minced garlic			

Brown meat (drain fat if you're using OTHER BEEF). Cover meat with Worcestershire sauce, then spices and minced garlic. Add chopped mushrooms, bell peppers and onions. Add tomato paste, tomato sauce and diced tomatoes. Cook on simmer until well mixed.

Kathy Stovall
3 Sons Cattle
Petrolia, TX

Piquant Cocktail Meatballs

2	lbs lean ground beef	1/4	teaspoon pepper
1	cup corn flakes crumbs	1/2	teaspoon garlic powder
1/3	cup dried parsley flakes	1	can jellied cranberry sauce
2	eggs	1	(12 ounce) bottle chili
1/3	cup ketchup		sauce
2	tablespoons soy sauce	2	tablespoons firmly packed
2	tablespoons dried minced		brown sugar
	onions	1	teaspoon lemon juice

Heat oven to 350 degrees. In a large bowl, combine beef, corn flake crumbs, parsley, eggs, ketchup, soy sauce, onions, pepper and garlic powder. Blend well. Form mixture into small meat balls (about the size of a walnut). Arrange meat balls in a 15"×10"×2" pan.

In medium sized saucepan, combine cranberry sauce, chili sauce, brown sugar and lemon juice. Cook over moderate heat, stirring occasionally, until mixture is smooth and cranberry sauce is melted. Pour over meatballs. Bake uncovered 30 minutes. Serve in a chafing dish with toothpicks. Can be made the day before and I think they are better if you do!

This was my Grandma's recipe and was always prepared for Christmas Eve. As a little girl, I remember thinking how grown up I was eating "cocktail meatballs" with the grown-ups before supper.

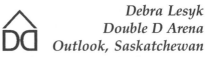

Debra Lesyk
Double D Arena
Outlook, Saskatchewan

Longhorn Mean and Lean Ground Meat and Calavazos

1	large onion, chopped	3-4	medium squash, sliced
2	tablespoons butter	1/4	cup picante sauce
2	cloves garlic, chopped		salt and pepper
2	lbs ground Longhorn meat		

Sauté onion in butter in skillet. Add garlic and ground meat. When meat is brown, put squash on top of meat. Add picante sauce and salt and pepper. Simmer until the squash is done.

Norma Holmes
H and H Longhorns
Robstown, TX

Italian Meatballs

1	lb Longhorn lean ground beef	1	(2 ounce) can sliced black olives
	Italian seasoning	1	small pkg shredded mozzarella cheese
	garlic powder		
	salt and pepper	4	servings of prepared white rice.
1	tablespoon dried onion		
1	jar Ragu Chunky Garden Style spaghetti sauce		

Crumble ground beef into bowl and sprinkle lightly with seasonings and dried onion; mix well. Form meat mixture into half-dollar size balls. Flatten meatballs slightly and brown in skillet. After meatballs are done, lower heat and put in jar of spaghetti sauce, olives and cheese. Cover and simmer on low heat for 10 minutes or until sauce is heated and cheese melts. Serve on rice.

Lani Fairchild
Fairchild Ranch
Stephenville, TX

Mimmy's Meatballs

SAUCE:

3/4 cup chopped onion
3-4 cloves garlic, finely
       chopped
small amount of margarine
6   (48 ounce each) tomato
       sauce
1   tablespoon brown sugar

1   teaspoon Italian seasoning
1/2 teaspoon comino seed
1 1/2 teaspoons black pepper
1/3 cup ketchup
1/4 teaspoon celery seed
1/4 teaspoon salt

MEATBALLS:

2   lbs lean ground beef
1   cup fine bread crumbs
4   cloves garlic, finely
       chopped

2   eggs, beaten
milk, as needed to combine
       mixture

Sauté onion and garlic in margarine. Add the tomato sauce and seasonings and heat to boiling, then turn down to simmer. Cook about 30 minutes. Mix meatballs and shape into about 2" diameter meatballs. Drop into hot sauce and cook for at least 1 hour.

Crockpot directions: Make sauce and heat on high while making meatballs. Drop in meatballs and turn to low and cook for 8 hours.

Lean Longhorn ground beef is great in this recipe. This is my son's favorite dish — nice to have in the crockpot after working with cows all day!

Judy Coats
JHC Longhorns
Heart of Texas Longhorn Association
Hutto, TX

Grama's Swedish Meatballs

1	lb Longhorn ground beef	1/4	teaspoon ground cloves
1	teaspoon salt	1/4	teaspoon nutmeg
1/2	teaspoon pepper	3	slices of bread soaked
1	onion, finely chopped		in milk
1/4	teaspoon allspice	1	egg, beaten

Combine all ingredients and make into small (bite-sized) balls. Brown and cook in skillet. Make gravy from drippings or serve with a cream sauce or BBQ sauce. Also can be served alone.

This was my Grama's recipe. It became my Mom's recipe and she is a grama now, so I guess it's still Grama's Swedish Meatballs.

Lyn Lewis
Flying Diamond Ranch
Ordway, CO

Meatballs

1	lb lean ground meat	1	carrot, grated
	salt and pepper	1	(10 1/2) can cream of celery
1	onion, grated		soup
1	potato, grated	1/2	can water

Mix the meat, salt, pepper and grated vegetables together in a bowl. Shape mixture into small balls and put into a baking dish. Mix soup and water. Pour over the meatballs. Cover and bake 35-40 minutes at 325 degrees.

A fast, easy main dish. Great use of Longhorn lean beef!

Judy Coats
JHC Longhorns
Heart of Texas Longhorn Association
Hutto, TX

Cowboy Sloppy Jo's

3	lbs hamburger	3	tablespoons vinegar
1	green pepper, chopped	1	small bottle ketchup
1	large onion, chopped	1	(12 ounce) bottle chili sauce
3	tablespoons sugar	3	teaspoons salt
3	tablespoons mustard		chili powder to taste

Brown hamburger. Add rest of ingredients and simmer 30 minutes. Serve on buns.

Loretta Miller
Tim Miller Ranch
Great Bend, Kansas

Spinach Fandango
(or How to get your family
to eat Spinach!)

2	lbs ground lean beef	1	(10½ ounce) can cream of
1	cup sliced mushrooms		celery soup
1	teaspoon oregano	2	cups sour cream or plain
	salt and pepper		yogurt
	garlic to taste		Mozzarella cheese, shredded
2	(10 ounce each) pkg		
	frozen spinach		

Brown beef with mushrooms, oregano, salt, pepper and garlic. Add spinach. Cook only until spinach is thawed. Stir in soup and sour cream (or yogurt). Pour into casserole dish and top with shredded cheese. Bake at 350 degrees for 30 minutes until cheese is golden and bubbly.

Debra Lesyk
Double D Arena
Outlook, Saskatchewan

Canned Texas Longhorn Beef

When you have your Longhorn butchered, have 25-50 lbs chunked into 1" cubes. Pack those beef chunks in quart jars. Do not add any water in the jars as the beef will make its own lean broth. Do add 1 teaspoon salt to each jar. Clean and wipe top of jars, then apply lids and rings. Put jars in pressure cooker for 90 minutes.

The end product can be eaten right out of the jar or with BBQ sauce for sand-wiches, stroganoff, stews, noodles and gravy, or whatever you want to do with it. It is especially good in Longhorn chili.

Jean Richardson
G-J Longhorns
St. Clair, MO
Show-Me Texas Longhorn Association

Peggy Smith's Texas Hash

1	large onion, chopped	1½	teaspoons salt
1	green pepper, chopped	¼	teaspoon pepper
3	tablespoons shortening	1	teaspoon chili powder
1	lb Longhorn ground beef	½	cup uncooked rice
1	(16 ounce) can tomatoes		

Fry onions and green pepper in shortening until yellow. Add meat and heat until it falls to pieces. Put in baking dish and add rest of ingredients. Bake about 45 minutes at 375 degrees or until done. (Keep covered while cooking.) Serves 4.

Peggy is one of my good friends and a very good cook.

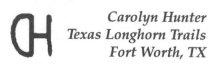

Carolyn Hunter
Texas Longhorn Trails
Fort Worth, TX

Carne Guisada

2	tablespoons oil	2	cups water or beef stock
2	lbs chuck or arm roast, cut into bite size pieces	1	tablespoon ketchup
2	tablespoons flour	2	teaspoons ground cumin
3	ribs of celery, chopped	1	teaspoon whole cumin seeds
1	medium onion, chopped	1/2	teaspoon chili powder
2	(or more) fresh jalapeños, chopped		

Heat oil in cast iron skillet, dust meat cubes with flour and brown. Add remaining ingredients and bring mixture to simmer. Cover skillet and simmer for several hours until meat is tender (begins to fall apart) and sauce is thick. Serve with soft flour tortillas.

Leslie P. Hathorn
Buzzard's Paradise
Jacksboro, TX

Grazeland Ranch Roast

3	lbs Texas Longhorn roast	2	tablespoons Louisiana type hot sauce
1	tablespoon black or lemon pepper	3	tablespoons Worcestershire sauce
1	teaspoon garlic powder	2	large potatoes, peeled and quartered
1	envelope dry onion soup mix	1	sweet onion, quartered
	juice of 1 lemon	3	carrots, cut in chunks

Place all ingredients in a crock pot, except potatoes, onion, and carrots. Cook on low heat overnight. Add potatoes, onions and carrots. Cook 2 more hours.

Bill and Tracey Hardin
Grazeland Ranch
McKinney, TX

Lemon Marinated Roast

3-4	lbs Longhorn beef, cut 1½" thick (chuck roast, top round or "London Broil"; eye of round also works, but leave it whole)	1	tablespoon lemon pepper
		1	tablespoon sugar
		1	teaspoon Worcestershire sauce
		1	teaspoon prepared mustard
½	cup lemon juice	¼	cup diced yellow onion or sliced green onions
⅓	cup oil		

Combine ingredients and marinate roast for several hours or overnight. Remove roast from marinade and grill over medium-hot coals for 10-15 minutes on each side for medium-rare. Boil reserved marinade for 2-3 minutes. Carve roast across grain into ½" slices, spoon marinade over.

Leslie P. Hathorn
Buzzard's Paradise
Jacksboro, TX

Dutch Oven Pot Roast

Put seasoning on the roast and then brown over hot coals. Be sure and brown meat on all sides. Put the roast in a Dutch oven. Add enough water to cover at least ³⁄₄ the height of the meat. Cut 2-3 onions into rings and place them on top and around the roast. Cut 4-5 carrots into small pieces and add to the meat and onions. Cook 3 hours with coals on top and bottom of Dutch oven. After 3 hours add chunks of potato and cook 1 more hour.

Options: Use beer instead of water and add any other vegetables you like.

J—
Jean Smith
Nance Ranch
Haslet, TX

Peppered Rib Roast

5-6 lbs unsliced ribeye	**coarse salt (margarita salt)**
pepper potpourri	**finely chopped garlic**

Liberally coat roast with pepper, salt and garlic. Place on rack above drip pan. Put meat thermometer in thickest area. Begin roasting in preheated 500 degree oven for 30 minutes, then reduce heat to 375 degrees and cook until thermometer reaches 140 degrees for rare, 160 for medium, and 170 for well done. (Estimate 15-20 minutes per pound.) Allow to rest 30 minutes after removing from oven. Slice to desired thickness. Serve with peppercorn sauce (below). Serves 6-8.

PEPPERCORN SAUCE:

1	teaspoon Worcestershire sauce	1/2	teaspoon pepper potpourri
1	teaspoon soy sauce	1/2	cup cold water
1	heaping tablespoon beef bouillon	2	tablespoons cornstarch
		1-2	tablespoons red wine (optional)
1 1/2	cups water	1/4	teaspoon garlic powder

In medium saucepan, combine first 6 ingredients. Simmer over low heat 5-15 minutes, depending on how hungry you are. Combine cold water and cornstarch. Add to saucepan slowly until desired thickness is reached. Serve over any beef, including beefburgers.

Duke and Linda
Flying Pig Ranch

---------------- ❖ ----------------

"Hap McGee of California had a large fleet of trucks. He came up with the idea of using the old truck tires for his fences. That worked for awhile until the tires filled with blowing sand and dust. Then his Longhorn cattle just walked over the fences."

—Linda Moore, Gainesville, Texas

Smoked Lean Longhorn Roast

2-4 lbs rump or sirloin tip roast from a Texas Longhorn (other cuts will also work, but won't be as tender)

Moore's or Dale's marinade or soy sauce

1-2 lbs thick cut bacon

handful of toothpicks

water smoker with hickory, pecan or oak wood (charcoal will do, but it's not hot enough)

1 (10½ ounce) can golden mushroom soup, optional

Marinate meat in marinade or soy sauce 6 -24 hours in the refrigerator. Place water pan over fire in smoker after starter fluid has burned off. Some flame is okay, smoker lid will smother later.

Wrap entire roast with bacon, attaching with toothpicks. Place on rack just above water and cover. Cook 30-45 minutes per pound, checking water <u>only once</u> after 2 hours. Add more water if needed. Don't keep opening lid to check or 1 hour per opening might need to be added to cooking time. Baste with leftover marinade at water refilling time. Cover and smoke. Meat will be done as bacon firms, not crisps. Remove bacon and serve to one side. Slice beef and serve.

Place leftovers in casserole dish, pour over a can of golden mushroom soup. Cover and refrigerate for a great microwaveable meal later.

Remember, smoked meat is red and juicy. It's probably more done than you think. It can be baked or microwaved after slicing to your liking.

Karl Kressman
Bascom, FL

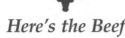
Longhorn Burgers on the Grill

As far as I'm concerned, the entire Longhorn carcass could be made into hamburger. I love Longhorn burgers cooked on the grill. Because the hamburger is so lean, the patties must be more than half cooked before I flip them over. The other side basically gets charred. This works out to "medium" and still juicy and delicious. I invite people for grilled Longhorn burgers all the time, then serve the burgers on plates WITHOUT buns and condiments! I won't let anyone spoil the taste with all that other stuff. (Salads, etc. are allowed on the plate with the beef patties, but nothing ON the burger.) My guests think me daft until they taste the Longhorn and then understand why I insist they not surround it with that ucky bread or that nasty yellow goopy stuff!

Rebecca Moeller
Cross M Texas Longhorns
Socorro, NM

Tastee Sandwich

1	heaping teaspoon Accent	3	heaping teaspoon cream style horseradish
5	lbs ground beef (85-90% lean)	3	teaspoons Worcestershire sauce
8	ounces measuring cup	3	teaspoons salt
4	ounces ketchup	1/4	teaspoon pepper
3	heaping tsp mustard		

Add Accent to the hamburger. All the spices should fill the 8 ounce measuring cup. Mix thoroughly until all ingredients are completely mixed. Put hamburger in kettle and add 8 ounce cup of spices. Fill cup with warm water (rinsing around to get all the seasonings out) and pour over meat. Add Accent directly onto meat. Take a wooden spoon and stir all the ingredients in kettle. Put the kettle on the stove over low heat and stir constantly with wooden spoon for about 15 minutes or until meat is broken apart finely. Then increase the heat by 1/4 until it comes to a boil. Let simmer about 25 minutes. Stir with wooden spoon every few minutes.

Tavern Sandwiches

2	lbs hamburger	1/4	cup ketchup
1	medium onion, chopped	1	teaspoon chili powder
1	(10 1/2 ounce) can tomato soup		pepper to taste
1	teaspoon salt	1/2	teaspoon Worcestershire sauce

Brown meat and onion. Add other ingredients and simmer. Water can be added if this Sloppy Joe sandwich spread becomes dry. Serves 4.

Great for family gatherings. Can be left in a crock pot for multiple servings.

COOK *Georgia M. Cook*
Cook Longhorn Ranch
Ree Heights, SD

Pretzel Burgers

3	lbs ground beef	2	tablespoons chopped onion
1/4	teaspoon salt	2	tablespoons chopped green pepper
1/2	cup very thin pretzel crumbs	1	egg, beaten
1/3	cup Italian dressing	1/8	teaspoon pepper

Combine all ingredients. Shape into patties. Grill on medium flame setting of gas grill about 5 minutes on each side or until they reach desired doneness.

Helpful Hint: *To prevent your hamburger patties from shrinking and drying out while grilling, simply grate a potato up real fine and add to the mix when seasoning your hamburger. It has no taste and your burgers stay moist, go farther, and won't shrink as bad.*

S *David and Patricia Smith*
The Running S Ranch
Frost, TX

Hamburger Foldovers

1-2 lbs hamburger	1 can Pillsbury Big Country
1/4 cup onion, chopped	Buttermilk biscuits
1/4-1/2 cup BBQ sauce	1 to 2 cups Colby or Longhorn cheese, grated

Brown hamburger and onions in skillet. Mix in BBQ sauce. Pat out biscuits into rectangles. In center, put a spoonful each of meat mixture and grated cheese. Fold over biscuits and seal closed. Bake at 350 degrees until biscuits are done - about 20 minutes.

Karen King
S/K Ranch
Granbury, TX

Tracey's Chicken Fried Steak

6 ribeye or strip Longhorn steaks (1/4-1/2" thick - tenderize with meat hammer)	1 1/2 cups milk
	2 cups flour
	1 tablespoon cayenne pepper
canola oil	2 teaspoons black pepper
2 eggs, beaten	4 ounces finely crushed saltine crackers

Tenderize steaks. Heat canola oil in Teflon skillet on medium. Mix eggs and milk in medium bowl. Place flour, cayenne and black pepper in a pile on wax paper and mix together. In a separate pile, place cracker crumbs. Cover steaks in flour mixture, then dip in egg mixture. Remove and cover with cracker crumbs. Fry on medium until meat is thoroughly cooked (approximately 15 minutes per steak). Remove from heat and cover with cream gravy.

Tracey Hardin
Grazeland Ranch
McKinney, TX

Chicken Fried Steak

2 lbs round steak, tenderized	pepper
seasoned salt	2 eggs, beaten
garlic salt	1/2 cup milk
	flour
	oil

Trim all fat and gristle from steak. Cut in small pieces. Season with seasoned salt, garlic salt and pepper on both sides. Beat eggs and milk together. Dip steak into flour, then eggs, then flour again. Heat oil and turn heat to low. Cook 15 minutes on first side until brown. Turn without puncturing crust. Cook 10 minutes on second side. Drain on paper towel. Keep warm while making gravy.

A hit with everyone, anytime.

3h
*Lorene Graves
Dayton, TX*

Beef Burgundy

2 1/2- 3 lbs round steak or extra good stew meat, cut into 1" cubes	1/2 teaspoon salt
	dash of pepper
flour	2 cups beef consommé
4 tablespoons oil	1/2 teaspoon dill weed
2 medium onions, chopped	1 cup Burgundy
1 clove garlic, chopped	1 cup mushrooms

Flour meat and brown well. Add onions, garlic, salt and pepper. Add rest of ingredients. Cook until tender (1 1/2 hours). Can be made ahead of time, and even frozen.

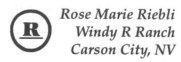

*Rose Marie Riebli
Windy R Ranch
Carson City, NV*

French Broil

1-2	flank steaks	1	clove garlic, minced
1/2	cup oil	1 1/2	teaspoons salt
1/2	cup Burgundy wine	5	drops Tabasco
2	tablespoons minced onion		

Score both sides of the steak in a diamond pattern about 1/8" deep. Combine all ingredients in a large, shallow baking dish. Coat steaks with marinade and turn four times during a 2 hour period of marinating in the refrigerator. Remove steak from the marinade and broil for 7 minutes on each side. To serve, cut steak diagonally into thin slices.

Dee Carlisle
Rocking C Ranch
Jewett, TX

Beef Scallopini

1	cup sliced mushrooms	1/2	cup chopped onions
	butter	1/2	cup chopped celery
1	lb round steak	1	cup beef broth
	flour	2	tablespoons parsley
	salt and pepper	2	cloves garlic
1/2	cup oil	1	cup dry Marsala wine

Brown mushrooms in small amount of butter and set aside. Pound meat until very thin and flat. Cut into small pieces. Coat with flour seasoned with salt and pepper, then fry in preheated oil, (a few pieces at a time) until brown. Remove cooked pieces to bowl. Pour out excess oil and brown onions and celery in same pan. Add beef broth, parsley, garlic and simmer 10-15 minutes. Add wine and simmer 10-15 minutes. Add meat and mushrooms, and heat through - about 10 minutes. Serve with pasta. Serves 4

Ruth Hoffman
Seven T Ranch
Metairie, LA

Sam's Steak Marinade

3	tablespoons Worcestershire sauce
3	tablespoons olive oil
3	tablespoons Tabasco sauce

lemon juice
Kosher salt
cracked black pepper

Mix first 3 ingredients in bowl. Dredge steaks in bowl. Put steaks on platter and sprinkle with Kosher salt and cracked black pepper to taste. Let steaks marinate anywhere from 10 minutes to 14 days. (Refrigerate if marinating for long period.)

2h

Sam Wirick
Dayton, Ohio

Osso Bucco (Braised Veal Shanks)

Note: I use Longhorn beef shanks, cut 3" long. This makes a nice presentation.

1	cup hot olive oil	2	(16 ounce) cans peeled tomatoes, with liquid
4	large soup shanks		
flour		1	tablespoon ketchup
1	large onion, thinly sliced	2	tablespoons chopped parsley
3	bay leaves		
2	carrots, sliced	3	cloves crushed garlic
1	celery ribs, sliced	1	tablespoon grated lemon zest
1/2	cup dry white wine (or beef broth)		
		1/2	teaspoon each salt and pepper

In a large pot, heat oil, dredge shanks in flour and brown. Remove shanks from pot and set aside. Add onion, bay leaves, carrots, celery and wine. Simmer 5 minutes or until most of the liquid has evaporated. Add browned shanks, tomatoes and ketchup. Cover and simmer 1 1/2 hours. Stir in parsley, garlic, salt and pepper. Simmer 5 minutes. Serve over rice or pasta noodles.

Sue Brown
Greene County Cattle Company
Lucedale, MS
Dixie Texas Longhorn Association

Longhorn Beef Bourguignon

2	lbs cubed steak	2	cups red Burgundy
1/2	teaspoon salt	2	tablespoons Brandy
1/2	teaspoon pepper	2-3	cups chopped onion
dash of thyme		butter	
1	bunch fresh parsley, chopped	1/4	lb sliced mushrooms
1/2	bay leaf	2	cups beef broth
3	tablespoons olive oil	2	cloves garlic, mashed

Place meat and the next 8 ingredients in a bowl and marinate for 4 hours in refrigerator. Strain and dry meat, reserving marinade. Sauté onions in butter until golden, then strain onions from skillet. Fry mushrooms in skillet until golden, then return onions to pan. In another pan, sauté meat until brown. Add boiling beef broth to the meat. Strain marinade and add to meat with the garlic. Cook on low until meat is tender. Add mushrooms and onions to the meat and cook, covered, another 30 minutes. Serves 6-8.

"People who fly into a rage always make a bad landing." — Will Rogers

Vicki Helms
Belleville, IL
Heartland Texas Longhorn Breeders Association

Italian Beef in the Crockpot

5	lbs roast, cut up	1	teaspoon garlic salt
3	beef bouillon cubes	1/2	cup Italian dressing

Place roast, bouillon cubes, garlic salt and dressing in crockpot. Add enough water to cover beef. Cook on low about 7 hours.

Put it in a pot; go to work and forget it! Serve hot garlic bread and salad or serve over rice. Great for sandwiches.

3h
Lorene Graves
Dayton, TX

Braised Steak and Onions

1½   lbs beef round steak,   salt and pepper
     cut ¼" thick
flour
2   tablespoons cooking oil

salt and pepper
2   small onions, chopped
½   cup beef broth

Cut meat into serving-size portions. Coat with flour. In skillet, brown meat in hot oil. Remove meat to shallow baking dish. Season meat with salt and pepper. Add onions to the skillet. Cook slowly, over medium-low heat, stirring occasionally, until onions are tender and well-browned. Place onions atop meat. Add broth to skillet, stirring to loosen crusty bits in pan. Pour over meat and onions. Cover and bake at 325 degrees for 1 to 1¼ hours.

S/K
Karen King
S/K Ranch
Granburry, TX

Steak Diane

4   sirloin strip steaks
salt
pepper
dry mustard
4   tablespoons butter

3   tablespoons lemon juice
1   teaspoon snipped chives
1   teaspoon Worcestershire
     sauce

Pound steak to ⅓" thickness. Sprinkle one side with salt, pepper and dry mustard and pound into meat. Repeat on other side. Melt butter in skillet. Add meat. Cook 2 minutes on each side. Place on hot platter. To skillet, add lemon juice, chives and Worcestershire sauce. Bring to a boil. Pour over meat.

Dee Carlisle
Rocking C Ranch
Jewett, TX

Beef Tips with Rice

4	slices bacon, fried	2	lbs beef tips
flour		2	cups beef bouillon
2	teaspoons salt	1	cup milk
1	teaspoon pepper		hot cooked rice

Fry bacon until crisp and drain, reserving drippings. Set both aside. Combine flour, salt, and pepper. Dredge beef tips in mixture. Brown in reserved bacon drippings in a heavy skillet. Add bouillon. Cover and simmer 1 hour or until beef is very tender. Add milk, cover, and simmer 30 minutes. Serve over rice. Serves 7.

Prepare before church, then reheat for lunch. Serve with green salad and you've got it made.

3h   *Lorene Graves*
Dayton, TX

Caldillo

The shearing crews used to come out and camp by the creek bed during shearing season. Robert's grandfather, who loved Mexican food, would often go down there to eat with them. He described this recipe to the family and this is Robert's grandmother's rendition from 1944.

Cut 1 large round steak in small cubes. Cut 2 large potatoes and a large onion in small cubes. Fry the potatoes and onion in 2 tablespoons bacon grease or oil. When slightly browned, add the meat. Cook until meat turns gray, stirring alot. Add 2 tablespoons flour. Stir well and then add chopped tomatoes and some hot peppers (we use *Rotel*). Add enough water to barely cover and stir often to keep from sticking. Cook over low heat for about 3 hours.

You want to have about as much potatoes as meat. This is good with a pot of pinto beans, crackers or tortillas and vegetable salad. Use a heavy pot. It cooks more slowly, and doesn't stick as badly.

R3   *Kim Richey*
Triple R Ranch
San Angelo, TX

Swiss Steak

10-12 pieces of round steak   **oil**

Pound round steak with flour until fibers are broken down. Brown steak in oil on both sides. Cover with sauce (*see recipe below*) and bake in slow oven for at least 2 hours, adding additional tomato juice if needed. Turn meat occasionally.

SAUCE:

1 **(10 ounce) can tomato puree**	1 **tablespoon lemon juice**
1/2 **cup ketchup**	1 **teaspoon celery seed or 1 cup chopped celery**
1 **tablespoon vinegar**	3 **tablespoon brown sugar**
1 **tablespoon dry mustard**	1-2 **cups tomato juice**
1/4 **cup water**	2 **teaspoons salt**
1 **tablespoon Worcestershire sauce**	1/4 **teaspoon pepper**
1 **onion, chopped**	1 **(10 1/2 ounce) can tomato soup**

Combine all ingredients.

La Nelle Staggs
Broken S Ranch
Arkansas Texas Longhorn Association
Washington, AR

Easy Smothered Steak

1 **large round steak, cut up**	1 **envelope dry onion soup mix**
1 **(10 3/4) can cream of mushroom soup**	

Line a 13"×9"×2" baking pan with heavy-duty foil, allowing excess foil to stand up around edges. Place steak on foil. Spread mushroom soup over steak, and sprinkle with dry soup. Seal foil tightly. Bake at 325 degrees for 1 hour. Serves 5.

Lorene Graves
Dayton, TX

D Bar D Swiss Steak

2	lbs round steak	1	medium onion, chopped
flour		1	teaspoon oregano
salt and pepper		2	tablespoons chopped
2	tablespoons oil		parsley
3	ribs celery, chopped	1	(8 ounce) can tomato sauce
2	cloves garlic, minced	1	cup red wine
1	small green pepper, cut into slices	1	can ripe olives

Cut steak into serving-size pieces. Pound with flour that is seasoned with salt and pepper. Brown in oil in Dutch oven, seasoning to taste. Remove meat. Add celery, garlic, green pepper, onion, oregano, and parsley. Cook until lightly browned. Return the meat to the Dutch oven and add the tomato sauce and wine. Simmer about 1½ hours or until tender when pierced with fork. Add olives and let cook an additional 10 minutes. Serve with rice or mashed potatoes.

$$\frac{D}{D}$$

Carol Davis
D Bar D Longhorns
Jackson, CA

Emil Marks Steak

My father never would touch as much as a toaster inside the house, but outside he could cook anything. His steaks were absolutely delicious, tender, cooked through, with no extra grease.

Get a Dutch oven. Use steak at least 2-3" thick, cut almost to fit the Dutch oven. Put salt in the bottom of the Dutch oven so that there is salt all over the bottom. Heat the salt. Just before it scorches, throw in the meat. Put the lid on the Dutch oven, and place it over the camp coals. Check in about 15 minutes. When it is cooked half way through on one side, flop it over. Cook. There will be no grease in there. Salt acts as a heat conductor and will cook that steak all the way through and retain all the juices.

LH7

Maudeen Marks
LH7 Ranch
Barker and Bandera, TX

Texas Longhorn Lean Ranchero

Voted most favorite at the Beef Industry Council's "Best of Beef Cookoff"

2 lbs Texas Longhorn lean round steak	2 (15 ounce each) cans Mexican-style stewed tomatoes
flour	
salt and pepper	2 (8 ounce each) cans tomato sauce
paprika	
2 tablespoons canola oil	1 tablespoon chili powder
1 cup chopped onions	1 cup water
1/2 cup chopped bell peppers	Longhorn Cheddar cheese, shredded
	fresh cilantro

Cut Longhorn lean steak into strips or cubes. Roll meat in flour seasoned with salt, pepper, and paprika. Brown meat in hot oil in heavy skillet. Add onions, peppers, tomatoes, tomato sauce, chili powder and water. Cover tightly and simmer slowly for about 1 hour. To serve, arrange steak on hot serving platter. Cover with sauce, and garnish with shredded Longhorn Cheddar cheese. Place platter under broiler long enough for cheese to melt. Garnish with fresh cilantro. Serve with rice, buttered noodles, or mashed potatoes. Serves 6-8.

Donna Jackson
Stonewall Valley Ranch
Austin, TX

———————— ❖ ————————

"Our first cow was a black Peeler cow with his wine glass brand on her hip. We traded two pickup loads of hay for her, and though her "moonblindness" quickly became total blindness (when we unloaded her the poor thing ran right into a tree). She got along well in the pastures traveling with the other Longhorns. We quickly bought two young steers at .15/# for friends to help her. She raised several calves for us and could be talked through the pens whenever we gathered in the spring and fall. However, she was about as far from a pet as you could get."

—T.D. & Sid Kelsey, T Lazy S Ranch, Pompeys Pillar, Montana

Indian Beef Kabobs with Corn

1/3	cup water	1/4	teaspoon sugar
1/3	cup commercial mango chutney	1/8	teaspoon garlic powder
1	teaspoon curry powder	1	lb lean, boneless sirloin
1/2	teaspoon ground ginger	2	large ears fresh corn, cut into 1" pieces
1/2	teaspoon ground cumin	1	large purple onion, cut into 8 wedges

Place first 7 ingredients into container of an electric blender or food processor, cover, and process until smooth. Set aside. Trim fat from steak, and cut steak into 24 cubes. Combine steak cubes and chutney mixture in a large zip-top plastic bag. Marinate in refrigerator 2 hours. Remove steak from bag, reserving marinade. Thread steak cubes, corn, and onion alternately on skewers. Coat grill rack with cooking spray; place on grill over medium-hot coals. Place kabobs on rack and cook 6 minutes on each side or to desired doneness, basting with reserved marinade. *Yield:* **4 servings**

(From Cooking Light Magazine - 1990)

Leslie Moseley
The Woodlands, TX

Quick Smothered Steak

Note: Adjust amounts of ingredients according to amount of meat used.

Tenderize steak with meat cleaver. Cut steak into strips or cutlet size pieces. Season a bowl of flour with salt and pepper. (*I use the pepper first, then cover the pepper with salt.*) Prepare a bowl of water. Dip steak pieces into the flour, then water, then flour. Fry in skillet in canola oil as if for fried steak. Sprinkle 3-4 tablespoons of the seasoned flour over the fried steak and oil mixture. Turn steak over, stirring in flour. Pour remaining water over steak to make gravy. Water may need to be adjusted at this time. Simmer until gravy is the right consistency. Season gravy to taste. Serve with Mrs. Porter's Ranch Biscuits and mashed potatoes.

Windelyn Tharp
Duewall Farm
Caldwell, TX

Texas Longhorn Steak Kabobs

2	tablespoons soy sauce	12	ounces boneless Texas
2	tablespoons honey		Longhorn sirloin steak,
1	teaspoon ground ginger		trimmed and cut
1	clove garlic, crushed		into 1" cubes
1	teaspoon lemon juice	8	cherry tomatoes
1/4	teaspoon crushed hot red	4	large mushrooms, cut in half
	pepper flakes	1	green bell pepper, cored,
			seeded, and cut into
			8 squares

In shallow glass dish, combine soy sauce, honey, ginger, garlic, lemon juice and red pepper flakes. Mix well. Add beef and stir to coat. Cover with plastic wrap and refrigerate for 1-2 hours, stirring occasionally. Remove beef from marinade. Using four 10" metal skewers, alternately thread beef, tomatoes, mushrooms and bell pepper. Place on grill. Grill, turning 2 or 3 times and brushing with leftover marinade until meat is medium-rare and vegetables are lightly browned. Place on serving plates and serve immediately. Serves 4.

Ed Durr, Jr.
Heaven View Farm
Amite, LA

Saucy Beef over Rice

2	tablespoons flour	1/2	cup water
1	envelope onion soup mix	1/4	teaspoon pepper
1	(14 1/2 ounce) can stewed	1	lb sirloin steak, cut in strips
	tomatoes	1	large Reynolds oven bag

Preheat oven to 350 degrees. Shake flour in bag. Place in 13"×9"×1" baking pan. Add soup mix, undrained tomatoes, water and pepper to bag and shake to blend ingredients. Add beef to bag. Turn bag to coat beef. Close bag with nylon tie and cut slits in top. Bake until beef is tender - about 45 minutes. Serve over hot rice. Serves 3.

Lorene Graves
Dayton, TX

Great Grandfather's Meat Cooker (1880 and up)

This is another old ranch recipe. This was used to cook all kinds of meat for large gatherings.

First, he dug a hole about 3 feet by 2 feet and 18 inches deep out back by the kitchen. In this he built a fire, and let it burn down to coals.

1	small ham	1/2	cup salt
1	shoulder	1/2	cup honey
2	sets of ribs	1/2	cup molasses
salt and pepper			

Rub meat well with salt and pepper. Then rub in honey and molasses mixed. Wrap all in white canvas sack, then wrap in wet tow sacks. Lay on red hot coals. Cover all in dirt and pack down. Leave all day or all night. Remove all wrapping and put meat on table. It is best served with sauerkraut and pepper sauce.

R3
Kim Richey
Triple R Ranch
San Angelo, TX

Easy Beef Stroganoff

1¹/₂	lbs round steak, cubed and browned	1	(10³/₄ ounce) can cream of mushroom soup
1	clove garlic, chopped	1	can water
2	tablespoons Worcestershire sauce	1	pkg wide noodles
		olives	
1	(1¹/₂ ounce) can tomato soup	1	cup grated mild Cheddar cheese
1	cup sour cream		

Simmer first 6 ingredients for 1 hour or until tender. Cook noodles. Chop olives and cheese to spread on top.

3h
Lorene Graves
Dayton, TX

30 Minute Longhorn Stroganoff

2-4 lbs lean Longhorn
     hamburger, frozen
Moore's or Dale's marinade
     (soy sauce if you can't find)
1/4 stick butter
1   medium to large Vidalia
     onion, chopped

1   box Hamburger Helper
     (Stroganoff flavor)
salt and pepper
1/2-1 cup Ranch dressing
1/2 lb cheese, optional

Partially thaw meat, just enough to cut or break into thumb-sized pieces. Brown in deep non-stick pan on high heat, while adding 3-4 tablespoons of marinade, butter, and diced onion. Add salt and pepper. Cover and reduce heat with lid cracked a little. Brown until most, but not all, marinade is cooked up. Don't stir too much as lean beef will break apart.

Follow basic directions on Hamburger Helper box. (Lean beef won't need draining and omit 1 cup water.) Add in optional cheese and ranch dressing when nearly done. (Or dressing can be added to taste when serving.)

A few "cat head" biscuits on top of this makes complete meal to satisfy the heartiest appetite.

After a couple days of refrigerating, this dish is even tastier and is easily microwaveable. Be sure to add enough meat. One lb hamburger isn't enough to find a hoofprint of a cow!

K^K *Karl Kressman*
     Bascom, FL

Suzanne's Goulash

1½	lbs ground round steak	1	(16 ounce) can stewed
1	small onion, diced		tomatoes
½	green pepper, chopped	1	(16 ounce) can pinto beans
1½	teaspoons salt		grated Cheddar cheese
1	teaspoon chili powder		crushed tortilla chips

Combine meat, onion, green pepper, salt and chili powder in a skillet. Cook until meat is browned. Add tomatoes and beans. Simmer about 15 minutes. Serve topped with cheese and tortilla chips. Serves 6-8.

Suzanne Graves Hickman (daughter of Blackie Graves)
Dayton, TX

3h

Campout Stroganoff

1	lb ground beef	5-6	ounces sour cream
2	medium potatoes, diced	¾	cup mushroom soup
1	large onion, diced	½	cup water from potatoes
4	cloves garlic, finely diced		

Brown ground beef in skillet while boiling potatoes in another pot. If not using Longhorn beef, be sure to drain the meat. Add all other ingredients (including potato water) and heat. Serve with green beans, applesauce, and hot bread.

Mike C. Moore
Dallas, TX

TIPS

MEAT

To slice meat into thin strips, partially freeze and it will slice easily.

A roast with the bone in will cook faster than a boneless roast—the bone carries the heat to the inside of the roast more quickly.

Never cook a roast cold—let stand for at least an hour at room temperature. Brush with oil before and during roasting—the oil will seal in the juices.

To freeze meatballs, place them on a cookie sheet until frozen. Place in plastic bags and they will stay separated so that you may remove as many as you want.

VEGETABLES

Potatoes soaked in salt water for 20 minutes before baking will bake more rapidly.

Let raw potatoes stand in cold water for at least half an hour before frying to improve the crispness of French fried potatoes.

OTHER

Don't despair if you've oversalted the gravy. Stir in some instant mashed potatoes and you'll repair the damage. Just add a little more liquid to offset the thickening.

Make ice cubes of tea so that when you're serving this iced beverage, it will not be weakened when cubes melt.

For juicier lemons, soak in hot water a few minutes before using.

Buttermilk adds a piquant flavor to soups. Try it in canned tomato, cream of mushroom, celery and pea soups for creamy texture and gourmet flavor.

Butter can be frozen successfully. It maintains quality for about 2 months.

In storing egg yolks, put in a jar and cover with water, and put on lid. Any moisture proof container will work.

Other Critters

LONGHORN LEAN!

How meats compare nutritionally
(information based on 3.5 oz. serving)

Meat	Calories	Protein (gms)	Fat (gms)	Cholesterol (mgs)
Ground Beef	289	24.1	20.7	90.0
Lean Ground	272	24.7	18.5	87.7
Chicken, dk	205	27.4	9.7	93.8
Lamb chop	216	30.0	9.7	95.8
Pork loin	190	28.6	9.8	79.6
Pork chops	202	30.2	8.1	82.7
Lamb leg	191	28.3	7.7	89.7
Pot roast	210	33.0	7.6	101.0
Venison	207	33.5	6.4	4.0
Turkey	170	29.3	5.0	76.6
Top round	180	31.7	4.9	84.6
Chicken, lt	173	30.9	4.5	85.7
Longhorn	**140**	**21.88**	**3.7**	**61.5**

Source: Longhorn data: *"Nutrient Density of Beef From Texas Longhorn Cattle;"* Texas A&M; 1987. Other data: USDA, *USA Today* 11/29/91, and Pope Labs, Inc.-Dallas, TX.

Longhorn Bill's Bachelor Dinner

One whole chicken, less feathers and guts (*Ya' gotta tell most bachelors that whole chickens don't mean <u>whole</u> chickens.*)

Place chicken in pan doggie style or missionary style, don't matter. Cover lightly with foil. Cook three hours and thirty minutes at 250 degrees. Remove foil and cook 30 minutes at 350 degrees.

If you choose, you can add spices and/or salt and pepper or garlic or all of the above before cooking. THIS IS SIMPLE and GOOD! If you have been brandin', plan on one chicken per hand.

> *Bill Jowell*
> *Rafter L Ranch*
> *Midkiff, TX*

Chicken in Crockpot

1	(10³/₄ ounce) can cream of chicken soup	1	(10³/₄ ounce) can cream of mushroom soup
1	(10³/₄ ounce) can cream of celery soup	1¹/₂	cups Minute Rice
		6	chicken breasts
		1	cup diced celery

Mix all soups and rice in the crockpot. Put chicken on top. Add celery and cook 4 hours on low.

Another quickie! Delicious!

> *Lorene Graves*
> *Dayton, TX*

Chicken and Sausage Gumbo

2	cups roux	1	onion, chopped
1	fryer or hen, cut into pieces	¹/₂	cup onion tops, chopped
			parsley
2	lbs smoked sausage, sliced		salt and pepper
			red pepper

In a large pot, put about 3 quarts water. When hot, add 2 cups of roux. Stir constantly until well dissolved. When boiling, add chicken, sausage, onions, onion tops and parsley. Season to taste. For fryer, cook about one hour. If hen is used, cook until meat is tender.

Poppy Seed Chicken

3-4	lbs cooked and boned chicken	1	small package roasted almonds
8	ounces sour cream	1	stick margarine
1	(10³/4 ounce) can cream of mushroom soup	3	tablespoons poppy seeds
1	(10³/4 ounce) can cream of celery soup	one	roll crushed Ritz crackers

Mix chicken, sour cream, soups and almonds. Place in a 15"×10"×2" dish which has been sprayed with cooking spray. Melt margarine and combine with poppy seed and crackers and sprinkle this over the casserole. Bake at 350 degrees until hot.

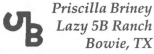

Priscilla Briney
Lazy 5B Ranch
Bowie, TX

Chicken Parmesan

4	boned chicken breasts, seasoned with salt and pepper	¹/2	cup bread crumbs
¹/2	stick butter, melted	¹/2	cup Parmesan cheese
			dash of garlic salt

Preheat oven to 350 degrees. Salt and pepper chicken and dip in melted butter, then roll in mixture of bread crumbs, Parmesan cheese and garlic salt. Place in baking dish and cover tightly with foil. Bake for 1 hour covered and 30 minutes uncovered. Serves 2 generously.

This dish is especially good served with Norma's Fettucine.

Norma Jean Blake
Double B Cattle Company
Dry Creek, LA

Foil-Wrapped Chicken Chinese

2	whole breasts of chicken or 1 breast and 2 thighs	1	teaspoon chopped parsley
2	cloves garlic, crushed or finely cut	1	tablespoon honey
1	tablespoon minced fresh ginger (or chopped preserved ginger)	2	tablespoons olive oil
		2	tablespoons sherry
		2	tablespoons plum sauce (from Chinese store)
1	teaspoon salt	½	cup soy sauce
			Quilted foil

Bone chicken with sharp knife and cut into pieces about 1" wide and 1½" long. You should get 20-24 pieces from the whole chicken breast, about 6-8 from the thigh. Mix all other ingredients into a sauce in large bowl, add chicken and marinate 30 minutes or longer.

Place each piece of chicken on a square of quilted foil, cut 7"×7", add a little marinade, and wrap each package securely, folding envelope fashion. Grill over hot coals about 7 minutes each side. Serve in foil wrappers, letting each guest unwrap his own. This makes about 3-4 dozen small bites, perfect for appetizers. To serve as an entree, use whole chicken parts, boned or not, as you like. Marinate and wrap as above, using 14" squares of foil. Grill 12-15 minutes on each side. Serves 4-6.

XIT *Ginny Boyce*
Almendra Longhorns
Manteca, CA

---❖---

"They prefer, too, to range in the country where they have been raised and when shipped north continually try to go south to their old home. One old steer which escaped and headed south, wandered into a farming community and was chased by dogs and men until he finally came to bay on a large bridge and refused to budge. He stopped all traffic and no one passed across the bridge until night came and the steer had slipped out into the woods."

— Forest Ranger Earl Drummond
Wichita Mountains National Wildlife Refuge
Cache, Oklahoma (1939)

Chicken and Spaghetti

1	large hen	2	tablespoons Worcestershire
1	stick margarine		sauce
2	large onions, chopped	1	small bottle ketchup
1/2	rib celery, chopped		Chili powder
3	small bell peppers, chopped		black pepper
			garlic salt
3	(10 1/2 ounce each) cans tomato soup	1	package spaghetti
			grated cheese for topping

Cook hen and debone, reserving stock. Melt margarine and sauté onions, celery and bell peppers until wilted, but not brown. Add enough stock to cook until tender. Add tomato soup and other seasonings. Add chicken and as much stock as needed. Add this to the spaghetti that has been cooked. Spread grated cheese on. Bake only long enough to set.

Delicious!

Chicken and Seafood Gumbo

6	tablespoons shortening	2	tablespoons black pepper
6	tablespoons flour	1	chicken, cut in serving pieces
1	onion, minced		
1/4	cup celery, diced	2	dozen oysters
1	green pepper, chopped	1	lb shrimp
1	cup chopped parsley		crabs
6	cups hot water	1/2	teaspoon gumbo file'
2	tablespoons salt		rice

Heat shortening on high. Add flour and stir constantly, until brown. This brown fat and flour is a roux. Add onions, celery, green pepper and parsley and cook until wilted. Add 6 cups hot water. Mix well to dissolve roux. Season with salt and pepper. Bring to a boil, add chicken and switch to a low heat and cook until chicken is tender (about 2 hours). Then add oysters, shrimp, and crabs. Let cook for 15 more minutes. Add file'. Serve over rice.

Julia Child's Chicken Wellington Recipe

I have always been a big fan of Julia Child. I had the great honor of having her on one of my flights into Denver. She was going to the Aspen Food Festival. I told her the reason I thought Glen married me was because of her Beef Wellington Recipe. She wrote her Chicken Wellington recipe on a United Airline cocktail napkin and gave it to me with a little note on how much she enjoyed our visit. I still have the original napkin recipe with her note. By the way, Julia Child is a big supporter of the Beef Industry and thinks everyone should eat good beef and use real cream.

Side note: *Always have a nice glass of wine whenever you're cooking—it soothes the soul!*

Boneless, skinless chicken breasts, flattened very thin	**garlic**
	Boursin cheese
	mushrooms, sliced
salt and pepper	**puff pastry or Crescent rolls**

Rub chicken with salt, pepper and garlic. Place 1 slice of cheese (Mozzarella works well, seeing as Boursin cheese is pretty scarce in Ordway, CO.) and about 1 tablespoon sliced mushrooms in flattened chicken breast and fold chicken like a diaper. If you have a favorite puff pastry recipe, use it. Otherwise, Pillsbury crescent rolls work really well. Unroll crescent rolls, using 2 to make a square. Put stuffed chicken in pastry, seam side of chicken down. Fold pastry around stuffed chicken like a diaper, and pinch pastry together. Bake at 350 degrees until brown, about 35-40 minutes. Make a sauce with chicken stock, flour, butter and cream. When your sauce is thickened, add about 1/4-1/2 cup brandy. Do not overcook brandy!

Bon Appetit!

Lyn Lewis
Flying Diamond Ranch
Ordway, CO

Herb Baked Fish

1	lb cod or haddock or halibut, thawed		dash oregano
1	cup milk	1/4	teaspoon garlic salt
2	tablespoon flour	1/8	teaspoon thyme
1/4	teaspoon salt	1/4	cup chopped green onion
1/8	teaspoon pepper		paprika

Place fish in 10"×6"×1" baking dish. Dot with butter. Blend milk with flour. Cook over medium heat until bubbling, stirring constantly. Add other ingredients and cook for 1 more minute. Pour this over the fish. Sprinkle with paprika and bake at 350 degrees for 25 minutes.

Beer Battered Fish

1	package hush puppy mix	1	can warm beer
1/2	cup flour		

Mix flour and hush puppy mix. Add beer and mix. Let stand for 1 hour. In bag, add flour to coat fish by shaking well. Shake off excess. Dip fish in beer batter and deep-fry until golden brown. Drain and serve.

Lorene Graves
Dayton, TX

Skillet Fried Trout and Hush Puppies

Clean fish and roll in corn meal. Fry in a large skillet of hot shortening on an open camp fire. After the fish are cooked, hush puppies are fried in the shortening remaining in the frying pan. Hush puppies are made by mixing 2 cups corn meal, 1 cup milk or water, 1 teaspoon salt, 2 teaspoon baking powder, and one onion, finely chopped. Shape into pones and fry until well brown.

Campfire Baked Trout

Save your larger fish for this overnight cooking. Clean fish and remove heads. Season inside and out with salt and pepper, then roll separately in waxed paper, folding ends in, and wrap in thick wet newspaper. Dig trench for each fish just deep enough to allow 1" of earth on top. Bury bundles, build the campfire over the trenches and leave until breakfast time.

Crawfish Pie

2	lbs peeled crawfish tails	4	tablespoons flour
1	teaspoon seasoned seafood salt	3¹/₂	cups water
¹/₂	teaspoon cayenne pepper	¹/₄	cup tomato paste
¹/₂	cup butter	2	tablespoons lemon juice
1	cup chopped onions	¹/₄	cup chopped green onions
¹/₂	cup chopped celery	¹/₄	cup parsley, chopped
¹/₂	cup finely chopped bell pepper		Enough pie pastry prepared for double crusts on 8 (6 ounce each) pie tins or plates.
5	garlic cloves, minced		

Sprinkle crawfish with salt and pepper and set aside. Melt butter in a heavy saucepan over medium heat and add next 4 ingredients. Stir until onions are limp and clear. Add crawfish and cook over low heat for 5 minutes. Add flour which has been dissolved in the water. Add tomato paste and lemon juice. Stir and cook until thickened. Add green onions and parsley, stirring well. Line the little individual pie plates with the pastry. Pour crawfish mixture into pie shells and cover with another layer of pastry. Pinch edges together or use fork tines to seal edges. Cut 2 slits in top of each pie. Bake at 350 degrees for 15 minutes. Reduce heat to 300 degrees and bake for another 10 minutes until crusts are golden brown. Serves 8.

Crawfish Etoufee

1	stick margarine	1	(10 ounce) can Rotel
2	onions, chopped		tomatoes
1	bell pepper, chopped	3	cups water
2	ribs celery, chopped		salt and pepper
1/2	clove garlic		garlic powder
2	(8 ounce each) cans	1-2	lbs peeled crawfish tails
	tomato sauce	1/2	cup green onion tops,
1	(10³/4 ounce) can golden		chopped
	mushroom soup	2	tablespoons parsley
			rice

Melt margarine in Dutch oven. Add chopped onions, bell pepper, celery and garlic. Sauté until light brown. Add tomato sauce, mushroom soup, Rotel, and water. Add salt, pepper and garlic powder to taste. Cook over low heat 1½-2 hours, stirring often to keep from sticking. Then add crawfish, green onions, and parsley. Cook another 20 minutes. Serve over rice.

Crawfish Fettucini Casserole

3	onions, chopped	1	pint cream or half-and-half
3	celery ribs, chopped	1	lb Velveeta, divided
2	bell peppers, chopped	1	lb fettucini noodles,
2	cloves garlic, chopped		boiled "al dente"
3	sticks margarine	2	tablespoons jalapenos
1/4	cup flour		salt and pepper
4	tablespoons dried parsley		Parmesan cheese
3	lbs peeled crawfish tails		

Sauté first 7 ingredients together for 15 minutes. Stir often. Add crawfish. Cook 15 minutes, stirring often. Add cream and ½ of Velveeta and all jalapenos. Add salt and pepper and cook for 30 minutes. Stir often. Add cooked noodles. Put in greased casserole dish. Top with Parmesan and remaining Velveeta. Bake at 350 degrees for 15-20 minutes.

Note: Shrimp may be substituted for crawfish.

Crawfish Janie

1	medium onion, chopped	1	lb peeled crawfish tails
2	stalks celery, chopped	1	(10³/₄ ounce) can cream
1/2	medium green pepper,		of mushroom soup
	chopped	1	(10 ounce) can Rotel
1/4	stick butter	1	lb Rotini macaroni, cooked
1	lb Velveeta cheese	salt	

Sauté onion, celery and green pepper in butter. Melt the cheese and mix with vegetables and remaining ingredients. Pour mixture into a large casserole and bake at 350 degrees for 35-40 minutes.

Boiled Crawfish

4	gallons water	1/2	cup vinegar
1	box salt	3	celery ribs, if desired
cayenne red pepper (plenty)		several potatoes, washed	
3	package crab boil		and not peeled
4	whole onions	8	lbs crawfish
4	lemons, cut in half		

Bring water to a hard boil in a large pot and add all ingredients except crawfish. Let boil until potatoes are tender. Add clean washed crawfish. Cover and let boil rapidly for about 6 minutes. Remove with strainer. When water boils again, you may add more crawfish.

❖

"Stampede"

"Longhorns on the stampede are as quick as a flash. They move as one animal although they may be bunched in a tight mass. Old timers say that the trail herd often got into the habit of stampeding on drives and would run night after night. They could be stopped by halting the drive for a few days, turning them loose on the range, and leaving them alone until they calmed."

— Forest Ranger Earl Drummond, Wichita Mountains National Wildlife Refuge, Cache, Oklahoma (1939)

Crawfish Creole

1	stick butter or margarine	1	teaspoon salt
2	large cloves garlic, minced	1	teaspoon sugar
1	cup chopped onions	1	lb cooked and peeled crawfish tails
1-2	cups chopped celery	1	cup white rice, cooked according to the package directions
1/2	cup chopped green pepper		
1	tablespoon flour		red pepper sauce
2	cans (15 1/2 ounce each) stewed Mexican-flavored tomatoes		

In a large pot, melt butter and sauté garlic, onions, celery and green peppers until wilted. Stir in flour until completely moistened. Add tomatoes, salt, and sugar; stir until mixed. Simmer 10 minutes. Add crawfish tails and heat just until hot. Serve over rice with red pepper sauce if desired. Serves 6.

Manale's Shrimp

1 lb shrimp	lemon juice
olive oil	Tabasco
cracked black pepper	Worcestershire sauce
salt	butter

Place whole shrimp, in shells, in single layer in oven-proof dish. Drizzle olive oil on top of shrimp. Pepper shrimp until they are black. (When you think you have enough pepper, add more!) Add lots of salt, lemon juice, Tabasco, and Worcestershire sauce. Remember you are seasoning through the shells. Cut up lots of butter and place pats on top of shrimp. Broil shrimp until they are cooked, about 15-20 minutes.

Serve with warm French bread. Great with cold beer and green salad. Base the amount of shrimp on the number of guests.

Kay Florence
Lazy K Ranch
Winnsboro, TX

Clam Bake

6	dozen cherrystone clams	15	frozen mini ears corn-on-the-cob
3	fryers, cut up		
	salt and pepper	2	large onions
15	small red potatoes	2¹/₂	large lemons
1-¹/₂	packages carrots	4	lbs raw shrimp in shells
		1	stick margarine

Clean clams by scrubbing shells with brush, discarding any clams with a broken shell or with the mouth open. Scrub potatoes and carrots, do not peel. Corn on cob need not be thawed. Cut the lemons and onions into eighths. Separate the chicken pieces, using only the breasts, thighs and drumsticks. In the bottom section of a large clam or lobster pot, as it is sometimes called, fill half full of water, then set the other section on top. Put a layer of clams, a layer of the large pieces of chicken, salt and pepper, another layer of clams, a layer of potatoes, another layer of clams, a layer of carrots, a layer of small pieces of chicken, salt and pepper, more clams, then a layer of onions and half the lemons, then the shrimp and top with remainder of lemons. Slice the margarine and put on top. Cook over medium flame for 2-2¹/₂ hours.

To serve, pour top section of clam pot into large trays. In the bottom section is a delicious broth. Strain and serve in cup to drink along with the clam bake. One pot serves 15 people.

Braxton Blake
Double B Cattle Company
Dry Creek, LA

Salmon Loaf

1	(16 ounce) can salmon	1¹/₄	cups grated cheese
1	egg, beaten	¹/₂	cup evaporated milk
¹/₂	teaspoon salt	1	cup bread crumbs
3	tablespoons melted butter	1	tablespoon lemon juice
¹/₈	teaspoon pepper	¹/₂	teaspoon dill

Mix all ingredients and place in bread pan, and bake for 30 minutes at 350 degrees. Serve hot or cold.

Low Country Boil

3-4	packages crab boil	5	lbs beef sausage, cut in 2" lengths
½	lb salt		
5-8	small red potatoes, washed and whole	2	dozen sweet corn-on-the-cob
2-3	lbs small onions, whole	5-10	lbs shrimp (30-36 count per lb), not peeled
3-4	lemons, cut in fourths		

For this you need a good hot cooker and at least a 5 gallon heavy pot. Cooks in 30 minutes from the time the water boils.

Add crab boil and salt to water and bring to boil. Add whole potatoes, onions and lemons. Cook for 10 minutes. Add sausage and cook for 5 minutes. Add corn and cook for another 3 minutes. Add shrimp last. It is very important not to overcook shrimp. They should be done within final 3 minutes. Turn heat off and let food sit in seasoned water for 10 minutes. Strain onto a very large "make do" serving tray lined with absorbent paper or cloth.

This is finger food. You will need lots of paper towels, paper plates, cocktail sauce, ketchup, hot sauce, whatever. Your choice. Several garbage containers for plates and trash.

I hope you try this. We use it often, never throw any away. You can get new friends with this food.

Joe Graddy
Graddy's Longhorn
Cottonwood, AL

Hot Shrimp

4	lbs shrimp	pepper, cracked or coarse ground
	Wishbone Italian dressing	1 lb butter

Wash fresh shrimp. Cover with dressing and marinate overnight in covered container in refrigerator. Drain shrimp, leaving wet with dressing. Place in large baking pan. Cover with butter and pepper. Use pepper liberally. Bake 45 minutes (or less, depending on the oven) in 400 degree oven. Stir occasionally.

Oven Shrimp

2	lbs shrimp in the shell	4	tablespoons lemon juice
1	stick butter	8	bay leaves
1	large bottle Italian Wishbone dressing	2	teaspoons Worcestershire sauce
1	onion, sliced		salt and pepper
2	lemons, sliced		garlic to taste.

Place shrimp in large baking pan. Blend all other ingredients and pour over shrimp. Bake at 400 degrees for 12-15 minutes. Basting sauce may be eaten with French garlic bread or hard rolls.

B
C
Bubbles and Brenda Choate
Judsonia, AR

Pickled Shrimp

1½	lbs shrimp		paprika
¾	cup corn oil	2	onions, sliced thick
1	tablespoon celery seed	¾	cup tarragon vinegar
1	teaspoon Worcestershire sauce	1	teaspoon garlic powder
5-6	dashes Tabasco	2	tablespoon capers and juice
	Salt and pepper		Parsley flakes

Boil shrimp in seasoned water for 8-10 minutes, depending on size of the shrimp. Peel. Mix all other ingredients and pour over shrimp. Marinate for 6-8 hours before serving. Keep refrigerated. Use within 4-5 days.

3h
Sharon Wilson
(granddaughter of Blackie Graves)

Shrimp Casserole

1	stick butter	1	(10 ounce) can onion soup
1	lb shrimp	1	(10³/₄ ounce) can cream of
1¹/₂	cups rice		chicken soup
1	(10 ounce) can Rotel	1	onion, chopped
	tomatoes	1	bell pepper, chopped

Melt butter and mix all ingredients. Pour into a large casserole. Bake at 350 degrees for 1 hour.

Shrimp and Sausage Jambalaya

4	tablespoons flour	1	quart cleaned raw shrimp
1/2	cup oil	2	lbs sausage
3	large onions, chopped	1/2	cup chopped parsley
1	large bell pepper,	1	cup cooked rice
	chopped		garlic powder
garlic			salt and pepper

This is cooked best in iron pot. Brown flour in oil. Add onions, bell pepper and garlic and cook until tender. Add shrimp and cut up sausage (cut in cubes). Cook until done. Add water to make thick gravy. Add parsley. Fold rice into gravy and let set until gravy is absorbed. Salt and pepper to taste. Enjoy!

Salmonettes

1	(14 ounce) can salmon,	1/8	teaspoon pepper
	drain and save liquid	1	teaspoon baking powder
1	egg, beaten	1/4	cup reserved salmon juice
1/2	cup sifted flour	oil	

Mix salmon, egg, flour and pepper. Add baking powder stirred in reserve salmon juice. Form into croquettes. Fry in hot oil 30 seconds and eat as soon as you can!!

Crabmeat Mornay

¹/₄	lb butter, not margarine	1	tablespoon Accent
1	small bunch shallots	¹/₄	tablespoon salt
¹/₂	cup finely chopped parsley	3	tablespoons sugar
2	tablespoon flour	1	small can mushroom stems and pieces
1	pint heavy cream		Tabasco to taste
¹/₂	lb grated Swiss cheese	1	lb fresh or frozen crab meat
¹/₄	tablespoon red pepper		Cornstarch
5	tablespoons sherry		Water

Melt butter in iron skillet and sauté shallots and parsley. When done, stir in flour (well blended with heavy cream). Heat until smooth. Add cheese and cook at very low simmer until cheese is melted. Add pepper, sherry, Accent, salt, sugar, mushrooms, and Tabasco. Simmer gently 5 minutes. Add crab meat. Make a paste of cornstarch and water, and add very slowly to above, stirring constantly until mixture reaches desired thickness. Serve in patty shells.

Norma Jean Blake
Double B Cattle Company
Dry Creek, LA

Shrimp Fettucine

3	sticks margarine	1	pint cream
3	onions, chopped	1	lb jalapeno cheese
3	bell peppers, chopped	¹/₄	cup flour
3	ribs celery, chopped	1	lb fettucine noodles
	parsley		grated cheese
4-5	cloves garlic, chopped		Parmesan cheese
3	lbs peeled shrimp		seasonings to taste

Sauté onions, bell peppers, and celery in margarine. Add parsley, garlic and shrimp and cook for 10 minutes. Add cream, cheese and flour. Simmer for 30 minutes. Boil and drain noodles, add to the shrimp mixture and stir well. Pour mixture in a large casserole dish and top with grated cheese and Parmesan cheese. Bake at 350 degrees for 20 minutes.

Oyster Rockefeller Casserole

2	sticks butter or margarine	1	teaspoon anise flavored
1/2	teaspoon thyme		liqueur (Absinthe)
1/2	cup green onions,	1/4	cup fresh parsley, chopped
	chopped fine	3	(10 ounce each) package
3/4	cup bread crumbs		chopped spinach
2-3	dozen oysters, drained		Salt, black pepper, white pepper
			and red pepper to taste

Melt butter; add thyme and green onions. Sauté for about 2 minutes. Add bread crumbs and sauté until crumbs are toasted. Add drained oysters and simmer until oysters curl up on edges. Add parsley and liquor (Absinthe, Pernod or Herbsaint) to oyster mixture. Cook frozen spinach according to directions; drain well. Add to oyster mixture, and mix well. Bake for 20-25 minutes in 425 degree oven. Season to taste.

May be served in oyster shells or individual servings or can be used as dip with Melba Toast.

Note: If liqueur is unavailable, boil 1½ tablespoons anise seed in ½ cup water for 10 minutes, strain, then use liquid.

Shrimp and Crab Casserole

1/2	cup diced celery	1	lb crabmeat
1/2	cup diced onion	2	lbs boiled shrimp
1/2	cup diced bell pepper	2	cups cooked rice
1/4	cup salad oil	1	tablespoon Worcestershire
1	(10 ounce) Rotel tomatoes		sauce
1	(10¾ ounce) can cream	1/4	teaspoon paprika
	of mushroom soup		green onions, chopped
1	(6 ounce) can sliced		parsley
	mushrooms		buttered bread crumbs

Sauté celery, onions, and bell pepper in salad oil. Add Rotel, cream of mushroom soup, sliced mushrooms and simmer for 5 minutes. Add rest of ingredients, season to taste and place in casserole dish. Sprinkle with buttered bread crumbs and bake in 350 degree oven for 25 minutes.

Grilled Salmon Filets

1	lb salmon filets, cut 1" thick		1/4	teaspoon salt
1	tablespoon oil		1/4	teaspoon pepper
1	tablespoon chopped fresh thyme or 1 teaspoon dried thyme		1	clove garlic, minced

Cut salmon into 1"×1¹/₂ pieces. Brush with oil. In a small bowl, combine thyme, salt, pepper and garlic. Mix well and rub on salmon. Cover and refrigerate for 1 hour. Heat grill. Thread salmon on metal skewers. When grill is heated to medium heat, grill 4-6" from coals. Cook 8-10 minutes, turning once. Fish will flake easily with a fork when done. Serves 4.

Sheryl Johnson
J 5 Longhorns
Molalla, OR

❖

"Over the years we became good friends with Carolyn and Jack Phillips. Jack called one night and said "Ol' Tex was down. You've always loved the old bull. If you can get here before he dies, you can have him." Texas was tough and he recovered, bred our cows for three years and even gave us some semen. Tex died while I was working on the maquette for Texas Gold, and his bones are in the Phillips steer in the monument."

—T.D. & Sid Kelsey, T Lazy S Ranch, Pompeys Pillar, Montana

(Note: Jack Phillips was the third president of the TLBAA and operated Battle Island Ranch at West Columbia, Texas. the "Tex" he refers to is the bull Texas Ranger JP whose pedigree is included in many Texas Longhorn cattle and was the first A.I. Certified TLBAA Bull. The Texas Gold , sculpted by Kelsey, is the 1-¹/₃ times life-size monument that rests on TLBAA property in the Stockyards area of Fort Worth).

Lamb Chops with Mint Sauce

8	lamb chops	1/2	cup chopped mint leaves,
salt and pepper			divided
1/4	cup vinegar	1/4	cup lemon juice
1	cup water, divided	1 1/2	teaspoons sugar
		1/2	teaspoon salt

Fry or grill lamb chops to taste. Heat vinegar and 1/2 cup water to boiling and pour over half the mint leaves. Let stand 15 minutes. Strain. Add remaining water, lemon, juice, sugar, and salt. Chill. Add remaining mint leaves, and serve with lamb. Yields 1 3/4 cups sauce.

S/K
SuzAnn Spindor
S/K Ranch
Fort Worth, TX

Lamb with Honey Mustard and Rosemary

2	tablespoons honey	2	tablespoons cider
3	tablespoons oil	1	teaspoon rosemary
2	tablespoons Dijon	salt and pepper	
	mustard	1 1/2- 2 1/2 lbs rack of lamb	
1	tablespoon dry mustard	1/2	cup dry cider
2	tablespoons vinegar		

Whisk the honey and oil together, then beat in the rest of the ingredients, except 1/2 cup cider, until thick and creamy. Rub the lamb all over with this mixture and bake at 400 degrees for 20 minutes (rare) to 30 minutes (well done). Remove lamb to a warm plate, add the 1/2 cup cider to the juices left in the pan and stir until bubbling. Strain and pour over the lamb.

John Wells
Rafter J Ranch
Red Bluff, CA

Lamb Curry Pie

2	lbs lamb, shoulder or breast	2¹/2	teaspoons salt
1	onion, diced	2	tablespoons flour
1	tablespoon shortening	1	teaspoon curry powder
3	cups hot water	¹/4	cup hot water
¹/4	teaspoon thyme	3	cups cooked rice

Cut lamb into 1" cubes. Brown lamb and onion in shortening. Add hot water, thyme and salt, and simmer 1¹/2 hours or until meat is tender. Combine flour and curry powder; add cold water and mix to a smooth paste. Add to lamb. Line greased baking dish on sides and bottom with rice, pressing rice firmly into place. Fill center with lamb mixture and bake in a 350 degree oven for 20 minutes. Serves 6.

❖

"The reason that my husband Noah got involved with Texas Longhorns was that he always loved preserving things that were close to extinction. He felt that the Texas Longhorns were close to that point. He bought his first ones (a bull and two heifers) from Mr. Carter McGregor of Wichita Falls, Texas, on our way to Lawton, Oklahoma, for a TLBAA convention in 1971. Back then, the TLBAA membership was listed on a legal sheet of paper, and we kept that folded up in our car. Whenever we traveled, we'd pull it out and call ahead to Longhorn breeders in that area to see if we could come by. Not one ever told us, 'no'. Now in his eighties, Noah just loves standing in the pasture among his cattle. As he watches them, he remembers all the good friends that we have met through the Longhorn cattle.

—Melba Oliver
Saddle Rock Ranch
Enterprise, Alabama

❖

Frikkadels (pronounced Frick-a-dels; A recipe from South Africa)

2	lbs lean ground lamb	2	teaspoons salt
1/2	cup bread crumbs, pulverized in food processor		freshly ground black pepper
		1/4	cup vegetable oil
1/2	cup onions, chopped in food processor	1	cup Swanson's beef broth or other beef broth (if you use 3 lbs lamb, increase
2	eggs, lightly beaten		to 1 (14 ounce) can broth)
1/4	teaspoon ground nutmeg	1-2	tablespoons flour
1	teaspoon ground coriander	1-2	tablespoons cold water

Combine lamb, bread crumbs, onions, eggs, nutmeg, coriander, salt, and a little pepper in a large bowl. Knead mixture as if making a meat loaf. When well mixed, divide in portions and process through a food processor so mixture is smooth and fluffy. Shape into patties about 3" in diameter and 3/4" thick. You should have 10-12 patties. (Moisten hands with cold water to make patties if mixture sticks to fingers.)

In a heavy 12" skillet, heat oil over moderate heat. Brown patties 5 or 6 at a time, regulating heat so they color evenly and richly without burning. Remove patties from skillet to a plate as they are browned.
Pour off fat remaining in skillet and add beef broth. Bring to boiling point, scraping brown bits from sides and bottom pan. Return patties to skillet along with any juice on the plate. Reduce heat to low, cover partially and simmer 30 minutes. With slotted spoon or spatula, transfer the frikkadels to a heated platter and cover with foil to keep them warm while making gravy.

Skim as much fat as possible from the liquid in the skillet. Make a smooth paste of flour and water. Whisk into liquid in pan. Use only as much as needed to make gravy the consistency you like. (Although traditionally made of lamb, frikkadels may be made with beef or pork as well, or any combination of the three.)

Mary Elizabeth Scott
Copa de Vino Ranch
Goliad, TX

Baked Ham

Use Swift's Premium ham. Score fat. Rub in all the brown sugar you can and stud with cloves. Make a paste of 8 cups of flour and water. Roll out and wrap ham. Save a piece of the dough to patch with as the steam will force holes through the dough. Put ham in roaster and add a little boiling water to keep from burning. Roast 5 or 6 hours, more if necessary depending on the size of ham. Break off dough, and put ham in oven to brown. A little sweet pickle juice is good poured over ham before putting in oven to brown.

Will Rogers Recipe
Dog Iron Ranch
Claremore, OK

Short Ribs and Sauerkraut

What you need is ribs, salt, pepper, garlic, sauerkraut, tomato sauce (8 oz can) or can of whole tomatoes and an onion.

HOW TO DO IT:

Place ribs in a roaster pan with a small amount of water. Salt and pepper. Put in 350 degree oven and braise. Remove and add garlic, chopped onion, tomato sauce and sauerkraut. Return to oven until ribs are done. I use fresh garlic, several cloves. I also use a large can of kraut or a couple of small ones.

They ain't no leftovers with this dish. Just rib bones.

S
David Smith
The Running S Ranch
Frost, TX

Sauerkraut and Ribs

| 2 | lbs of meaty pork ribs | 1 | quart sauerkraut |
| 1-2 | apples, peeled and sliced | 1/2 | cup brown sugar |

Brown ribs in oven until golden in color. Place ribs in baking dish and cover with sliced, peeled apples, then add sauerkraut and brown sugar. Cover with lid or foil and bake in moderate oven for 3 hours. Add water if needed. Serve with mashed potatoes.

Rosalie Brackebusch
Divernor, FL

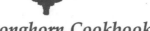

Pork Stew with Pepper Dumplings

1	tablespoon olive oil	1	tablespoon cornstarch
1	(10 ounce) package yellow pearl onions, peeled, divided	1	(1 lb) butternut squash, peeled, halved, seeded, and cut into 1" cubes
12	small mushrooms	1	cup unsifted all-purpose flour
1½	lbs boneless pork loin or shoulder, cut into 1¼" cubes	1	teaspoon baking powder
3½	cups water, divided	¼	teaspoon cracked black pepper
1	teaspoon salt, divided	½	stick butter, cut into small pieces
⅛	teaspoon ground black pepper	¾	cup milk
		12	broccoli flowerets

In 9" cast-iron skillet, heat oil over medium-high heat. Add 12 onions and the mushrooms; sauté until lightly browned on all sides—about 5 minutes. Meanwhile, chop remaining onions. Remove onions and mushrooms to small bowl and set aside. Add pork to skillet; sauté, turning occasionally, until pieces are browned on all sides. Add chopped onions and sauté, stirring constantly, until onions are lightly browned. Add 3 cups water, 1/2 teaspoon salt and the pepper; heat to boiling over high heat. Reduce heat to low; cover and cook 45 minutes.

In 1-cup measuring cup or small bowl, combine remaining 1/2 cup water and the cornstarch. Stir cornstarch mixture into pork mixture in skillet; add squash and the reserved onions and mushrooms. Cover and heat stew to boiling over high heat; reduce heat to low and cook 15 minutes, stirring occasionally. Meanwhile, heat oven to 400 degrees. In medium-size bowl, combine flour, baking powder, the remaining 1/2 teaspoon salt, and the cracked pepper. With pastry blender or 2 knives, cut butter into flour mixture until coarse crumbs form. With serving spoon, stir milk into flour mixture until soft dough forms. Spoon dough around edge of skillet.

Bake stew 15 minutes. Remove from oven, stir broccoli into stew in center of skillet. Return to oven and bake 5-10 minutes longer or until dumplings are browned and broccoli is crisp-tender.

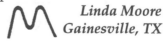

Linda Moore
Gainesville, TX

P.K. Pork Loin

1	large rolled pork loin roast		Tony Chachere's Creole seasoning (green can)
1	jar whole jalapenos (I like to use fresh)		olive oil

Unwrap roast and brush all 4 sides with olive oil. Halve jalapenos vertically; place jalapenos along flat side of roast. Cover (pack) completely with Creole seasoning. Re-tie roast with kitchen string and sprinkle outside of roast heavily with seasoning. Bake at 350 degrees for 1^{1}/$_{2}$ hours, uncovered.

This is a rich roast and rather spicy. It is a Christmas tradition at our house, and I love it because it is so easy.

Pat Harrell
Full Circle Ranch
Strawn, TX

Ham Stroganoff

3	cups cooked ham, diced	1	cup sour cream
1/2	cup chopped onion	1/3	cup milk
2	tablespoons butter	1/2	teaspoon paprika
1/2	cup sliced ripe olives	6	pastry shells
1	(10³/4 ounce) can cream of chicken soup	1/3	cup toasted slivered almonds

Sauté ham and onion in butter until onion is tender. Stir in olives. Combine soup, sour cream, milk and paprika until smooth and add ham. Cook and stir over medium heat until heated through. Spoon into pastry shell. Sprinkle top with almonds.

Beverly Sorem
Flying S Cattle
Nevada, IA

Sunset Silhouette

He stood and watched her graceful movement,
though he had no time to waste.
She noticed he was watching,
but she never showed a trace
Of interest in him watching her,
but it wasn't attitude.
She politely just ignored him
not wanting to be rude.
The sun was slowly going down,
the clouds and sky were pink
Her shadow, and her silhouette,
made him sigh and think.
How many other cowboys watched?
Had she taken their berth too?
Because she really was quite splendid
and she didn't have a clue.
Then he remembered about supper,
his wife would have it ready now.
So he forked off an extra flake,
she's his favorite Longhorn cow.

—Charlotte Thompson, Adel, Oregon

Living Off
The Land

❖

"Texas Gold"

Texas Longhorns are often referred to as Texas Gold because the cattle were the only thing that men returning from the Civil War could use to make a living. It is also the name of a magnificent work of art. A gift of artist and rancher T.D. Kelsey and his wife, Sidni, to the Texas Longhorn Breeders Association of America, "Texas Gold" is one of the largest cast bronze statues in the world. Seven Texas Longhorn steers and an outrider stretch across a base that measures 29 feet by 13.8 feet. Though roughly one-third larger than life-size, each figure remains anatomically correct and true to scale. Eleven feet tall, the bronze weighs seven tons. The cattle represent the seven "families" of Texas Longhorns: Wichita Mountains Wildlife Refuge, Yates, Phillips, Marks, Butler, Wright and Peeler. Each steer has a heart, just as the cattle themselves did. "Texas Gold" is the focal point of the two-acre TLBAA property at the corner of North Main and Stockyards Boulevard in Fort Worth."

❖

Mincemeat

1	lb venison, cooked and ground or chopped	2	cups brown sugar
3/4	lb suet, finely chopped or ground	2	cups peeled, cored, and finely chopped apple
1	lb black currants	1/4	cup fresh lemon juice
1	lb golden raisins	1/2	cup dry sherry
1	lb dark raisins	2	cups Cognac
1	cup chopped glaceed pineapple	1/2	teaspoon ground nutmeg
1	cup chopped glaceed cherries	1 1/2	teaspoons ground cinnamon
1	cup chopped mixed glaceed fruits	1/2	teaspoon ground allspice
1/2	teaspoon salt	1/2	teaspoon ground cloves
			Grated peel of 1 orange
			Grated peel of 1 lemon

Mix all ingredients together and place in large crock or glass jar. Cover and let stand in refrigerator at least 1 month before using. If mixture becomes dry at any time, add more sherry.

Grilled Dove Breast

Jalapeño pepper
apple

dove breast
bacon

Insert small piece of jalapeno pepper into 1/2 cavity of dove breast and small piece of apple into other half. Cut pieces small enough to fit cavities. Wrap in bacon, securing with toothpicks. Lightly salt and pepper. Grill to taste. <u>Don't overcook</u>!

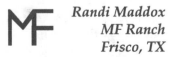

Randi Maddox
MF Ranch
Frisco, TX

Venison Jerky

This is a great recipe for venison jerky. It also works on any other cut of beef, wild hog, even wild turkey.

Take your meat and cut with the grain in strips about 1$^{1}/_{2}$" thick. Make a brine of 1 cup TenderQuick to 6 cups water in plastic or glass bowl. Place meat in brine for 48 hours in refrigerator. Stir once and ensure meat is covered. After 48 hours, drain meat and place in boiling water. Wait until water boils again, then remove from heat. Drain meat, place on cookie sheet and season with your favorite mix. I use coarse pepper, red crushed pepper (some) and a pinch of sage. Cover all surfaces of meat. Do this while it is still hot.

While you are doing this, get a fire started in your favorite smoker/ BBQ pit. Set it so it's not too hot and mainly smoke. Mesquite is my favorite. Smoke for 2-4 hours depending on your taste. Remove from pit and place in glass bowl for drying a couple of days. I put the bowl on top of the refrigerator for about a day and a half. After that place your jerky in plastic bags and throw in the refrigerator.

No need to freeze. Slice across the grain for guests. Or on the trail, if you have good teeth, chew off a chunk. Enjoy!

Nancy Kerry
Heartland Ranch

❖

"Long drives, even up to 30 miles in a single day, do not appear to be injurious to Longhorns as in the case of domestic livestock. They can "take it" without the shrinkage and harm which comes to the beef breeds. Neither do the cows and calves bellow like the domestic cattle when they are being handled; and where Longhorns are fed, they quickly learn to come upon call. A "feeder" call brings them in from long distances on a brisk trot, whereas domestic cattle would have to be driven from any great distance."

— *Forest Ranger Earl Drummond, Wichita Mountains National Wildlife Refuge, Cache, Oklahoma (1939)*

Marinade for Deer Steak

1/3	beef bouillon	1/3	can beer
1/3	tomato juice		

Combine all ingredients and pour over deer. Marinate for 6-8 hours in refrigerator. Cook as desired.

MF *Randi Maddox*
MF Ranch
Frisco, TX

Dove and Wild Rice

12	doves	1	cup bouillon cubes
2	sticks butter, divided	1¼	cups water
1	onion, chopped	1	package wild rice
1	bell pepper, chopped	1	can mushrooms

Fry dove in butter. Place in large baking pan. Fry onion and pepper in remaining butter. Pour over dove. Mix bouillon cubes and water until dissolved. Pour rice, bouillon, and mushrooms over dove and bake 1½ hours at 325-350 degrees.

VYZ *Laney Weise*
Lazy LYZ Ranch
Voca, TX

Quail Barbecue

6-8 quail	barbecue sauce

Marinate quail by placing in large glass bowl. Pour enough chilled barbecue sauce over quail to cover. Cover bowl and refrigerate 24 hours. Turn birds at least once to marinate completely in sauce. Remove quail from sauce and place on outdoor grill or in outdoor smoker. Cook until tender and done throughout, basting frequently with sauce. If an outdoor smoker or grill is not available, place quail in baking pan and bake at 350 degrees for 30 minutes or until tender, basting with sauce.

S/K *SuzAnn Spindor*
S/K Ranch
Fort Worth, TX

Quail-Rice Magnifique

6	quail breasts	1/2	cup chopped parsley
salt and pepper		3	cups chicken broth
6	tablespoons butter	8-10	drops Tabasco
1	cup shredded carrots	1	cup long grain rice
1/2	cup chopped green onion	3	slices bacon, halved

In skillet, brown quail breasts which have been seasoned with salt and pepper, in butter. Remove and set aside. In same skillet, sauté carrot, onion, and parsley until tender, stirring frequently. Add chicken broth, more salt and pepper and Tabasco. Put rice in large flat 13"×9"×2" baking dish, add liquid mixture and stir. Top mixture with quail breasts and place a strip of bacon across each. Cover with foil and bake at 350 degrees for about 1 hour or until liquid is absorbed by rice. Remove bacon slices to serve.

2B

Norma Jean Blake
Double B Cattle Company
Dry Creek, LA

Venison Steak Rolls

6-8	venison steaks	1/4	cup flour
1/4	teaspoon black pepper	1/4	cup butter or margarine
3	green onions, chopped	1	envelope dry onion soup
1	rib celery, chopped		mix
1	cup grated aged Cheddar or Swiss cheese	1/4	cup red wine
		1	cup water

Pound steaks with meat mallet until flattened. Sprinkle with pepper. Mix onions, celery and cheese; place about 2 tablespoons of mixture in center of each steak and roll tightly. Use wooden pick to secure if necessary. Dredge each steak roll in flour. Melt butter in frying pan and brown steak rolls. Reduce heat. Stir in onion soup mix, wine, and water. Sprinkle any leftover cheese mixture over top of steaks. Cover and cook on low 20 minutes or until tender. Serve on bed of white rice and garnish with celery leaves.

Roasted Wild Turkey with Cranberry Sauce

1	whole, wild turkey, dressed and skinned		oil
		1	(10 ounce) jar currant jelly
2	tablespoons brown bouquet sauce	1/4	cup whole cranberry sauce
		1/4	cup white raisins
2	tablespoons melted butter	2	tablespoons vinegar
1	turkey-size cooking bag		dash ground cinnamon

MICROWAVE METHOD:

Dry turkey with paper towel. Brush with a mixture of brown bouquet sauce and melted butter. Cut 1/2" wide strip from open end of cooking bag. Place turkey in bag and set in roasting dish. Lightly oil inside of bag over breast to prevent sticking. Add 1/2 cup water. Close bag by tying open end with the plastic strip. Make a slash in the bag near the closure. Microwave on medium for 11 minutes per pound or until a meat thermometer or probe reaches 170 degrees. Let turkey stand 10 minutes before removing from bag. Mix jelly, cranberry sauce, raisins, vinegar, and cinnamon in 2 cups glass measuring cup. Cover with paper towel and cook on high for 1 1/2 minutes. Serve over turkey slices, or spoon over whole bird.

CONVENTIONAL OVEN METHOD:

Follow directions on cooking bag box for roasting turkey in oven. To make sauce, heat ingredients in saucepan.

Chicken Fried Venison

6	round steaks, tenderized by pounding with meat mallet		salt and pepper
		2	eggs and 3 tablespoons water, beaten together
	flour		oil

Coat steaks in flour seasoned with salt and pepper and dip in egg mixture. Coat again with flour. Fry in hot oil until crispy and browned. Sprinkle with salt and pepper again if desired.

Special Thanksgiving Turkey

STUFFING:

1	tablespoon butter	1½	cups cranberries
1	cup finely chopped onion	2	cups breadcrumbs
1	cup chopped mushrooms	2	large bunches parsley, cleaned and chopped
1	cup chopped walnuts		
1	cup chopped celery	1	teaspoon paprika
1	cup finely diced spicy sausage	2	teaspoons oregano
			salt and pepper
		1	beaten egg

Melt the butter in a skillet and lightly fry the onions, mushrooms, walnuts, celery, sausage, and cranberries. Stir in the breadcrumbs and the remaining ingredients and set aside.

THE BIRD:

1	(8-10 lbs) turkey	2	cups water
1	lemon, sliced	2	vegetable stock cubes
½	bottle Cognac	2	bay leaves
1	bottle Madeira or sherry	1	teaspoon fresh nutmeg
2	tablespoons melted butter	1	tablespoon basil

Stuff the turkey cavity loosely. Bake any leftover stuffing in a separate dish. Place turkey in a deep roasting pan and arrange the lemon slices between the wings, thighs, and drumsticks. Pour the Cognac, Madeira, and melted butter over the turkey and add the water to the liquid in the bottom of the pan. (This ensures there'll be no flames!) Add the stock cubes and bay leaves to the liquid and sprinkle with nutmeg and basil. Roast the turkey in a preheated 450 degree oven, basting every 20 minutes. Cover with foil after the first hour of cooking. Allow 20 minutes per pound plus an extra 20 minutes.

Florine Matthews
Matthews Longhorns
Bristow, OK

Baked Quail in Rice

4	quail, dressed and ready for baking	1	cup uncooked wild rice
4	tablespoons butter	2¹/₂	cups chicken broth
1	cup grated carrot	¹/₂	cup white wine
¹/₂	cup chopped green onion	¹/₂	teaspoon seasoning salt
¹/₄	cup finely chopped parsley	2	slices bacon, cut in 4 pieces

In deep skillet, brown birds in butter. Remove birds and set aside. In same pan, sauté carrot, onion, and parsley until limp. Add rice, chicken broth, wine and salt; stir well. Place quail on top of rice and lay a bacon strip atop each quail. Cover and cook over low heat for 30 minutes or until quail are tender. Sprinkle with additional salt.

Fried Quail or Dove

Clean birds thoroughly. Place in a large bowl and cover with whole milk. Soak in milk 30 minutes to an hour. Reserve 2 cups of milk. Remove and sprinkle birds with black pepper. Coat each bird with flour. Fry in 2" of hot oil in a 10" skillet. Cover and cook until browned. Drain on absorbent paper and sprinkle with salt. Make cream gravy by draining all fat from pan except for 4 tablespoons. Stir ¹/₄ cup flour into hot fat to make a smooth paste. When flour mixture starts to bubble, add 2 cups of the milk used to soak the birds. Cook and stir until thickened and smooth. Add salt and pepper to taste.

Venison Marinade

¹/₃	cup honey	¹/₄	cup soy sauce
2	teaspoons fresh grated ginger	1	cup dry white wine
		1	teaspoon dry mustard

Mix all ingredients well while warming in a pan. When mixture is cool, marinate any cut of venison or other wild game. Marinate from a couple of hours to overnight in refrigerator. Then prepare meat in any way you would like. Also good for beef, steak, broiled steak, etc.

Jean Smith
Fort Worth, TX

Barbecued Buffalo, Elk, and Venison

Buffalo, elk and venison make good barbecue meat when prepared in a barbecue oven or in a good barbecue pit. If the meat comes from an old animal, it should, by all means, be placed in Venison Marinade for 2-3 days prior to the barbecue. This is not necessary when meat from anything up to a three-year-old animal is used. Bear in mind the longer and slower the cooking and the barbecuing in your oven, the better your meat will be. It is the mixture of the spices and the flavor of the smoke that makes a good barbecue. Also, it is essential to baste often. In barbecuing the game cuts, it is advisable to first lard your cuts of meat with lardons made of salt pork strips. In barbecuing for large parties or picnics, meats should be cut in chunks of 10-15 lbs roasts and barbecued very slowly. Six to eight hours is not too much for these sized roasts. Serve sliced with barbecue sauce.

Jean Smith
Fort Worth, TX

Sauce for Wild Game

1	lb corn oil margarine	2	cloves garlic, finely chopped
⅔	cup sherry or red wine		
2	tablespoons Worcestershire sauce	½	cup chopped parsley
		2	teaspoons salt
2	tablespoons soy sauce	1	cup water

Combine all ingredients in heavy saucepan and bring to boil. Lower heat and simmer 30 minutes. Brush on meat surfaces halfway through and at end of cook time. This is enough sauce to cook 16 chickens or 4 turkeys and is good when used to smoke any kind of beef, ham, pork or lamb.

Betty Cooper
Lady Cow Puncher Ranch
Leesville, LA

Spicy Baked Venison

1-	1½ lbs venison, cut into ¾" cubes	1	green bell pepper, seeded and sliced in strips
1	(1⅜ ounce) package dry onion soup mix	2	cups fresh tomatoes, cored or 1 (16 ounce) can tomatoes
2	tablespoons butter or margarine	2	tablespoons Worcestershire sauce
8	ounces fresh mushrooms, sliced	2	sprigs parsley
		1	tablespoon cornstarch

Place venison in bottom of a 2 quart baking dish. (If cooking this at the deer camp, omit the casserole dish and place the layered mixture in the center of a large sheet of heavy duty foil. Seal and bake in camp oven or on campfire coals.) Sprinkle onion soup mix over top of venison; dot with butter. Layer mushrooms and pepper strips on top. In a blender or food processor, puree tomatoes. Add Worcestershire sauce, parsley, and cornstarch and blend until mixed with tomatoes. Pour tomato mixture over venison mixture, wrap a heavy piece of foil under and over casserole, sealing dish very well at top and sides. Bake in the oven at 350 degrees for 2-3 hours until venison is very tender. Remove foil and serve. Hot rolls, cornbread or rice go very well with this dish.

Buffalo Stew

1	buffalo (large)	salt and pepper
2	rabbits (optional)	

Cut the buffalo into bite-sized pieces. This should take about 2 months. Add enough gravy to cover. Cook over a kerosene fire for about four weeks at 465 degrees. This will serve 3,777 people. If more are expected, two rabbits can be added, but this should be done only if necessary, as most people do not like to find hare in their stew.

Oven Dried Marinated Jerky

2 lbs boneless meat (lean cuts of beef, venison or white meat of chicken or turkey)	¹/₄ teaspoon pepper
	¹/₄ teaspoon garlic powder
	¹/₂ teaspoon onion powder
¹/₄ soy sauce	1 teaspoon hickory flavored salt
1 tablespoon Worcestershire sauce	1 teaspoon brown sugar (Art's secret ingredient)

Trim and discard all fat. Slice meat with the grain. Make strips ¹/₈-¹/₄" thick and as long as possible. Combine all spices and coat meat thoroughly. Let stand in refrigerator for 2-3 days, shaking or stirring to coat thoroughly. Drain meat, arrange on racks or hang from racks. Bake at 175-225 degrees about 8 hours or until dried. Turn once during cooking.

J-J   *Jody Nelson*
J-J Longhorns
Salix, IA

❖

Each year since 1943, except once during W.W.II, the Wichita Mountains National Wildlife Refuge has sold their surplus Texas Longhorns at public auction. In 1946 "Buyers and Connie Hill, the auctioneer, were on the west side of a woven wire big-game fence that joined the wooden corral system. The sale cattle were moved around this fenced area by Drummond and a couple of others on horseback. Buyers sat on wooden ammunition boxes borrowed from Fort Sill. There was no shade. The auctioneer, standing between the buyers and the fence, cried the auction without benefit of a PA system. Most of the adult animals sold were destined for the slaughter house. Some of the calves went to farmers and ranchers to be fed out for beef at the home, or for sale. A few were destined to be held as Longhorn breeding stock. The average price for a six-month-old calf was $35."

—*Julian A. Howard*
Wichita Refuge Assistant Manager following World War II. (1991)

Venison Pot Roast

1¹/₂	lbs venison	2	teaspoons instant beef bouillon
¹/₄	teaspoon black pepper		
3	tablespoons flour	1	tablespoon browning sauce
3	tablespoons vegetable oil or bacon drippings	3	carrots, scraped and cut in 3" pieces
1	large onion, peeled and thinly sliced into rings	2	large potatoes, peeled and sliced
1¹/₂	cups water	¹/₂	teaspoon salt
¹/₂	cup wine		

Sprinkle roast with pepper and dredge in flour. Heat oil in large heavy frying pan and brown roast on both sides. Top roast with onion rings. Pour water and wine over all. Reduce heat and stir in bouillon. Pour browning sauce on top of roast. Cover and cook on low 2 hours. If roast becomes dry, add more water. Add carrots and potatoes, sprinkle with salt. Cover and cook 1¹/₂-2 hours until roast is tender. Place roast on heated platter and arrange vegetables around roast.

Make a gravy by mixing ¹/₄ teaspoon salt and 2 tablespoons flour with ¹/₂ cup cold water and ¹/₂ cup milk and 2 tablespoons Worcestershire sauce. Stir or shake in tightly covered jar until flour is completely dissolved. Pour into pan with roast drippings. Cook on high heat until mixture starts to boil. Reduce heat and stir until thickened and smooth. Season to taste. Serve over roast and/or on the side. Serves 4.

Note: *To vary, omit potatoes and serve over cooked white rice.*

❖

"The most important economic trait of the Longhorn cross cow, to me, is that she gets a calf every 12 months and I almost never have a dry cow. The cattle also go well with my Spanish meat goats. The cattle play the role of guard dog. We've never lost any goats in the pastures where the cows had calves.'

—**Agricultural economist Robert Kensing**
Menard, Texas

Mexican Venison Scramble

1	cup diced cooked venison steak	2	tablespoons shortening
3	tablespoons chopped onions	1	can whole kernel corn
		1½	cups tomato juice
1	tablespoon green pepper	½	teaspoon chili powder
		1¼	teaspoons salt

Sauté meat, onion, and green pepper slowly in shortening until browned. Add corn, tomato juice and seasonings and simmer in covered skillet for 30 minutes. Serve with brown rice.

SPECIAL HINTS:

Oven cooking bags are excellent for cooking wild game because they hold in juices and cook with moist heat. Buy bags according to the size of the meat or bird and follow the directions on the package.

Wild turkeys are flavorful, juicy and tender when cooked in a turkey size oven cooking bag. For ease of preparation, skin the turkey before putting in the bag instead of trying to remove all the pin feathers. The bird will still remain juicy if you follow the cooking bag directions.

Salt meat after it is cooked in order to have a moist and juicy product. Salt draws moisture out during cooking.

Experiment and try different kinds of herbs and spices for seasoning wild game.

Slow cookers are very good for cooking wild game. The long, slow cooking leaves a very tender, juicy product. Also, they are portable and travel well to the hunter's camp.

Canned soups, especially the creamed and tomato varieties, added to wild game and birds during cooking will provide flavor and moisture.

Grind lean venison and a small amount of fat pork or fat beef (about 10%) to make an excellent ground meat for meat loaves and hamburger patties.

Something For Your Sweet Tooth

❖

Son-Of-A-Gun-In-A-Sack

When the coosie wanted to return a favor to a cowhand who had brought in some dry firewood (or cow chips) off the range, or if there was a special occasion, he would make this boiled suet pudding. He would add raisins or dried apples if available. Some sources say it got its name because it was so difficult to make and others because it was so good.

2	cups flour	1	teaspoon ground cinnamon
1	cup dried fruit such as raisins	1/4	teaspoon ground cloves
1	tablespoon soda	1/4	teaspoon ground nutmeg
1	cup bread crumbs	1	cup ground beef suet
1	teaspoon salt	1	cup canned milk
1	cup molasses		

Mix dry ingredients together. Add suet and mix well. Stir in milk and molasses until well mixed. Pour mixture into a cloth sack and tie with a string. Place in a large pot of boiling water, cover and boil gently for 2 hours. Serve warm with sweetened canned milk or cream if available.

—Campfire Cooking **by Jalynn Burkett**
Texas Longhorn breeder and County Extension Agent
Fort Worth, TX

❖

Sour Cream Banana Bars

1½ cups sugar	1½ cups mashed bananas, about 3 large
1 cup sour cream, do not use light sour cream	2 teaspoons vanilla
½ cup butter or margarine, softened	2 cups flour
	1 teaspoon baking soda
2 eggs	¾ teaspoon salt
	½-1 cup chopped nuts

Heat oven to 375 degrees. Grease and flour a 15"×10"×1" pan. Mix sugar, sour cream, margarine and eggs in a large bowl on low speed for 1 minute. Beat in bananas and vanilla on low speed. Beat in flour, baking soda and salt on medium speed for 1 minute. Stir in nuts. Spread batter in pan and bake until light brown, about 20-25 minutes. Don't overbake. Frost with Browned Butter Frosting.

BROWNED BUTTER FROSTING:

¼ cup butter	1 teaspoon vanilla
2- 2½ cups powdered sugar milk or half-and-half	

In medium saucepan, heat butter over medium heat until a light delicate brown. Remove from heat. Add powdered sugar, milk or half-and-half to desired consistency. Add vanilla.

Frost when cool and add more nuts if desired. I use English or Black walnuts. Cream cheese frosting is also very good.

Cheryl Carlson
Crown-C Ranch
St. Marys, KS

Cherry Winks

3/4 cup shortening	1/2 teaspoon baking soda
1 cup sugar	1 cup chopped pecans
2 eggs	1 cup chopped dates
2 tablespoons milk	1/3 cup maraschino cherries
1 teaspoon vanilla	2 1/2 cups corn flakes
2 1/4 cups flour	maraschino cherries for
1 teaspoon baking powder	garnish, optional
1/2 teaspoon salt	

Cream shortening and sugar; add eggs, milk and vanilla. Sift flour, baking powder, salt and baking soda and blend slightly. Add pecans, dates and cherries. Mix well. Shape into balls with about 1 teaspoon of dough for each. Crush 2½ cups corn flakes and roll balls in flakes. Place on greased cookie sheet and top with ¼ piece of cherry if desired. Bake at 375 degrees for 10-12 minutes.

This recipe is very good as is, but I especially like it for my Christmas gift baskets. Sometimes for Christmas I use both red and green cherries.

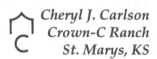

Cheryl J. Carlson
Crown-C Ranch
St. Marys, KS

Longhorn Sweets

3/4 cup sugar	cinnamon and nutmeg to taste
1 stick margarine	1 teaspoon vanilla
3/4 cup canned milk	1 can biscuits, halved
3/4 cup whole milk	

Bring all to boil except biscuits. Place halved biscuits in 13"×9"×2" cake pan. When mix boils, pour over biscuits and bake at 350 degrees until done.

Donna Roberson
Rocking R Ranch
Tahoka, TX

Fruit Roll

1	lb marshmallows	1	package dates
1/2	cup Pet milk	1/2	lb raisins
1/2	cup milk	1	large bottle red maraschino
1	lb graham crackers,		cherries, drained and halved
	divided	1	large bottle green
1	quart shelled pecans		maraschino cherries,
1/2	lb shelled walnuts		drained and halved

Melt marshmallows in milk in top of double broiler. Crumble graham crackers into small crumbs, reserving 1½ cups in large flat dish. Pour hot milk-marshmallow mixture over nuts, dates, raisins, cracker crumbs and cherries. Mix well and shape into several rolls. Roll in remaining crumbs until well-coated. Wrap each roll in waxed paper and then again in foil. Put into refrigerator and store for several months. Slice with very sharp knife.

Note: Put your graham crackers through the food processor. This really speeds up the process. You can also melt your marshmallows in some milk in the microwave. It's really a lot easier if you have someone help you roll these and wrap them. Your hands get very sticky. I also coat my hands with butter and this seems to help when making the rolls.

J— *Jean Smith*
Fort Worth, TX

Yummy Bars

1	cup sugar	1	(6 ounce) package
1	cup white Karo syrup		chocolate chips
1/2	cup chunky peanut butter	1	(6 ounce) package
6	cups Special K cereal or		butterscotch chips
	corn flakes		

Mix sugar and Karo and just bring to a boil. Add peanut butter. Mix with cereal. Press mixture down hard in a 13"×9"×2" buttered pan. Over hot water melt chocolate and butterscotch chips. (I use all chocolate). Spread over mixture in pan. Cool and cut in squares.

Zucchini Bars

2	cups sugar	2 1/2	cups flour
4	eggs	1/2	teaspoon each - baking
1/2	cup vegetable oil		powder, baking soda, salt
2	teaspoon cinnamon	2	cups unpeeled shredded
1	teaspoon vanilla		zucchini

Heat oven to 350 degrees. Lightly grease a 17"×11"×1" jellyroll pan. Beat sugar, eggs, oil, cinnamon and vanilla in a large bowl with a hand mixer until well blended. Add flour, baking powder, baking soda and salt. Stir in zucchini. Spread evenly in prepared pan. Bake 25-30 minutes.

FROSTING:

1/2	stick margarine, softened	1	teaspoon vanilla
1	(3 ounce) package cream cheese, softened	2	cups powdered sugar walnuts

Mix margarine, cream cheese, vanilla and powdered sugar. Garnish with walnuts.

J-J

Jody Nelson
J-J Longhorns
Salix, IA

---------------- ❖ ----------------

"Our country is steep and rough. Actually it's what you might call good goat country. It's up and down, and cattle must travel over two miles to water. Texas Longhorns are the only breed of cattle that have ever been able to range some of the ground on our ranch."

—*Don Akehurst*
Ellensburg, Washington

Jean's Butter Sticks

1	stick of butter	1	cup milk
2¹/₂	cups flour	3¹/₂	teaspoons baking powder
1	tablespoon sugar	1¹/₂	teaspoon salt
¹/₄	teaspoon baking soda		

Melt butter in a jelly roll pan. Mix all other ingredients, roll out, and cut into strips. Dredge strips through the butter, covering all sides. Bake at 425 degrees until golden brown. You can add garlic and parsley, or cinnamon, or roll in cinnamon sugar.

These are good hot or cold, which is good because the cowboys and the chuck wagon don't always meet at the appointed time.

Note: *Out here in West Texas, we use radios to communicate. Mrs. Demere (Jean) is easily the best cook in our county, and she feeds 6-8 hungry cowboys that work on their ranch at noon every day. Everyday, around 11:30, those radios (and many others, including ours!) are tuned to channel 1 to get her version of Hee-Haw's "Hey Grandpa, what's for dinner?"*

R3 *Kim Richey*
Triple R Ranch
San Angelo, TX

❖

"Milling"

"If forced by riders when Longhorns are alarmed, they will sometimes begin to circle in a closely packed bunch. This is known as "milling". Riders handling Longhorns in such a situation usually cut off a small bunch of the animals and crowd them until they enter the gate. Others in the herd generally follow.

"Milling" Longhorns often stampede when frightened by a slight noise. Even a shout or loud talk might start them. For this reason, riders spoke soft and low to the herd and frequently sang to quiet them. Many a Texas and Oklahoma cowpuncher probably got his reputation as a crooner from the practice he received by singing to a steer herd."

— Forest Ranger Earl Drummond
Wichita Mountains National Wildlife Refuge
Cache, Oklahoma (1939)

Pumpkin Pie Squares

1	cup flour	2	eggs
1/2	cup quick oatmeal	3/4	cup sugar
1/2	cup brown sugar	1/2	teaspoon salt
1/2	cup butter	1	teaspoon cinnamon
2	cups pumpkin 1/2		teaspoon ginger
1	can evaporated milk	1/2	teaspoon cloves

TOPPING:

1/2	cup chopped nuts	2	tablespoons butter
1/2	cup brown sugar		

Combine flour, oatmeal, brown sugar and butter in large mixing bowl. Mix until crumbly. Press into ungreased 13"×9"×2" pan. Bake at 350 degrees for 15 minutes. Combine pumpkin, milk, eggs, sugar, salt, cinnamon, ginger and cloves in bowl. Beat well. Pour into crust and bake at 350 degrees for 20 minutes. Mix nuts, brown sugar and butter. Sprinkle over pumpkin filling. Bake 15-20 minutes longer. Cool in pan and cut in 2" squares. Serve with whipped cream.

Linda Krukow
4K Longhorns
Hampton, IA

White Brownies

1/3	cup butter, melted	1	teaspoon baking powder
1	cup brown sugar	1/8	teaspoon salt
1	egg, unbeaten	1	teaspoon vanilla
1	cup flour		chopped nuts

Mix all ingredients together. Pat into 8"×8"×2" pan. Bake at 350 degrees for 25 minutes.

Should vegetarians eat animal crackers?

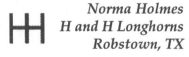

Norma Holmes
H and H Longhorns
Robstown, TX

Chocolate Lovers Dessert

1	box brownie mix	1	large Cool Whip
1	large box chocolate instant pudding	1	bag Skor candy pieces (or 35 Skor bars, chopped)

Prepare brownies as directed and cool. Break into chunks. Mix pudding as directed and then layer pudding with Cool Whip, Skor candy bars and brownies. Repeat layers. One batch serves 6, but recipe may be doubled or tripled.

Margie Deal
D & M Ranch
Read Oak, TX

Chocolate Turtle Brownies

1	(12 ounce) package semisweet chocolate chips, divided	1	cup granulated sugar
		1/4	teaspoon baking soda
		1	teaspoon vanilla
1	stick butter or margarine, cut into pieces	1/2	cup chopped pecans
		12	caramels
3	eggs, beaten	1	tablespoon milk
1 1/4	cups flour		

Melt 1 cup of the chocolate chips and the butter in large, heavy saucepan over low heat, stirring constantly until smooth. Remove from heat; stir in eggs. Add flour, sugar, baking soda and vanilla; stir well. Spread batter into greased 13"x9"x2" baking pan; sprinkle with remaining chips and nuts. Bake in preheated 350 degree oven for 20-25 minutes or until wooden toothpick inserted in center comes out slightly sticky. Melt caramels and milk on high in microwave for 1 minute. Continue to cook in 10-20 second intervals, stirring after each, until smooth. Drizzle over warm brownies. Cool in pan.

"Humor is the good-natured side of truth."—Mark Twain

Vicki Helms
Belleville, IL
Heartland Texas Longhorn Breeders Association

Ozark Apple Pie

1	egg, beaten	¹/₄	teaspoon salt
³/₄	cup sugar		dash cinnamon
¹/₂	cup flour	1	cup finely chopped apples
1¹/₂	teaspoons baking powder	¹/₂	cup chopped nuts

Mix eggs and sugar and beat until thick. Add flour, baking powder, salt and cinnamon. Fold in apples and nuts. Bake in buttered 9" pie plate.

Serve with ice cream or whipped cream.

Nancy Meade
Windmill Longhorn Ranch
Milo, Iowa

Never-Fail Pie Crust

1¹/₃	cups flour, divided	1	teaspoon salt
²/₃	cup Crisco	¹/₄	cup water

Blend 1 cup flour, Crisco and salt together with fork or pastry blender. Mix ¹/₃ cup flour and water into a paste and add to the first mixture. Blend well and roll out on a floured board.

Beverly Sorem
Flying S Cattle
Nevada, IA

Alamo Pie

1	can Eagle Brand Milk, low fat is fine	whipped cream or low fat dairy topping
³/₄	cup maple syrup	toasted coconut
¹/₂-³/₄	cup chopped pecans	baked pie crust

Bring milk and syrup to a boil. Cook about 8 minutes until thick. Cool. Add pecans and place mixture in pie crust. Top with whipped cream and sprinkle with toasted coconut. Keep refrigerated.

Priscilla Briney
Lazy 5B Ranch
Bowie, TX

Jeff Davis Pie

6	eggs yolks	1/4	teaspoon cloves
2	cups sugar	1/4	teaspoon nutmeg
2	tablespoons flour	3	cups half-and-half, divided
1/2	teaspoon allspice		butter, the size of an egg
1 •	teaspoon cinnamon	2	unbaked pie crusts

In a mixing bowl, mix together egg yolks, sugar, flour, allspice. cinnamon, cloves and nutmeg. Add 1/2 cup of the half-and-half, and mix real well. Heat the rest of the half-and-half and butter until it is just good and warm, and pour into the bowl with the egg mixture. Mix well again. After all is well-mixed, pour into pie crusts and bake in 325 degree oven until set. This is just a version of an egg custard, treat it the same.

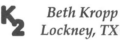
Beth Kropp
Lockney, TX

Voodoo Pecan Pie

4	eggs	1	cup dark or white Karo syrup
1	cup sugar		
1	stick margarine vanilla	3/4	cup semi-sweet chocolate chips
2	jiggers Bourbon	1	cup pecans
		1	unbaked deep dish pie crust

Combine all ingredients and pour into crust. Bake until set in 300 degree oven. When cool, cut into sections and put Cool Whip or ice cream on it.

---------------- ❖ ----------------

"Texas Longhorn cattle are as good as the best, and better than the rest in this part of the country. That's the way I see it."

J.W. Isaacs
Alvin, Texas
Sixth President of the TLBAA

Never Soggy! Pie Crust

²/₃	cup shortening	1	teaspoon salt
2	cups flour	¹/₂	cup cold water

Cut shortening into flour and salt mixture. Gradually add cold water. Divide into 2 crusts. Roll out one crust and place in 9" or 10" pie pan. Roll the second crust out. Using a pizza cutter, cut this crust into narrow strips. Braid and lay around edge of pie. Bake with filling for 1 hour at 350 degrees.

Kathy Stovall
3 Sons Cattle Company
Petrolia, TX

Dick, Martha and Maryellen's Raisin Pie

1¹/₂ cups dark raisins
1¹/₂ cups golden raisins
Boiling water to cover raisins
1   cup sugar
¹/₄ cup flour
juice from 1 fresh lemon

zest of 1 lemon (use only the yellow)
1   package Pillsbury prepared pie crust (2 crusts)
vegetable oil cooking spray
1   egg yolk
1   tablespoon milk

Combine dark and golden raisins in a large bowl and cover with boiling water. Let stand for 15 minutes. Drain in a colander. Discard the water. Return the raisins to the bowl. Add sugar, flour, lemon juice and zest. Mix and set aside for 10 minutes to thicken. Spray a 9" metal pie pan with vegetable spray. Place the pie crust in the pan without any overhang. Punch holes in the top crust on a flat surface with a pastry tip or a drinking straw (about 10-12 rows of holes). Fill the prepared crust with the raisin mixture. Add the top crust. Tuck the top crust under the bottom crust around the edges. Refrigerate 30 minutes. Heat oven to 425 degrees. Mix egg yolk and milk in small bowl. Brush the pie crust sparingly with the mixture. Place on a baking sheet and bake 20 minutes. Then reduce temperature to 375 for 35-40 minutes. If pie starts to get too brown, cover it with a piece of foil. Remove from oven and cool on wire rack. Easy and delicious!

Custard Egg Pie

This pie makes its own crust!

4	eggs, well-beaten
4	tablespoon flour
1/2	cup sugar
1	teaspoon vanilla

1/2	teaspoon nutmeg
1/4	teaspoon salt
2	cups milk

Beat all together. Grease and flour 9" pie pan. Bake at 325-350 degrees until lightly brown and set, about 45 minutes.

J-J
Jody Nelson
J-J Longhorns
Salix, IA

Buttermilk Pie

3	eggs, well-beaten
1/2	cup butter, melted
1/2	cup buttermilk
1/2	teaspoon vanilla

1 3/4	cups sugar
1/4	cup flour
1/4	teaspoon salt
	unbaked pie crust

Mix eggs, melted butter, buttermilk, and vanilla. Add sugar, flour and salt. (A wire whisk works best.) Bake in pie crust for 1 hour at 350 degrees. Cover edges of crust with foil until last 15-20 minutes to keep edges from becoming too brown.

Marilyn Wood
Wild Wood Ranch
Lindale, TX

❖

"In our area, the temperature sometimes drops to 30 degrees below zero, lasting for three to four days. These Longhorns cows are very intelligent. As soon as they see bad weather coming, they head off for the rough country to bed their calves down."

—*Charles Miller*
Sunnybrook Cattle Co.
Fort Collins, Colorado

Sweet Potato Pie

2	cups cooked sweet potatoes, mashed	1/4	teaspoon salt
		1/2	teaspoon cinnamon
1/2	cup butter or margarine, softened	1/2	teaspoon ground nutmeg
		1/2	teaspoon ground ginger
2	eggs, separated	1/2	cup milk
1	cup firmly packed brown sugar	1/4	cup sugar
		1	9" unbaked pie crust

Combine sweet potatoes, butter, egg yolks, brown sugar, salt, cinnamon, nutmeg and ginger. Stir in milk and mix well. Beat egg whites on high speed with an electric cup mixer for 1 minute. Gradually add 1/4 cup sugar, 1 tablespoon at a time, beating until stiff peaks form. Fold egg whites into sweet potato mixture. Spoon mixture into pie crust. Bake at 400 degrees for 10 minutes. Reduce heat to 350 degrees and bake for 45 minutes or longer until set.

Sour Cream Raisin Pie

3/4	cup sugar	1	cup sour cream
2	tablespoon flour		raisins
3	egg yolks	1	baked pie crust

Cook sugar, flour and egg yolks in saucepan over very low heat and stir continually. (This will scorch very easily.) Cook until lightly boils and thickens. Fold in sour cream and raisins. Remove from heat and add to pie crust. (If you want a thick filling, you may want to make 1 1/4 recipes.)

Top with Cool Whip or make egg white meringue.

Beverly Sorem
Flying S Cattle
Nevada, IA

Blueberry/Banana Pie

1	frozen deep dish pie crust	1	can blueberry pie filling
2	medium bananas, sliced		Cool Whip

Bake pie crust according to directions. When cool, add sliced bananas to pie crust, and top with blueberry pie filling. Cover pie filling with Cool Whip (as much as desired).

This is great for unexpected company or when you need to take a dessert somewhere in a hurry. Doesn't have to be chilled. I also use fresh strawberries when in season. This will require Strawberry pie filling. I got this recipe from Florine Matthews, Bristow, Oklahoma.

Linda Moore
Manteca Ranch
Gainesville, TX

Cherry-O-My Pie

1	(8 ounce) package cream cheese	1	can cherry pie filling
1⅓	cups Eagle Brand Sweetened Condensed Milk		graham cracker crust (store bought or I use crushed graham crackers, brown sugar and butter and cook
1	teaspoon vanilla		for 10 minutes at 350
⅓	cup fresh or bottled lemon juice		degrees)

Soften cream cheese and whip until fluffy. Gradually add condensed milk, vanilla and lemon juice, continuing to blend until smooth. Pour into prepared crust and refrigerate for 2-3 hours. Cover with cherry pie filling and chill again. This is Robert's favorite dessert and always good, especially in the summer.

R3

Kim Richey
Triple R Ranch
San Angelo, TX

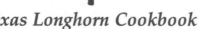

Nutty Chocolate Chip Pie

1	cup sugar	1	cup melted, unsalted butter
1	cup brown sugar, packed	1/2	cup chopped pecans
1	cup flour	1/2	cup chocolate chips
2	large eggs, slightly beaten	1	10" pie unbaked pie crust

Mix sugar, brown sugar and flour together. Stir in eggs, then the butter, combining well. Fold in nuts and chips. Spread in crust and bake at 325 degrees for 60-70 minutes. Pie is done when knife inserted in center comes out clean.

When it rains, why don't sheep shrink?

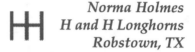

Norma Holmes
H and H Longhorns
Robstown, TX

Grand-Ma Cookies

1	cup sugar	1 1/2	cups oatmeal
1	cup brown sugar	1	teaspoon soda
1	cup Crisco oil	1/2	teaspoon baking powder
2	eggs	1	cup chocolate chips
1	tablespoon vanilla	1	cup almond bark chips
1 1/2	cups flour	1	cup flaked coconut
1 1/2	cups corn flakes	1	cup chopped pecans

Cream sugars and oil. Add eggs one at a time and beat well. Add vanilla. In a separate bowl add all other ingredients. Stir well to get all mixed and stuck together real well. Mix with sugar mixture. It will be pretty stiff. Drop by spoonfuls on a lightly greased cookie sheet. Bake at 325 degrees for 15-20 minutes or until light brown. Cool and remove from cookie sheet. Eat and ENJOY!!!!!

Everyone's grandchild except mine loves these cookies, but mine prefers peanut butter cookies!

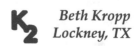

Beth Kropp
Lockney, TX

Tea Cakes

3¹/₂ cups self-rising flour	1 teaspoon vanilla
1¹/₂ cups sugar	³/₄ cup milk
¹/₄ cup butter Crisco	2 eggs, beaten
¹/₄ cup butter	

Mix flour, sugar and Crisco. Add butter, vanilla, and milk. Add eggs and blend well. Form mixture into small balls and place on greased cookie sheet. With a fork dipped in flour, make a criss-cross design, flattening the ball of dough. Bake 8-10 minutes or until light brown at 350 degrees.

JM *Vonda Burden*
Town Creek, AL

No Bake Peanut Butter Cookies

1 cup white sugar	2 cups peanut butter
1 cup white corn syrup	4 cups chow mein noodles

Bring sugar and corn syrup to a boil, and add peanut butter. Add noodles. Drop on wax paper in spoonfuls, allow to cool, then eat, and eat, and eat!

No Bake Cookies

1 package almond white bark	2¹/₂ cups Rice Crispies
	2¹/₂ cups Planters Dried Peanuts
1 cup chocolate chips	1 cup miniature marshmallows
2¹/₂ cups Captain Crunch	

Melt almond bark and chocolate chips in microwave for 2-3 minutes. Stir frequently, so as not to burn. In a large bowl mix cereals, peanuts and marshmallows. Combine with almond bark and chocolate chips. Drop by the spoonful on wax paper. This makes several dozen depending on the size of the spoonful. This hardens very quickly.

Yummy!

Butter Bittersweets

1	cup powdered sugar	1/2	teaspoon salt
1	cup soft butter	2	cups flour

Cream sugar and butter and salt. Add flour. Using 1 teaspoon dough each, shape into balls. Place 2" apart on cookie sheet, sprayed with cooking spray. Make thumbprint in each. Bake at 350 degrees for 10-12 minutes until edges are golden brown.

FILLING:

1	cup powdered sugar	1	(3 ounce) package cream
1	teaspoon vanilla		cheese, softened
2	tablespoons flour	1/2	cup chopped pecans
		1/2	cup coconut

Cream powdered sugar, vanilla, flour and cream cheese. Add pecans and coconut. Fill each cookie with 1/2 teaspoon filling as soon as cookies are out of the oven.

GLAZE:

1/2	cup chocolate chips	2	tablespoons butter
2	tablespoons water	1/2	cup powdered sugar

In a small saucepan, melt chips with water and butter. Stir constantly. Remove from heat. Add powdered sugar and blend until smooth. Drizzle over top of cookies. Makes 2 1/2 dozen fabulously rich gourmet cookies.

Velna Jackson won a blue ribbon premium at the Gillepsie County Fair with this recipe.

     Stonewall Valley Ranch
Austin, TX

Lite Chocolate Chip Cookies

1	stick margarine	2 1/4	cups flour
3/4	cup sugar	1	teaspoon baking soda
3/4	cup brown sugar or honey	1/2	teaspoon salt
1	teaspoon vanilla	6-12	ounces lite semisweet
2	eggs, beaten		baking chips

Heat oven to 375 degrees. Cream margarine and sugars. Add vanilla and eggs. Stir in flour, baking soda and salt. Gradually add chips. Bake for 8-10 minutes.

Orange Slice Cookies

1	cup sugar	1	teaspoon baking powder
1	cup packed brown sugar	1/2	teaspoon salt
1	cup shortening	2	cups quick cooking
2	eggs		oatmeal
1	teaspoon vanilla	2	cups candy orange slices,
2	cups flour		chopped
1	teaspoon baking soda	1	cup flaked coconut

In a large bowl, cream sugars and shortening till fluffy. Add eggs and vanilla. Beat well. Stir together flour, baking powder, baking soda and salt. Stir into creamed mixture. Stir in oats, candy and coconut. Using about 1 tablespoon of mixture for each, roll into 1" balls. Place on a greased cookie sheet. Bake at 350 degrees for 10-12 minutes or until lightly browned. Makes 6 dozen.

❖

"A Texas Longhorn steer will stop more people than a dead man."

—Col. Eddie Wood
Payday Ranch
Wynnewood, Oklahoma

Ole Tyme Fig Cookies

2	cups sugar	1	teaspoon vanilla
2	eggs	1/2	teaspoon nutmeg
1/2	cup butter flavor Crisco	1/2	teaspoon cinnamon
3 1/2	cups flour	1	cup fig preserves
1	teaspoon baking soda	1	cup pecans, chopped

Cream sugar, eggs and shortening until creamy. Add the rest of the ingredients and mix well. Drop by teaspoonfuls far apart on a greased cookie sheet. Bake at 350 degrees until light brown. Makes 7-8 dozen.

You can use more spices (to taste). I use a pint of fig preserves (mash if whole). If preserves have a lot of juice, you may have to add a little at a time. Happy eating!

Cow Patties

1	cup shortening	2	teaspoons baking soda
1	cup margarine	2	teaspoons baking powder
2	cups brown sugar	2	cups oatmeal
2	cups sugar	1	(6 ounce) package chocolate chips
4	eggs		
1	teaspoon vanilla	1	(6 ounce) package butterscotch chips
1	cup chopped pecans		
4	cups flour	2	cups crushed corn flakes

Cream shortening, margarine and sugars. Add eggs and beat well. Gradually stir in the remaining ingredients. Drop by teaspoonfuls on ungreased cookie sheet. Bake at 325 degrees for 10-12 minutes. Makes several dozen.

❖

"Ate terrapin and dog meat, and was glad to get it."

—*Trail Driver Ben Drake (1879)*

Chocolate Cashew Crunch Cookies

1/2 stick unsalted butter	1/2 cup finely chopped cashews
1/3 cup brown sugar	1 1/2 teaspoons vanilla
1/4 cup corn syrup	1 (6 ounce) package
1/3 cup flour	chocolate chips

Preheat oven to 350 degrees. Butter and flour cookie sheet. In sauce-pan, melt butter over medium heat. Add brown sugar and corn syrup. Bring to a boil over medium heat, stirring until sugar dissolves (3-5 minutes). Remove from heat and stir in flour, cashews, and vanilla. Drop 1/2 teaspoon mounds 2" apart using small spatula to flatten mounds into circles. Bake 8-10 minutes. Rotate back of pan to front of oven after 4 minutes. Cool 30 seconds, then transfer to wire rack to cool. Melt chocolate chips and dip cooled cookie half way.

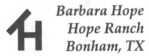

Barbara Hope
Hope Ranch
Bonham, TX

Almond Cookies

graham crackers	1/2 cup sugar
1 stick butter	1 package slivered almonds
1 stick margarine	

Put 8 graham crackers (broken into fourths) on greased cookie sheet that has sides. Boil butter, margarine and sugar for 3 minutes. Add slivered almonds. Mix and pour over graham crackers. Bake at 350 degrees for 10 minutes. Take spatula and immediately put on waxed paper.

S/K
Karen King
S/K Ranch
Granbury, TX

Peanut Clusters

1　lb white chocolate or almond bark	1　(13 ounce) package salted peanuts
1　(12 ounce) package chocolate chips	

Combine white chocolate or almond bark and chocolate chips in top of double broiler and melt (or use microwave oven.) Then, add salted peanuts. Combine and drop on waxed paper, by spoonfuls and let harden. Keep refrigerated.

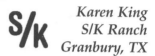

Karen King
S/K Ranch
Granbury, TX

Mayonnaise Chocolate Cake

1　cup sugar	1½　teaspoons baking soda
2　cups flour	1　cup cold water
¼　cup cocoa	1　cup Hellmann's mayonnaise
1½　teaspoons baking powder	1　teaspoon vanilla

Mix together first 5 ingredients. Add water, mayonnaise and vanilla. Mix for 2 minutes. Makes 2 8" layers or 9" square cake. Bake at 325 degrees for 30 minutes. (Lower oven to 300 degrees for glass pan.)

FROSTING:

½　stick margarine, room temperature	½-¾ box powdered sugar dash salt
2　tablespoons cocoa	1　teaspoon vanilla
3　tablespoons milk	

Mix well. Spread on cake.

Connie Goodman
Dalgood Longhorns
Houston, TX

2 Dump Cake

2	cups flour	1	(20 ounce) can crushed pineapple
2	cups sugar		
2	teaspoons baking soda	1/2	stick butter
2	eggs	1	cup chopped pecans

Mix all ingredients together. Bake at 350 degrees for 30-35 minutes.

ICING:

1	(8 ounce) package cream cheese, softened	1	(1 lb) box powdered sugar
1 1/2	sticks butter, softened	1	teaspoon vanilla

Mix all ingredients and spread on cake.

Roop Ranch
Keatchie, LA

Vanilla Wafer Cake

1	stick margarine, softened	1/2	cup milk
2	cups sugar	1	small can coconut
6	eggs	1	cup chopped pecans
1	(12 ounce) package vanilla wafers, crushed fine		

Preheat oven to 350 degrees. In a large bowl, cream the margarine and sugar with a mixer. Add eggs one at a time. Beat well after each addition. Add vanilla wafers, alternately with milk to creamed mixture. Add coconut and pecans. Place batter in greased 10" bundt cake pan. Bake at 350 degrees for 1 hour.

This is very good. One of Blackie's favorites!

Lorene Graves
Dayton, TX

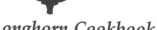

Mom's Chocolate Cake

½ cup buttermilk	pinch of salt
1 teaspoon baking soda	1 stick margarine
2 cups sugar	½ cup shortening
2 cups flour	1 cup water
4 tablespoons cocoa	2 eggs
1 teaspoon baking powder	1 teaspoon vanilla
½ teaspoon cinnamon	

Mix buttermilk with baking soda and set aside. Sift sugar, flour, cocoa, baking powder, cinnamon and salt together. Bring margarine, shortening and water to a boil. Pour over flour mixture. Add buttermilk and soda mixture. Mix well. Beat eggs and add to batter. Add vanilla. Bake in greased loaf pan for 20-25 minutes at 350 degrees.

ICING:

1 stick margarine	1 box powdered sugar, sifted
¼ cup milk	1 teaspoon vanilla
4 tablespoons cocoa	1 cup chopped pecans
pinch of salt	

Bring margarine and milk to a boil. Add cocoa and salt. Mix well. Remove from heat and add sifted sugar. Add vanilla. Spread thin layer over hot cake. Add pecans to remainder of icing and finish spreading over cake.

My mother has been baking this cake for us ever since I can remember and no family get-together is complete without one (or more)! When my husband and I got married last year, mother volunteered to bake one for the groom's cake. My sister, my mother and I wound up baking five chocolate cakes for the wedding reception. The wedding cake was a big hit, but the chocolate cakes were gone before we knew it!

My husband and I raise Texas Longhorns, and a week before our wedding we got to know firsthand just how tough Longhorns are. There is no better way to say it. They're tough and they are born that way. We have living proof. One day when working in the pasture, we noticed all the cows clustered around something pink on the ground. On closer inspection, that pink think turned out to be a tiny premature calf. It was late November and cold outside. We

bundled the calf up and headed for the barn. The calf was a tiny heifer with almost no hair and she was barely breathing.

We warmed her as best we could then moved her to the house for better care. She weighed a mere 14.9 pounds, and as close as we could estimate was at least two months premature. She was so weak, she could barely lift her head, but we felt she deserved every chance at survival that we could give her. We started her on electrolytes and milk. She managed to take about one ounce every two hours. The next day I milked her mother so she could get some colostrum and we continued the round-the-clock feedings. She gained strength steadily.

The calf was born six days before our wedding date. By the third day, we had decided to postpone the honeymoon because of our new arrival. Her name just naturally became "Honeymoon".

We came very close to losing the calf on the third day. Her lungs were failing and filling with fluid. Fortunately, since I am a veterinarian, I was able to start her on IV fluids and medication to clear her lungs. She was definitely doing her part in her fight for survival. She tried to nurse the bottle every time we offered it to her and by the fourth day was standing and tottering around our kitchen. She spent the first three weeks of her life in our whirlpool bathtub, which worked as the perfect "corral" for her.

When she got big enough and grew a little hair, we moved her to the heated tack room in our barn. By then we were able to reduce her feedings to 4-5 times per day and she was gaining weight on a steady basis.

"Honeymoon" is close to weaning age by now and weights nearly 500 pounds. I still find it hard to believe that she survived against such odds. She had the strongest will to live and is definitely "Texas Longhorn" tough. She runs to the barn every time I go near it for her bottle, which John or I am still giving her three times a day. I asked John the other day how he thought we should wean "Honeymoon". He said, "That's simple enough. We'll just stop feeding her." The next day he gave her all three of her bottles. We're still working on a solution!

Darlene Aldridge
Forest Creek Farms
Cypress, TX

Wilma's Wonderful Chocolate Cake

3/4	cup shortening	1	teaspoon vanilla
2	eggs, beaten	1/2	cup cocoa
1	cup sour milk or buttermilk	2 1/2	cups flour
2	teaspoons baking soda	1	cup boiling water

Mix and bake at 350 degrees for 30 minutes.

Note: This recipe can be converted to a spice cake by just adding 1 teaspoon cinnamon, 1 teaspoon nutmeg and 1/2 teaspoon cloves instead of cocoa.

CHOCOLATE FROSTING:

1 1/2	cups sugar	6	tablespoons margarine
6	tablespoons milk	1	cup chocolate chips

Boil sugar, milk and margarine for 30 seconds and add chocolate chips. Mix quickly and spread on cake.

Wilma Kastl
Herman, NE
Nebraska Texas Longhorn Association

Wilma turned 97 on May 11, 1998. She is an Associate Member of the NTLA. She still lives in her own home and is a retired schoolteacher and the oldest resident of Herman. She loves to visit the Longhorns every opportunity she gets.

Caramel Krazy Cake

3	cups flour	2/3	cup oil
2	teaspoons baking soda	1	teaspoon vanilla
1	teaspoon cinnamon	2	tablespoons vinegar
1	cup brown sugar	2	cups cold water
1	teaspoon salt	1	cup nuts, optional
3/4	teaspoon ground cloves		

Mix first 6 ingredients. Stir with all other ingredients in ungreased cake pan and bake at 350 degrees for 30-35 minutes.

Coconut Cake

1	package yellow cake mix	2	cups extra fine sugar
1	(12 ounce) package frozen coconut		(If you use regular sugar, blend well in blender first.)
1	(8 ounce) sour cream	1	(12 ounce) package Cool Whip

Bake cake mix in two round 9" pans. Mix coconut, sour cream and sugar and chill while cake is baking. When cool, cut both cake rounds in half horizontally. Set aside 1 cup of coconut mix and spread remaining mixture between cake layers. Mix the 1 cup of coconut mixture with Cool Whip and frost cake.

Refrigerate 3 days before eating this cake. It is worth waiting for. I would trade my husband off for this cake! It's the best.

B C *Brenda Choate*
Judsonia, AR

Snow Carnival Cake

Use a Betty Crocker cake mix and bake according to the directions on the box. Poke holes in top of cake with a wooden spoon handle while still warm. When cool, spread 2 (10 ounce each) strawberries, halved over the top. Next cover with 1 prepared and set package of instant vanilla pudding. Place a layer of Cool Whip over top and sprinkle with flaked coconut. Will keep weeks in the refrigerator. (If no one knows it is there!)

Quick Caramel Frosting

1/2	stick butter	1/4	teaspoon salt
1	cup brown sugar	2 1/2	cups powdered sugar, sifted
1/4	cup milk	1/4	teaspoon vanilla

Melt butter and stir in brown sugar. Cook 2 minutes over low heat stirring constantly. Add milk and stir until mixture comes to a boil. Remove from stove, and stir in salt and powdered sugar. Add vanilla. If too thick, add additional milk.

Black Russian Cake

1	box yellow cake mix	1	cup oil
1/2	cup sugar	4	eggs
1	(3 ounce) package instant	1/4	cup Vodka
	chocolate or chocolate	1/4	cup Kahlua
	fudge pudding	3/4	cup water

Mix all ingredients together on low speed for 1 minute, then beat at medium speed for 4 minutes. Bake in a large bundt pan at 350 degrees for 60-70 minutes. Cool cake in pan for 10 minutes. Turn out of pan and poke holes in cake.

GLAZE:

1/2	cup powdered sugar	1/4	cup Kahlua

Mix and spread over cake.

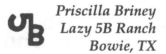
Priscilla Briney
Lazy 5B Ranch
Bowie, TX

Peanut Butter Cake

1	package banana cake mix	1/2 cup crunchy peanut butter

Mix cake mix as directed on package. Fold in peanut butter. Bake as directed in layers or sheet pan.

ICING:

1	cup peanut butter, crunchy	1/2	teaspoon nutmeg
		1/2	cup milk
1/3	cup powdered sugar	1	(8 ounce) package cream
1/2	cup honey		cheese, softened
1	teaspoon vanilla	1/2	cup chopped peanuts

Mix and spread on cake (and between layers if you use layer pans).

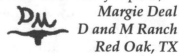
Margie Deal
D and M Ranch
Red Oak, TX

Apple Cake

2	eggs	1/2	teaspoon salt
1¹/₂	cups sugar	2	cups diced apples
1	cup flour	1	cup chopped pecans
2	teaspoons baking powder		

Beat eggs. Add sugar and continue beating until very thick. Mix flour, baking powder and salt together and add to egg mixture. Fold in apples and nuts. Pour into 8"×8"×2" greased baking pan and bake in 350 degree oven for 45 minutes. Cool in pan. Serve warm with whipped topping, topped with a maraschino cherry.

"I always like to hear a man talk about himself, because then I never hear anything but good."—Will Rogers

Vicki Helms
Belleville, IL
Heartland Texas Longhorn Breeders Association

Brown Sugar Apple Cake

1/2	cup shortening	1	teaspoon baking powder
1	cup sugar		dash of salt
2	eggs, beaten	1	teaspoon allspice
2	cups flour	1	cup milk
1	teaspoon baking soda	2	cups raw apples, chopped

Cream shortening and sugar. Add eggs. Mix all dry ingredients and add alternately with milk to mixture. Add apples.

TOPPING:

1	cup brown sugar	1/2	cup nuts

Mix sugar and nuts and spread over batter. Bake in 12"×8"×2" baking dish or pan. Bake in 350 degree oven for 40-45 minutes.

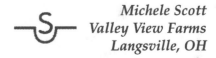

Michele Scott
Valley View Farms
Langsville, OH

Pumpkin Pie Cake

1	(29 ounce) can pumpkin	1/2	teaspoon nutmeg
4	eggs	1	yellow cake mix
1	can evaporated milk	1	cup melted butter or
1 1/2	cups sugar		margarine
1	teaspoon ginger		chopped nuts
2	teaspoons cinnamon		

Beat together first 7 ingredients. Pour into ungreased 13"×9"×2" pan. Sprinkle with the dry cake mix and nuts. Drizzle with margarine. Bake 1 hour (and no longer) at 350 degrees.

J-J
Jody Nelson
J-J Longhorns
Salix, IA

Home on the Range Bed and Breakfast Banana Nut Bread Cake

4	cups Original Pioneer Buttermilk Biscuit mix	1	teaspoon baking soda
4	smashed bananas	2	cups sugar
2/3	cup buttermilk (or 2/3 cup milk with 2 teaspoons vinegar)	3	eggs, beaten
		1	cup chopped pecans powdered sugar

Mix all ingredients together. Spray a bundt cake pan or 3 small loaf pans with cooking spray. Pour in batter and bake at 350 degrees for 40-50 minutes. Dust with powdered sugar for a great cake or loaves.

Stonewall Valley Ranch
Austin, TX

Banana Nut Cake

¹/₂ stick butter or margarine	1¹/₂ teaspoons baking soda
1¹/₂ cups sugar	2 cups flour
2 eggs, separated	1 cup mashed bananas
¹/₄ cup buttermilk	1 teaspoon vanilla
1 teaspoon baking powder	¹/₂ cup chopped nuts

Cream butter and sugar and egg yolks. Add buttermilk and dry ingredients, then bananas and vanilla. Beat egg whites until stiff and fold in last with chopped nuts. (I like pecans, but walnuts may be used.) Bake at 350 degrees about 30-40 minutes in 13"×9"×2" pan. Poke holes in cake with handle of wooden spoon. Icing should be spread on cake while still warm.

ICING:

1 banana	1 teaspoon vanilla
¹/₂ stick butter	1 (1 lb) box powdered sugar.

Mash banana with a little lemon juice. Melt butter and add vanilla. Add powdered sugar until thick (almost a box). Mix and spread over cake.

Marilyn Wood
Wild Wood Ranch
Lindale, TX

Gooey Cake

1 box cake mix	2 teaspoons vanilla
1 stick butter or margarine	2 eggs, beaten
2 eggs	powdered sugar
1 (8 ounce) package cream cheese, softened	

Beat first 3 ingredients and pour into greased 13"×9"×2" pan. Combine cream cheese, vanilla and eggs. Spread over the first layer and bake 35-45 minutes at 325 degrees. Sprinkle powdered sugar on top when cool. Cut into squares.

Carrot Cake

2	cups flour	2	teaspoons baking soda
2	cups sugar	1½	cups corn oil
2	teaspoons cinnamon	4	eggs
½	teaspoon salt	3	cups grated carrots
1	teaspoon baking powder	1	teaspoon vanilla

Mix all dry ingredients together. Add oil, eggs, carrots and vanilla and blend well. Bake in three 9" pans at 350 degrees for 30 minutes or until done.

FROSTING:

1	(8 ounce) package cream cheese, softened	1	box powdered sugar
		1	teaspoon vanilla
1	stick butter or margarine, softened	1	cup chopped pecans
			milk, optional

Cream the cream cheese and butter. Add sugar, vanilla and pecans. Blend well. Add milk if needed to spread.

Velma Slater
Slater Longhorns
Mexia, TX

❖

"When Walter Scott was elected president in 1971, there were only about 15 or 18 folks there at Lawton, Oklahoma, for the TLBAA convention. We met at the Holiday Inn, but the large meeting room was already taken. The only room left was the bar, the Lion's Den, so we took over one corner and had our election. We had so few members during those early years that we were hard put to find officers. It worked out to where "I'll take this office, if you'll take this one.' That's the way we were elected."

—J.W. Issacs
TLBAA President (1975-77)
Alvin, Texas

Chocolate Chip Carrot Cake

1½ cups flour	3 eggs
¾ cup sugar	¾ cup vegetable oil
½ cup packed light brown sugar	1½ teaspoons vanilla
1¼ teaspoons baking soda	2 cups grated carrots
1 teaspoon cinnamon	1 (12 ounce) package semi-sweet chocolate chips
½ teaspoon salt	½ cup chopped walnuts

Combine flour, sugars, baking soda, cinnamon and salt in large mixing bowl. Beat eggs, oil and vanilla in small bowl, then add to dry mix. Blend well. Stir in carrots, chocolate chips and nuts. Pour into 13"×9"×2" floured and greased pan. Bake at 350 degrees for 35-40 minutes. Cool completely.

CREAM CHEESE FROSTING:

1 (3 ounce) package cream cheese, softened	2 cups powdered sugar
¼ cup softened butter	1 teaspoon vanilla

Beat cream cheese and butter in small mixing bowl until smooth and well blended. Gradually add sugar. Stir in vanilla and beat until smooth.

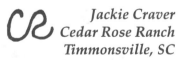

Jackie Craver
Cedar Rose Ranch
Timmonsville, SC

❖

"My favorite steer was Texas Star. He won the Steer Show at Denver in 1978, and was the only steer to win all four divisions. He was always a pet. He'd come watch me when I worked in the flower garden, and I'd talk to him, telling him how pretty he was. When he won at Denver, I went into the arena to accept the award. Star came running up, and everybody was worried about what he'd do. Well, he stopped about 12 feet from me, put his head up in the air, and just looked around as if to say, "Look at me and what I did".

—Carolyn Phillips, Battle Island Ranch, West Columbia, Texas

Mandarin Orange Cake

1	box yellow cake mix	1	(11 ounce) can mandarin
1/2	cup vegetable oil		oranges, including juice
4	eggs		

Combine all ingredients and mix on medium speed for about 3 minutes. Pour into 3 greased and floured cake pans. Bake in 350 degree oven for 20-25 minutes or until cake tests done.

ICING:

1	(12 ounce) carton	1	(20 ounce) can crushed
	nondairy whipped topping		pineapple, drained
1	(6 ounce) instant vanilla		
	pudding mix		

Combine all ingredients. Frost between layers and on top.

I made this for SuzAnn Spindor's birthday, and everyone at the TLBAA office loved it. Hope you do, too.

Shirley DuBose
North Richland Hills, TX
Texas Longhorn Breeders Association of America

Strawberry Delight Cake

1	box yellow cake mix	1	(16 ounce) package frozen
1	(11 ounce) cream cheese,		strawberries in syrup,
	softened		thawed
1	(8 ounce) carton Cool Whip,		
	thawed		

Prepare cake according to directions. Allow cake to cool, and split layers in half. Beat cream cheese, and add Cool Whip. Drain half of the syrup from strawberries. Add strawberries and 1/2 of syrup to cheese mixture. Beat well. Frost each layer and top of cake with frosting. Refrigerate.

This is better the second day.

Lorene Graves
Dayton, TX

Poor Man's Raisin Cake

1	cup raisins	1	teaspoon baking powder
2	cups water	1/4	teaspoon salt
1	teaspoon baking soda	1/4	teaspoon ground allspice
2	tablespoons shortening	1/4	teaspoon nutmeg
1	cup sugar	1/4	teaspoon cinnamon
2	cups flour	1/4	teaspoon ginger

Cook raisins and water down to 1 cup of juice. Add baking soda and shortening to liquid while warm. Add sugar and flour (enough to make a light batter, not stiff), baking powder, salt, ground allspice, nutmeg, cinnamon, and ginger. Mix well and bake at 350 degrees until done, about 20-25 minutes. (I like to use a 11"×7"×2" pan, greased.)

My step-mother made this cake when I was young. This recipe is over 75 years old. She said that back then, many families didn't have milk or eggs, so they made this cake. It's so good and takes no time to make, and it stays moist for days.

S *Patricia Smith*
Frost, TX
Heart of Texas Texas Longhorn Association

Cherry Chocolate Candy

2	sticks margarine	3/4	cup peanut butter
12	large marshmallows	1	large package salted
1	(6 ounce) package cherry		peanuts
	chips	1	teaspoon vanilla
1	(12 ounce) package		
	chocolate chips		

Combine margarine and marshmallows over on low heat. Bring to a boil and simmer for 5 minutes. Remove from heat. Add cherry chips. Combine chocolate chips and peanut butter and melt. Add peanuts and vanilla. Put 1/2 of the chocolate mixture in greased oblong pan. Pour cherry mixture in. Add rest of the chocolate. Chill and cut.

Flavored Divinity

3	cups sugar	1	package any flavored
1³/₄	cups white syrup		Jell-O
³/₄	cup water	¹/₂	cup flaked coconut
2	egg whites	¹/₂	cup nuts

Cook sugar, syrup and water to hard ball stage (225 degrees). Beat egg whites and Jell-O until fluffy. Pour syrup mixture into the egg whites slowly with electric mixer running and beat until it holds peaks. Add coconut and nuts. Drop on greased cookie sheet and chill. You must work fast as it sets rapidly. My favorite kind is Cherry Jell-O with Maraschino Cherries cut up and drained on paper towels and folded in with the coconut and nuts.

Makes a huge batch. This is a must for Christmas time, because it is so colorful.

Microwave Pralines

1	lb light brown sugar	2	tablespoons butter, use
1	cup whipping cream		real butter
		2	cups pecan pieces

Combine sugar and cream in large bowl, mixing well. Microwave on high for 14 minutes, stirring after 7 minutes. Add butter and pecans. Microwave on High 1-2 minutes or until a few drops form a soft ball in a cup of cold water. Working quickly, drop by large tablespoonfuls onto waxed paper. If necessary, return to microwave for a few minutes to soften the mixture. Do not beat after the soft ball test shows the consistency is correct. Spoon out immediately.

Marilyn Wood
Wild Wood Ranch
Lindale, TX

Donna Jackson's
Melt in Your Mouth Fudge

1	(12 ounce) package Nestle's semi-sweet chocolate chips	10	large marshmallows
		1	(5 1/3 ounce) can evaporated milk
1	teaspoon vanilla	2	cups sugar
1/2	cup melted butter, not margarine	1	cup walnut or pecan halves

In a mixer bowl, combine chocolate chips, vanilla, and melted butter. Set aside. In heavy pan (10" frying pan or iron skillet), slowly melt marshmallows, milk, and sugar. After they are melted, turn up heat to medium and bring to a bubbly simmer, stirring constantly. Begin timing at this point. Lower heat and keep at a bubbly simmer for exactly 6 minutes. Continue to stir constantly (scorches very easily). Pour this mixture over the chocolate mixture in the mixing bowl. Turn mixer to stir speed and stir for about 2 minutes, until butter is well incorporated and it looks a little thicker. At this point, add nuts. Pour into waxed paper-lined 9"×9" or 8"×8" pan. Cool overnight. Yields 80-1" squares.

Stonewall Valley Ranch
Austin, TX

Mama's Peach Cobbler

2/3	cup margarine	1/2	cup sugar
1 1/2	cups flour	3/4	cup milk
1	teaspoon salt	1 1/2	cups sweetened fresh peaches
2	teaspoon baking powder		

In 8"×8" baking dish (I use Pryex) melt margarine. Mix flour, salt, baking powder, sugar and milk. Pour over butter in baking dish. Top with peaches. Bake at 350 for 25-35 minutes.

This cobbler is not your traditional crust recipe. It is great!

SuzAnn M. Spindor
S/K Ranch/TLBAA Office
Saginaw, TX

Fudge

2 cups sugar	1 tablespoonful butter
1 cup milk	

Just before done beat until thick. Stir in nuts.

This recipe is from a Cook Book issued by The Woman's Home Mission Society of Mertzon, Texas in May 1913.

R3
Kim Richey
Triple R Ranch
San Angelo, TX

Stonewall Valley Ranch
Peach Fantasy

BOTTOM LAYER:

1½ cups flour	1½ cups finely chopped pecans
¾ cup butter, softened	

Mix ingredients until crumbly. Press into the baking dish that's been sprayed with cooking spray. Bake at 350 degrees for 15-20 minutes or until golden. Cool.

MIDDLE LAYER:

1 (8 ounce) package cream cheese, softened	1 (9 ounce) carton Cool Whip, divided
1 cup powdered sugar	

Beat cream cheese and sugar until smooth. Fold into $^1/_2$ of the Cool Whip (or whipped cream). Spread over cooled crust.

TOP LAYER:

4 cups fresh sliced peaches

Drain off juice and thicken it with cornstarch and stir it into peaches. Spread peaches over middle layer. Top with the other half of the Cool Whip (or cream). Refrigerate overnight.

Stonewall Valley Ranch
Austin, TX

Mom's Homemade Vanilla Ice Cream

6	eggs, separated	1/4	teaspoon salt
3	cups sugar	1 1/2	quart half-and-half
1	tablespoon vanilla		milk
2	tablespoons flour		

Beat the egg whites till fluffy, and beat the egg yolks in a separate bowl until lemon colored. Add sugar to egg yolks and beat. Add vanilla, flour, salt, half-and-half, egg whites and enough milk to reach the "Fill" line on the freezer can. Freeze cream in an electric or hand crank freezer.

Stonewall Valley Ranch
Austin, TX

Stonewall Peach Freeze

1	cup ice	1/2	cup sugar
2/3	cup milk	2	cups peaches, chopped
1	teaspoon vanilla		

Put ingredients in a blender and whirl till mixed and smooth. Serves 2.

One third of the nation's peaches are grown and shipped out of Stonewall, Texas. The third weekend in June is the Stonewall Peach Jamboree, in which the Stonewall Jacksons celebrate by riding their big saddle steers, Captain Twiggs, Talk of Texas, and Koolaid, and our wagon steers, Gee and Haw, in the Jamboree Parade. After the parade, these Stonewall Peach Freezes really hit the spot.

Stonewall Valley Ranch
Austin, TX

Amaretto Sauce

1	cup sugar	1	egg, beaten
1	stick margarine	1/3	cup amaretto liqueur

Cook sugar, margarine and egg in the top of double boiler, stirring constantly about 5 minutes. Add amaretto and simmer 2 minutes longer.

Aunt Jolene's Chocolate

1	cup chocolate wafer crumbs	1	quart peppermint ice cream, softened
3	tablespoons butter, melted	1/2	cup chocolate fudge topping

Combine crumbs and butter, press mixture into bottom and part way up sides of an 8" square baking dish. Freeze until firm. Spread ice cream over frozen crumbs. Cover with chocolate topping. Freeze several hours or overnight. To serve, place in refrigerator for about 20 minutes. Cut into squares.

Plum Pudding

1	quart seeded raisins	1	quart grape or other juice
1	pint currants	8	eggs, well beaten
1	pint finely cut citron	1	pint sugar
1	quart finely cut apples		nutmeg
1	quart finely cut suet		cinnamon
1	heaping quart bread crumbs		

Enough flour to make a stiff dough added to the above as given. Steam four hours. This makes four nice puddings. Reheat by steaming one when wanted, and serve with hard sauce made as follows:

Cream 1/4 lb of butter, gradually adding 3/4 lb powdered sugar, stirring and beating until like whipped cream. Flavor with vanilla and nutmeg.

Sallie Rogers McSpadden
(Will Rogers' sister)
Dog Iron Ranch
Claremore, OK

Out of the Kettles

1951 cattle round up, complete with chuckwagon and remuda. Pioneer Texas Longhorn breeder Graves Peeler (third from right). (From the archives of the Texas Longhorn Breeders Association of America.)

"The Dutch Oven"

"The Dutch oven was the main cooking utensil on the chuck wagon. It was used for frying, broiling, baking, boiling and storing items. There are even tales of how it was used as a stool for sitting and a pillow for sleeping. It was a deep vessel made of heavy cast iron, had a tight fitting flanged lid for holding hot coals and three legs that elevated it high enough from the ground so that a bed of coals could burn underneath. The Dutch oven was an English invention, but so many Dutch peddlers brought them to America in the 17th century for trade that they became known as the Dutch oven."

"The Coosie"

The chuck wagon cook was called a "coosie" (from the Spanish word *concinero* meaning male cook), "cookie", or sometimes even "old lady" or "gut robber". He was usually an aging cowboy hired for his ability to drive a wagon rather than his culinary skills. He was complete boss of the wagon and everything that pertained to it. He was paid more than the other hands because the success of the camp and the drive depended greatly on him. A cowhand earned about a dollar a day; the cook made twice that.

The coosie had other duties, too, such as serving as the doctor, the barber, and burying the dead (that's one reason the chuck wagon gear always included a shovel). His last duty of the day was to point the wagon tongue towards the North Star in order to provide the trail boss with an accurate compass at daybreak.

Chuck wagon cooks had a reputation of being cantankerous and probably had good reason because they worked long, hard hours under conditions that weren't the most desirable. Blistering heat, blue northers, soaking rain, lack of campfire fuel, stampedes and dust in the food were but a few of the coosie's troubles, but nevertheless, he and his chuck wagon provided a home on the range for the cowboy."

Santa Fe Green Chili Stew

3	lbs stewing beef, cut into cubes	3	tablespoons beef broth granules
2	medium onions, diced	1	tablespoon sugar
2	tablespoons vegetable oil	1	clove garlic, minced
1	(16 ounce) can pinto beans	1	cup shredded white Cheddar or Monterey Jack cheese
1	(10 ounce) can tomatoes, chopped	1	package small flour tortillas
1	cup water		
2	(4 ounce) cans green chilies, chopped		

Brown beef and onions in oil in a large saucepan. Add beans, tomatoes, water, chilies, beef broth granules, sugar and garlic. Bring to a boil. Reduce heat and simmer, uncovered, for 1 hour or until meat is tender. To serve, ladle into bowls and sprinkle with cheese. Serve with warmed tortillas. Serves 6-8. Double recipe for a crowd.

A tasty stew, can tame the most ferocious appetite, after a long trail ride or Longhorn roundup. (No, I didn't use our famous bull "Santa Fe Ring" to make this recipe.)

6+6 *Myrna Carpenter*
Stephenville, TX

Taco Stew

1¹/₂	lbs crumbled, cooked, drained ground beef	1	(16 ounce) can ranch beans
1	envelope Ranch Dressing	1	(16 ounce) can pintos with jalapeños
1	envelope Lawry Taco Seasoning	1	(15 ounce) can stewed tomatoes
1	(16 ounce) can corn		

Mix all ingredients. Cook in a crock pot all day.

Kim and Robert Richey
R3 *Triple R Ranch*
San Angelo, TX

Beef Stew Bourbonnais

1¹/₂ lbs cubed chuck	¹/₈ teaspoon pepper
1 tablespoon fat	¹/₂ cup ketchup
¹/₂ onion, chopped	basil
1 (10¹/₂ ounce) can	thyme
tomato soup	3 medium carrots, sliced
³/₄ cup dry red wine	4 medium potatoes,
¹/₄ cup water	quartered
¹/₂ teaspoon salt	

Brown cubed chuck in fat. Add onion and sauté until transparent. Add remaining ingredients except carrots and potatoes and simmer 30 minutes. Arrange carrots and potatoes on top. Simmer 2¹/₂ hours.

Karen King
S/K Ranch
Granbury, TX

Nance Ranch Stew

30 lbs Longhorn stew meat	10-15 lbs peeled potatoes,
10-15 onions, quartered	chunked
3 gallons canned tomatoes,	10 carrots, peeled and chunked
chopped	1-2 (10 ounce each) cans
1-2 heads cabbage, cut in	Rotel tomatoes
chunks	salt and pepper to taste
1 small jar crushed garlic	Chili powder to taste

Brown meat in large cast iron wash pot. Then add all ingredients except potatoes and carrots. Cook 3 hours and add potatoes and carrots and cook another hour. Add water as needed for liquid. Serves 200.

J—   *Jean Smith*
Fort Worth, TX

Five Hour Beef Stew

2	lbs beef cubes (may use venison)	3	tablespoons tapioca
1	cup chopped celery	1	tablespoons sugar
1	cup chopped onions	1	tablespoons salt
1	cup chopped carrots	3	tablespoons sherry
½	bell pepper		Pepper
		1	(15 ounce) can tomatoes

Mix all ingredients and bake for 5 hours at 300 degrees. May add potatoes if desired. Serve over rice if desired.

This was served for lunch at the 1997 Spring ATLA Show.

LaNelle Staggs
Arkansas TX Longhorn Association
Washington, AR

Longhorn Steer Stew

1	medium sized Longhorn steer	2	rabbits (optional)
			salt, pepper, and spices to taste

Cut Longhorn steer into bite-sized pieces. This will take a while so start early. Add enough water to cover; then cook for three weeks or until you run out of fuel. If you expect a lot of in-laws, add the rabbits—but do this only if necessary because some folks are cranky and don't like to find hare in their stew.

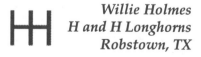

Willie Holmes
H and H Longhorns
Robstown, TX

E. Stonewall Jackson's
Chuck Wagon Stew

This is a favorite dish of guests to Stonewall Valley Ranch especially during the winter. It is served with Donna's Sour Dough Wheat Bread.

flour
salt and pepper
2 lbs Texas Longhorn lean round steak (may use chuck or lean stew meat), cubed
2-3 tablespoons canola oil
1 large onion, chopped
1 clove garlic, chopped or garlic powder

6 large potatoes, cubed
4 large carrots, cut into 1/2" slices
4 ribs celery, chopped
2 cups vegetable cocktail juice
3 dashes hot pepper sauce
2 bay leaves
2 tablespoons Tones Beef Soup Base or 1 package dry onion beef soup mix

Combine flour, salt, pepper and meat in a paper bag and shake bag to coat well. Brown meat in oil in a large pot or Dutch oven. When all meat has been browned, scrape the drippings loose from the bottom of the pot. Add at least 2 tablespoons flour and stir into drippings. Cover meat with water and bring to a boil, stirring constantly to prevent sticking. You should have a meat and gravy-like mixture. Next, add the onion, garlic, potatoes, carrots, celery, juice, hot sauce, bay leaves, beef soup mix and enough water to cover vegetables and meat. Stir mixture. Cover pot with lid. Reduce heat to low and let simmer for 2 hours or until the carrots and potatoes are tender. Stir stew occasionally and scrape bottom of pot so stew doesn't stick. This hearty stew will feed 8-10 hungry ranchers or cowboys.

The Stonewall Jacksons
Stonewall Valley Ranch
Austin, TX

Cowboy Stew

1	lb or more to taste of Longhorn beef or venison	1	(16 ounce) can chile style stewed tomatoes or chunky Mexican salsa hot or mild
1	large onion, coarsely diced		
1	(16 ounce) can whole kernel corn, drained	1	lb Cheddar cheese, grated
1	(16 ounce) can Ranch style beans	1	jalapeño pepper diced fine (optional)

Brown beef and onions and drain. Add corn, beans, and tomatoes or salsa. Simmer until stew thickens. Then incorporate cheese. Serve over cornbread or flour tortillas. (Add more corn and beans if you need to stretch stew.)

Leftovers are good in an omelet.

Amanda Page-Russell
Dallas, TX

Cowboy Stew

1½	lb ground beef	1	can stewed or Rotel tomatoes
1	large onion, chopped		
1	bell pepper, chopped		salt and pepper
1	can corn, undrained		garlic
1	(16 ounce) can Ranch style beans	2-3	potatoes, diced
1	package Taco Seasoning mix		chili powder to taste

Brown ground meat and drain. Add onion and pepper and sauté until tender. Add all other ingredients and simmer 1-1½ hours.

2h

Marcie Wirick
Dayton, TX

Baked Stew

1	cup diced carrot	salt and pepper	
1	large onion, diced	1	lb ground beef, use chuck
2½	cups tomato juice	3	cups diced potatoes
½	cup rice	½	cup water
1	cup diced celery		

Mix well. Place in casserole dish. Bake 1 hour at 350 degrees.

3h　　*Lorene Graves*
Dayton, TX

Green Chili Stew

2	onions, chopped	salt to taste	
1	tablespoon bacon	1-2	teaspoon cumin
	drippings	4-6	poblano peppers,
2	lbs deer meat, cubed		roasted and skinned
6-8	cups water	4	potatoes, cubed

Sauté onion in bacon drippings until clear. Add meat, water, salt and cumin. Simmer for at least 30 minutes. Add pepper (chopped) and potatoes. Cook until meat is very tender, about 1 hour.

Garnish with Cheddar cheese and serve. Serves 6.

So good! Love the Santa Fe flavor.

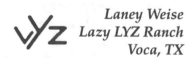 *Laney Weise*
Lazy LYZ Ranch
Voca, TX

Cauliflower or Broccoli Soup

4	tablespoons margarine	1	(10 ounce) can cream of
3	tablespoons flour		potato soup
3	cups milk	salt and pepper	
2	cups chopped, cooked	4	slices American cheese
	cauliflower or broccoli		

Melt margarine in saucepan, blend in flour until bubbly. Add milk, cauliflower or broccoli, soup and seasonings. Cook until thick and add cheese. Stir until cheese is melted.

Lazy LYZ Ranch Stew

4	tablespoons bacon grease		salt and pepper
1	tablespoon flour		cumin
1	large onion, cubed or sliced		water
		2	peeled, cubed potatoes
2	lbs cubed deer meat	1	canned jalapeño pepper

Melt grease in stew pot. Add flour and 1 cup water. Mix until paste forms. Add onion and sauté lightly. Add deer meat and continue to sauté. Add salt, pepper and cumin to taste. Cover mixture with water and cook approximately 45 minutes. Add potatoes and jalapeno pepper, and cook until tender (approximately 1 hour). <u>DO NOT USE CHILI POWDER.</u>

Serve with crackers or corn bread.

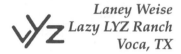

Laney Weise
Lazy LYZ Ranch
Voca, TX

Jalapeño-Potato Soup

1	medium onion, chopped	¹/₄ -¹/₂ cup coarsely chopped pickled jalapeños and juice
¹/₂	cup butter or margarine	
5	lbs russet potatoes, peeled and cubed	pinch of baking soda to prevent curdling
8	cups chicken broth	4 cups evaporated milk
1	teaspoon cumin	salt and pepper
		garnish: sour cream and chives

In a large stock pot, sauté onion in butter until tender. Add potatoes, chicken broth, and cumin. Cover and cook until potatoes are tender, about 20-30 minutes. When done, add jalapenos, baking soda, and evaporated milk. Coarsely mash potatoes with potato masher. Stir well and taste for salt and pepper. Simmer for 15 minutes, stirring frequently.

Marsha Proctor
Poolville, TX

Old Fashioned Cream of Tomato Soup

1 (40 ounce) can diced tomatoes	2 tablespoons sugar
	1 tablespoon chopped onion
1 (10½ ounce) chicken broth, undiluted	A pinch of baking soda
	1½ cups cream
1 tablespoon butter	½ cup milk

Mix tomatoes, chicken broth, butter, sugar, onions and baking soda. Simmer 1 hour. Heat cream and milk in double boiler. Add cream and milk to tomato mixture. Serve and enjoy!

Loretta Miller
Tim Miller Ranch
Great Bend, KS

Taco Soup

1 lb Longhorn lean ground beef	1 (16 ounce) can pinto beans
	1 (4 ounce) can chopped green chilies
1 onion, chopped	
1 package taco seasoning mix	1 (15 ounce) can stewed tomatoes
1 (16 ounce) can corn	

Brown meat and onions in Dutch oven. Stir in taco seasoning mix, then add all other ingredients. (Do not drain vegetables.) Simmer for 30 minutes. Serve with shredded cheddar cheese and corn chips or tortillas.

Lani Fairchild
Fairchild Ranch
Stephenville, TX

Texas Longhorn Steak Soup

1½ quarts water	1 tablespoon Worcestershire sauce
1½ lbs cubed Texas Longhorn beef	
	1 teaspoon garlic powder
1½ teaspoons Lawry seasoning salt	¼ cup beef bouillon granules
½ cup chopped onion	1 lb frozen mixed vegetables
	1½ sticks margarine or butter
½ teaspoon lemon pepper	1 short cup flour

Boil first 8 ingredients until the meat is tender. Add vegetables. In separate pan, melt butter and mix in flour. When mixed, add to soup. Add more water for desired consistency.

"Longhorn" Steak Soup

1-1½	lbs ground beef	1-2	quarts water
1	cup chopped onion	1	stick butter or margarine
1	cup chopped carrots	1	cup flour
1	cup chopped celery	1	can tomato sauce or wedges
2	cups frozen mixed vegetables	1-2	tablespoons beef base
			salt and pepper

Brown the ground beef and drain if necessary. Par boil all the vegetables and add to meat, including the water. Add all other ingredients. Simmer for an hour or so. The flour is for thickening. (I usually use corn starch instead of flour and thicken slightly.)

Leftovers keep well in the refrigerator for several days and the flavor is better the second day! I fix this a lot on cold winter days, or the days when I have hunters or woodcutters.

Cheryl J. Carlson
Crown C Ranch
St. Marys, KS

B. Stonewall Jackson's Green Chili Soup

2	lbs Longhorn lean ground beef	1	tablespoon salt
1	large onion, chopped	2-3	teaspoons garlic powder
1	(7 ounce) can chopped green chilies	1	teaspoon cumin
2	(10 ounce) cans Rotel tomatoes	2	large potatoes, cubed
		1-2	(16 ounce) cans Ranch style jalapeño beans
		2	quarts water

Brown meat and drain all excess fat. Cook onion with meat and add chilies and tomatoes. Let simmer a few minutes to blend flavors. Add seasonings. Add potatoes, beans and water. Simmer 1-2 hours. Serves 8.

The Stonewall Jacksons
Stonewall Valley Ranch
Austin, TX

Worcestered Longhorn Soup

1½	lbs Longhorn stew meat or chuck, cut into ½" cubes	1½	quarts chopped tomatoes, canned or fresh
2	tablespoons flour	½	cup Worcestershire sauce— yes, really ½ cup
1	teaspoon salt pepper	1	medium onion, chopped
1	teaspoon paprika	2	cloves garlic, minced
2	tablespoons oil	½	cup sliced carrots
2	quarts beef stock or water and beef bouillon	½	cup chopped celery
		1	cup diced potatoes

Dredge meat with flour seasoned with salt, pepper, and paprika; shake off excess. Brown meat on all sides in hot oil. Add beef stock, tomatoes, Worcestershire sauce, onion, and garlic. Bring to a boil. Reduce heat, and simmer covered until meat is almost tender, about 1½ hours. Add carrots, celery and potatoes. Simmer, covered, until the vegetables are tender, about 20 minutes.

$$\frac{\mathbf{D}}{\mathbf{D}}$$
Carol Davis
D Bar D Longhorns
Jackson, CA

Garlic Soup

1	whole bulb of garlic, minced	2	(28 ounce) cans whole tomatoes with juice, coarsely chopped
½	cup good quality olive oil		pepper to taste
2	tablespoons dried thyme		feta cheese
2	teaspoons beef bouillon, dissolved in 2 cups boiling water		

Sauté minced garlic in olive oil. Stir constantly, being careful not to brown. Add thyme, beef bouillon, tomatoes and juice. Simmer soup for 1 hour or longer over low heat, allowing flavors to blend. Pepper to taste and garnish with feta cheese.

Serve with French bread and a Greek salad. You can't miss!

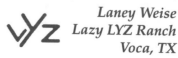
Laney Weise
Lazy LYZ Ranch
Voca, TX

Mexican Soup

2	lbs ground beef	1	(15 ounce) can of water
1	large onion, chopped	1	package taco seasoning mix
3	(15 ounce) cans stewed tomatoes	1	small package of Hidden Valley Ranch Dressing Mix
1	(15 ounce) can of yellow hominy, drained	1	(4 ounce) can of chopped green chilies
1	(15 ounce) can of kidney beans, drained	1	teaspoon cumin
1	(15 ounce) can of pinto beans, drained		

Brown meat and onions. Add vegetables and seasonings. Cook about 1 hour.

I did this recipe times ten for the Heart of Texas Spring Show. So you can make a big pot of this for a large crowd.

Kay Florence
Lazy K Ranch
Winnsboro, TX

Cheesy Chicken Soup

4	bouillon chicken cubes	1	onion, chopped
4	cups water	2	cups diced potatoes
6	chicken breasts	2	cups noodles
salt and pepper		1/2-1	lb Velveeta or mild Mexican Velveeta
2	cups diced carrots		
2	cups diced celery		

Make bouillon with 4 cups of water. Add chicken and salt and pepper. When chicken is done, remove from pot. Let cool and cut into small pieces. While the chicken cools, add carrots, celery, onion, potatoes to broth. Add noodles last 10 minutes of cooking time. Add Velveeta at end of cooking time.

Betty Baker
Sunrise Ranch
Liberty Hill, TX

Vegetable Soup

1	lb ground beef or shredded beef (cooked)	1	teaspoon salt
1	cup chopped onion		pepper
4	cups hot water	1/2	teaspoon Worcestershire sauce
3	carrots, sliced		
1	cup chopped celery	1	cup broken noodles, uncooked
4	bouillon beef cubes	1	(16 ounce) can green beans
2	cups canned tomatoes	1	(8 ounce) can corn

Cook all ingredients except beans and corn for 1 hour. Add beans and corn and heat thoroughly.

Jan and Howard Sears
J H Ranch
Leon, IA

My Broccoli Cheese Soup

	salt	butter
4	heads broccoli	flour
1	onion, chopped	milk
2	(14 ounce) cans light chicken broth	pepper
		bacon, optional
3-4	cup grated cheese	

Mix salt, broccoli, onion and broth and cook until broccoli is tender. Make white sauce using butter, flour, milk. Melt cheese into white sauce mixture, and stir into soup base. Pepper to taste. Add crumbled bacon, if desired.

 COOK

Georgia M. Cook
Cook Longhorn Ranch
Ree Heights, SD

Clam Chowder Soup

1	cup diced carrots	1	(10¾ ounce) can cream of chicken soup
4	cups dried potatoes		
1½	cups diced celery	1	cup grated cheese
1	medium onion, chopped		salt and pepper
2	cans minced clams		garlic salt
1	can evaporated milk		
1	(10¾ ounce) can cream of mushroom soup		

Cover vegetables with water and cook until nearly done. Add clams, milk and soups. Cover and simmer a few minutes. When heated thorough add cheese. Add salt, pepper and garlic salt to taste.

Judy Vyhnalek
Vyhnalek Longhorns
Dorchester, NE

Hamburger Minestrone Soup

1	lb ground beef	½	cup rice
1	cup finely chopped onions	1	bay leaf
1	cup chopped potatoes	½	teaspoon thyme
1	cup finely chopped carrots	¼	teaspoon basil
½	cup finely chopped celery	5	teaspoons salt
½	cup chopped cabbage	½	teaspoon pepper
1	(16 ounce) can tomatoes	1½	quart water
	Cheddar or Parmesan cheese		

Brown beef and onions. Add potatoes, carrots, celery, cabbage, tomatoes, rice and seasonings. Then add water, cover and simmer for 1 hour. Sprinkle with Cheddar or Parmesan cheese. Serves 5.

Mrs. James B. Rogers (Astrea)
Daughter-in-law of Will Rogers
Dog Iron Ranch

Ham and Vegetable Soup

6	cups water	1/2	cup sliced celery
	Knorr Chicken Flavor	1	cup diced potato
	Bouillon to taste	11/2	cups diced cabbage
11/2	cups diced turnips		(or more to taste)
1/2	cup diced or sliced carrots	1/2	teaspoon minced garlic
1	(13 ounce) can lima beans	1-11/2	cups diced smoked ham
1	(15 ounce) can Cannelloni		salt and pepper
	beans		dill

Bring chicken broth to a boil. Add turnips and carrots to pot and cook for about 5 minutes. Add beans, celery, potatoes, cabbage, garlic, and diced ham. Cook another 10-15 minutes or until vegetables are done to taste.

Ladle into soup bowls and salt and pepper to taste. Just before serving sprinkle with dill. Good with cornbread or other good bread.

I was hungry for vegetables one evening. Since Bob isn't very crazy about beef stew, this is what I came up with. Hope you enjoy it as much as we do.

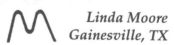

Linda Moore
Gainesville, TX

Taco Soup

1/2	lb ground beef	1	(12 ounce) can corn
1/4	cup onion, chopped	1	(14 ounce) can chicken
1	(16 ounce) can crushed		broth
	tomatoes	1	package taco seasoning
1	(16 ounce) can red or	1	package ranch dressing
	Ranch style beans		grated cheese

Brown ground beef, pour off grease, and combine all ingredients. Cook on low for 15 minutes. Serve in bowl, topped with grated cheese with corn bread or chips.

Pat Harrell
Full Circle Ranch
Strawn, TX

Taco Soup

1	lb. ground Longhorn meat	1	(16 ounce) can Ranch style beans
2	(8 ounce) cans stewed tomatoes	1	(12 ounce) can whole kernel corn
2	(10 ounce) cans Rotel tomatoes	1	package taco seasoning mix
1	(16 ounce) can pinto beans	1	package ranch dressing mix

Brown meat. Put in crock pot with all other ingredients for 2 hours on high.

To serve, break up tortilla chips and place in bottom of bowl. Fill with Taco Soup, and sprinkle with Mexican style cheese.

To really heat it up, try replacing 1 can of Rotel tomatoes with 1 can of extra hot Rotel tomatoes.

Best served on one of our coldest Texas days.

Carla Haberzettle
Texas Longhorn Breeders Association of America
Fort Worth, TX

Broccoli Cheese Soup

2	(10 ounce) package chopped frozen broccoli	3	(10³/4 ounce) cans cream of mushroom soup
1	stick margarine	1	small jar Cheese Whiz with jalapeño peppers
1	medium onion, chopped		
3	(10 ounce) cans Pet milk		

Cook broccoli (in boxes) in microwave for 10 minutes, turning twice. Sauté onions in margarine in microwave until onions are transparent. Cook Cheese Whiz in microwave until you can pour it. Add all ingredients to crock pot. Take hand mixer and mix well. Cook 30 minutes-1 hour or until hot.

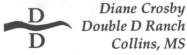

Diane Crosby
Double D Ranch
Collins, MS

Tortellini Minestrone

2 cans (10½ ounce) condensed beef broth	1 bag (16 ounce) frozen mixed cauliflower, zucchini, carrots, and red peppers
3½ cans water	
1 tablespoon instant tomato bouillon	1 can (10½ ounce) white kidney beans, rinsed and drained
1 bag (16 ounce) frozen cheese tortellini	
1½ teaspoon dried Italian seasoning	

Bring broth, water and bouillon to a boil in large covered saucepan or Dutch oven over high heat. Add remaining ingredients. When boiling, reduce heat to medium-low and simmer 6-8 minutes, or until tortellini and vegetables are tender.

French Market Soup
(9 bean soup)

BEAN MIX

USE 1 LB EACH:

large limas	kidney beans
small limas	split peas
black beans	navy pea beans
black-eyed peas	barley
garbanzo beans	lentils
pintos	

Wash two cups bean mixture and place in heavy 3 quart pot. Add 2 quarts water, a country ham bone, and 1 lb of ham chunks or trimmings. Boil slowly 2½-3 hours. Add the following and cook an additional 30 minutes:

1 (28 ounce) can tomatoes juice of one lemon	1 large onion, chopped fine
	1 clove garlic, chopped fine

Serve with cornbread and enjoy.

Just Out of the Oven

Fandango's Husker, owned by Dick and Jan Barnard, shares a greeting with Wilma Kastl, Herman, Nebraska's oldest resident.

"Sourdough Bread"

Sourdough transported in crocks or kegs provided the coosie with a start for leavened bread. It was also used to make cornbread, pancakes and cobblers. Many cooks prided themselves in how long they could keep a starter going. On chilly nights, the coosie would take the crock to bed with him to keep the cold from stopping the fermentation. Since he did not want to bother with a biscuit cutter, he pinched off pieces of dough, rolled them into balls and placed them close together in a heavily greased Dutch oven to rise and bake light and tender.

Baking bread in a Dutch oven over an open fire is no simple matter. You have to achieve an even balance of heat under and over the vessel so that the bread will rise properly and brown evenly on the bottom and top.

❖

"Only a fool argues with a skunk, a mule or a cook."

❖

If a cowboy went to the coffee pot to refill his cup and another cowhand hollered "man at the pot", this was a signal to go around and refill all cups extended out to him.

❖

When a cowhand went to a pot to fill his plate, he was very careful to handle the lid just right so it wouldn't touch the ground.

Eddie Wood's Biscuits

Automatically wake up at 6 a.m. each day. Try to get Joyce up. . . No luck. Put coffee on . . . smell of coffee still doesn't get Joyce up. Decide to make biscuits. Clear off the cabinet. Turn on the oven to 400 degrees. Put on gloves. Open freezer door and start digging behind all the boxes of diet food (never used) and containers of homemade peach ice cream. Finally, my hiding space . . . the Schwan's Southern Style Biscuits. Place biscuits on cookie sheet and put in oven. Hide package where I found it (She never looks at anything near diet food!) Oops . . . it's almost time for her to get up. Need to get lots of utensils and get them dirty. She's up!!! She must have smelled the biscuits. Here I go doing her work another day. Glad to do it. She always tells Jim Curry that I made biscuits for her. It's worth the trouble.

Eddie Wood
PayDay Ranch
Wynnewood, OK

Chuck Wagon Sour Dough Starter

1	package of dry yeast	2	tablespoons sugar
4	cups warm water	4	cups flour
	(105-115 degrees)	1	raw potato, cubed

Dissolve yeast in warm water. Then mix all ingredients in a 1 gallon crock or other non-metallic container. Cover with a close-fitting lid, and let the starter rise until light and bubbly on top, 12 hours in warm weather and longer in cool weather. Never let the starter get cold. Pour off 1 cup of starter to use to bake bread. Each time you use a cup of starter, you will need to feed the starter with 1 cup warm water, 2 teaspoon sugar, and enough flour to return the starter to its original consistency. Add more potato occasionally as food for the yeast when the original starter is getting low, but don't add more yeast. For best results, use starter often, otherwise, it will die. The starter improves with age, and can be used for breads, roll, pancakes, etc.

Chuckwagon Sour Dough Starter/ Donna's Sour Dough Starter

A Texas Longhorn cookbook would not be complete without some sour dough bread recipes like the ones the "cookies" used on the Longhorn trail drives. Donna Jackson is the bread baker in our home at Stonewall Valley Ranch. Here are some of Donna's secret recipes.

Donna's Sour Dough Starter (refrigerated)

2	packages dry yeast	2/3	cup sugar
1/2	cup warm water	3	tablespoons instant
1	cup warm water		potato flakes

Dissolve yeast in 1/2 cup warm water in medium mixing bowl. Stir in 1 cup warm water, sugar and potato flakes. Let mixture sit out all day, then refrigerate for 5-10 days. A 10-day schedule works fine. Remove from refrigerator and feed (see feeding instructions).

Now you are ready to use 1 cup of the starter to make bread. Return the rest of the starter in a covered glass jar or container to the refrigerator for 5-10 days. Before making a batch of bread, feed starter. You need to feed starter every 5-10 days whether you make bread or not.

FEEDING RECIPE:

1	cup warm water	3	tablespoons instant
3/4	cup sugar		potato flakes

Stir feeding ingredients into the starter. Keep at room temperature for 10-12 hours. Take off 1 cup of starter for baking and put the remainder into the refrigerator. Makes 2-3 cups starter.

Donna's Sour Dough Wheat Bread (or Labor of Love Bread)

On the day you wish to bake bread, take starter out of refrigerator in the morning and feed it. Let starter stand out all day (10-12 hours). That evening, stir up and pour off 1 cup starter for baking. Return remainder to refrigerator.

1	cup sour dough starter	1½	cups warm water
½	cup sugar	3	cups white bread flour
½	cup oil	3	cups wheat bread flour
½-1	tablespoon salt		

Stir to mix all ingredients until soft dough forms. Cover lightly with plastic wrap and let it rise all night in warm, draft-free place. The next morning, turn dough out on floured counter or board and divide into 2 or 3 small sections. Knead each section until ball forms enough to get into loaf pan. Spray loaf pans with cooking spray. Let loaves rise in warm place about 6-8 hours. Bake at 350 degrees for 30 minutes. Makes 2 or 3 loaves.

This bread is super, but it does take a labor of love to prepare and bake.

Donna Jackson
Stonewall Valley Ranch
Austin, TX

Aunt Ollie Rolls

1½	cups warm water	2	tablespoons shortening
1	package yeast	1	teaspoon salt
2	tablespoons sugar	2½	cups flour

Mix and knead for 1 minute. Let rise until doubled in size. Turn out on floured surface, knead and roll out. Cut and place on ungreased pan and let rise again. Bake at 425 degrees for 15 minutes.

I grew up on these rolls, and they just melt in your mouth. Bet you can't eat just one!

R3
Kim Richey
Triple R Ranch
San Angelo, TX

Garden Loaf Quick Bread

3	cups flour	4	eggs
1¹/₂	cups sugar	1	cup shredded zucchini
1	cup chopped walnuts	1	cup shredded carrots
4¹/₂	teaspoons baking powder	²/₃	cup vegetable oil
1	teaspoon salt	2	teaspoons grated lemon peel

In large bowl mix flour, sugar, walnuts, baking powder and salt. In small bowl beat eggs slightly, stir in zucchini, carrots, oil and lemon peel. Stir into flour mixture until flour is moistened. Spread batter into 2 greased loaf pans and bake at 350 degrees for one hour or until toothpick comes out clean. Cool on racks for 10 minutes and remove from pans.

Good with cheese spread.

Arlene Glinsmann
Rockville, NE

Tex-Mex Cornbread

1	cup cornmeal	¹/₄	cup bacon grease
2	eggs, well beaten	1	lb Longhorn ground meat
1	cup milk	¹/₂	lb grated cheese
¹/₂	teaspoon baking soda	4	jalapeño peppers, chopped
³/₄	teaspoon salt	1	large onion, chopped
1	(8 ounce) can cream style corn		

Mix the first 6 ingredients and set aside. Melt bacon grease and brown beef in a skillet, drain and set aside. Combine cheese, jalapenos and onion. Grease large iron skillet and heat. Sprinkle thin layer of cornmeal in skillet and brown slightly. Pour ¹/₂ batter in hot skillet. Add meat and cheese mixture and pour the remaining batter on top. Bake at 350 degrees for 45-50 minutes. Run spatula around edges before slicing and lifting out of skillet.

My family loves this dish!

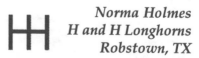

Norma Holmes
H and H Longhorns
Robstown, TX

Donna's Fresh Milled Wheat and Honey Bread

(Takes only an hour or two to make start to finish. It is sugar-free and very low fat.)

Donna uses a KTEC Kitchen Mill to grind her wheat fresh, and a Kitchen Champ to mix and knead the bread dough. Any mixer with bread dough hooks will also work.

9$^{1}/_{2}$ cups wheat (5 cup Montana Red Wheat and 4$^{1}/_{2}$ cup Golden 86 wheat) — Grind on medium coarseness to yield 14$^{1}/_{2}$ cup of fresh milled wheat flour

IN BREAD MIXER BOWL:

5$^{1}/_{4}$ cup hot tap water (105-115 degrees)

Add: $^{2}/_{3}$ cup canola oil
Mix in: $^{2}/_{3}$ cup honey
Mix in: 2 cups fresh ground wheat flour

ADD:

$^{1}/_{2}$ cup gluten
2 tablespoons dough enhancer

3 tablespoons instant yeast
2 cups fresh ground wheat flour

Continue mixing 1 minute. Let set 1 minute.

Start mixer and add: 1 tablespoon salt and allow to blend in for 1 minute. Add remainder of fresh ground wheat flour. Continue to mix for 7 minutes. Heat oven on "warm" setting. Place bread pans into oven. Remove pans when ready to load with dough and turn off oven. Next measure bread dough by weight. (1$^{3}/_{4}$ lb bread dough per large loaf pan.) Fold dough twice and roll out for each loaf and chop ends. Place in warm oven and let rise for 30 minutes. Now turn the oven on and set it to 350 degrees. Bake the bread at 350 degrees for 25-30 minutes. Makes 6 loaves.

Donna Jackson
Stonewall Valley Ranch
Austin, TX

Mrs. Porter's Ranch Biscuits

2	packages yeast	1/4	cup sugar
1/2	cup warm water	1	teaspoon salt
2	cups buttermilk	4	teaspoons baking powder
1/2	cup vegetable oil	1/2	teaspoon baking soda
4 1/2	cups flour		

Dissolve yeast in warm water. Mix buttermilk and oil. After yeast is foamy, add to buttermilk and oil mixture. Add liquid mixture to dry ingredients. Mix well. Knead gently on floured surface for a few minutes until dough is not too sticky and can be shaped into rolls. These rolls will be lighter if allowed to rise, but is not necessary. Bake in greased pan at 450 degrees for about 15 minutes. Makes 18-24 larger or 35-40 smaller biscuits. This dough may be refrigerated and rolls pinched off as needed. Will keep several days in the refrigerator.

While writing a history of our farm this year (1997-98) we found this brand that was registered to my great-grandfather, Rudolph Duewall. It was registered in Burleson County on June 1, 1883. We re-registered it on March 20, 1998. The Duewall Farm has been in our family since 1881.

Kenneth and Windelyn Tharp
 IIE *Duewall Farm*
Caldwell, TX

Fried Cornbread Patties

1	cup Aunt Jemima or Martha White self-rising corn meal mix	3/4	cup milk
		1	egg
		3	tablespoons oil

Combine first 3 ingredients. Mixture will be very thin. Put oil (I prefer olive oil) into a skillet. Heat oil until <u>very hot</u>. Using a large household tablespoon, dip and pour from spoon into hot skillet. Should cook about four cornbread patties to each skillet. Watch closely as it cooks very fast. Add additional oil as needed to cook remaining cornbread patties.

KY *Mrs. Bobby Barker*
Frankfort, KY

Sour Dough Biscuits

1	package dry yeast	6	cups or more flour
1	cup warm water	4	teaspoons baking powder
1/4	cup sugar	2	teaspoons salt
2	cups buttermilk	1/4	teaspoon baking soda
3/4	cup oil		

Dissolve yeast in water. Mix sugar, buttermilk and oil. Then add flour, baking powder, salt and baking soda. Knead a little, place dough in covered bowl in refrigerator or bake immediately. No need to let rise before baking. Bake at 450 degrees 15 minutes or until golden brown.

Ellen Goodnight
Married to relative of Col. Charles Goodnight
Mead, KS

Will Rogers Centennial Corn Bread

1	cup yellow corn meal	1	teaspoon salt
1	cup flour	1/3	cup soft butter
1	tablespoon baking powder	1	large or 2 small eggs
1	tablespoon sugar	1	cup milk

Combine all dry ingredients, mix well. Add butter, blend well. Add eggs and milk. Mix all together until just blended. Pour into well buttered 8"×8"×1" pan. Bake in a 400 degree oven for 25 minutes.

Two Hour Rolls

Cream 1/2 cup sugar and 1/2 cup shortening. Add 1 cup boiling water and beat. Add 2 beaten eggs. Dissolve 2 package yeast in 1 cup warm water. Mix 1 tablespoon salt and 6 cups flour. Mix all together (with spoon, you don't have to knead it!) Let rise 1 hour. Shape rolls and let rise another hour. Bake at 350 degrees for 14-20 minutes or until lightly browned. (It makes delicious raised donuts.)

COOK
Georgia M. Cook
Cook Longhorn Ranch
Ree Heights, SD

Dan's South of the Border Cornbread

1	lb ground Longhorn beef	1	cup buttermilk
1/2	lb pork sausage	2	cups grated Cheddar cheese
1	cup self-rising cornmeal	1	large onion, chopped
1/2	cup self-rising flour	4-5	tiny hot Mexican peppers,
3	tablespoons sugar		seeded and chopped or
2	cups creamed corn		6-8 jalapeño peppers
2	eggs, well beaten		
1/2	cup bacon grease		
	(or reserved grease		
	from meat)		

Fry beef and sausage together until brown. Drain; reserve grease from meat. While meat is browning, mix together cornmeal, flour, sugar, corn, eggs, bacon grease, and buttermilk. Pour 1/2 of batter into a lightly greased 13"×9"×2" inch pan sprinkled with cornmeal. Sprinkle cheese over batter, then the crumbled meat. Mix together chopped onion and peppers and sprinkle over meat. Pour remaining batter over top. Bake at 350 degrees for 1 hour.

J— *Jean Smith*
Fort Worth, TX

Beer Bread

3	cups self-rising flour	1	egg, beaten
1/4	cup sugar	1	tablespoon water
1	can Lite beer		melted butter

Mix flour and sugar and add beer. Watch it foam and mix just until blended. Pour into buttered loaf pan (preferably glass). Combine egg with water and brush top of loaf. Let rise 10 minutes. Bake at 350 degrees for 40-45 minutes. Brush with butter while hot.

Laney Weise
∨YZ *Lazy LYZ Ranch*
Voca, TX

Cornbread

1¹/₂	cups cornmeal	1	cup milk
¹/₂	cup flour	2	eggs, beaten
2	teaspoons salt	2	tablespoons shortening
¹/₄-¹/₂	teaspoon sugar	7¹/₂	or 8" iron skillet
4	teaspoons baking powder		

Preheat oven to 425 degrees. Combine dry ingredients in large bowl, stirring well with wooden spoon. (No need to sift-except for baking powder if lumpy.) Add milk and eggs and stir well. With stove burner at medium high, heat skillet and melt shortening. Remove skillet from heat and swirl to coat bottom and sides of pan. Pour remaining shortening into cornbread batter, stir quickly, and pour batter into hot skillet. Immediately put in oven. Bake 25-30 minutes. When done a toothpick should come out clean when inserted into the center. Let cool briefly before cutting. Serves 4-6.

This recipe makes a thick cornbread that rises high in the center and forms a circular crack as it bakes. My children called it a "hat". It is Walter's favorite. He makes it to go with pinto beans.

Double this recipe for a 10" skillet.

Mary Elizabeth Scott
Copa de Vino Ranch
Goliad, TX

Homemade Dinner Rolls

1	package dry yeast	¹/₂	cup butter or shortening
2	cups milk	4	cups self-rising flour
¹/₂	cup sugar		

Dissolve yeast in two cups warmed milk. Cream sugar with butter or shortening. Add yeast mixture. Add flour, one cup at a time. Mix well. Spoon into greased muffin tins. Bake at 350 degrees until golden brown.

Vonda Burden
Town Creek, AL

Stonewall Jackson's
Mexican Corn Muffins

1	cup cornmeal	1	egg, slightly beaten
1	cup unbleached white flour	1	cup whole kernel corn, drained
1/4	cup sugar		
2 1/2	teaspoons baking powder	1/2	cup chopped pimentos, or chopped green chilies or chopped jalapeño peppers, or a combination
1/4	teaspoon salt		
1	cup buttermilk or plain yogurt		
8	tablespoons melted butter		

Preheat oven to 400 degrees. Measure the cornmeal, flour, sugar, baking powder and salt into a mixing bowl. Make a well in the center and pour in the buttermilk or yogurt, butter and egg. Stir only until combined. Fold in the corn and pimentos or chilies or jalapeños. Fill each greased muffin cup with batter. Bake until firm and golden, about 20-25 minutes. Makes 12 muffins.

The Jacksons
Stonewall Valley Ranch
Austin, TX

Rhubarb Bread

1 1/2	cups brown sugar, packed	3	cups flour
3/4	cup sour milk or buttermilk	1 1/2	teaspoons baking soda
		1/2	teaspoon salt
2/3	cup oil	2	cups finely chopped rhubarb
2	eggs, beaten		
2	teaspoons vanilla	4	tablespoons sugar, divided

Combine sugar, sour milk, oil, eggs and vanilla and beat well. Add dry ingredients and mix well, then add rhubarb and blend. Do not overbeat. Pour into two greased and floured 9"×5"×3" loaf pans. Sprinkle 2 tablespoons sugar on top of each loaf. Bake at 325 degrees for one hour or until loaves test done. Cool 10-15 minutes and remove from pans to finish cooling.

Vernon and Corinne Bancroft
Pleasant Pines
Paton, IA

Mom's Refrigerator White Rolls

1	package dry yeast	1	teaspoon salt
1/4	cup warm water	1/4	cup sugar
3/4	cup milk, scalded	3	cups sifted flour divided
1/4	cup shortening	1	egg

Soften yeast in warm water (110 degrees). Combine hot milk, shortening, salt, and sugar. Cool to lukewarm. Add 1 cup flour, beat well. Beat in yeast mixture and egg, add remaining flour. Mix well, then place in greased bowl. Grease surface, cover, and store in refrigerator at least 2 hours or until needed. About 2 hours before serving, shape into biscuits on well-floured surface. Let rise in warm place until doubled in size (about 2 hours). Bake at 400 degrees for 12-15 minutes. Makes about 16 medium rolls.

Growing up, we always had homemade bread in the house. Every other Sunday, my mother, Lola McKeever, would be in the kitchen making 7 or 8 loaves for us to eat till the next baking day. She also used the dough to make one of our favorites, fried bread, and even made the world's best cinnamon rolls out of the dough. I was about 18 years old before I had my first store bought bread. It had been available in the stores for years, but my Dad preferred Mom's homemade. This recipe is as close as we'll ever come to those rolls. Hope you enjoy them as much as I do.

Shirley DuBose
Texas Longhorn Breeders Association of America
North Richland Hills, TX

Feather Pancakes

1	cup sifted flour	1/2	teaspoon salt
2	tablespoons sugar	1	egg, beaten
2	tablespoons baking powder	1	cup milk
		2	tablespoons vegetable oil

Sift together dry ingredients. Combine egg, milk and vegetable oil. Add to dry ingredients till moistened. Cook on hot griddle.

Allison Damrow
Roca, NE

Bacon Bread

1	lb. hickory smoked bacon	3	cans refrigerated biscuits
1	teaspoon vegetable oil	1/2	cup butter, melted
3/4	cup chopped green pepper	2	ounces shredded
3/4	cup chopped onion		cheddar cheese

Cook bacon until crisp, then drain, crumble and set aside. Place oil in skillet, heat and add green pepper and onion. Cook until tender. Cut biscuits in fourths and place in large mixing bowl. Add cooked vegetables, crisp bacon, butter and cheese. Toss until thoroughly mixed. Place in a 10" tube pan coated with cooking spray. Bake at 350 degrees for 30 minutes. Immediately invert onto large plate and serve warm.

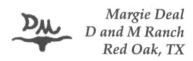

Margie Deal
D and M Ranch
Red Oak, TX

Pumpkin Bread

2/3	cup shortening	1 1/2	teaspoons salt
2 2/3	cups sugar	1/2	teaspoon baking powder
4	eggs	1	teaspoon cinnamon
1	(16 ounce) can pumpkin	1	teaspoon cloves
2/3	cup water	2/3	cup coarsely chopped nuts
3 1/3	cups flour	2/3	cup raisins
2	teaspoons baking soda		

Heat oven to 350 degrees and grease 2 loaf pans. Cream shortening and sugar thoroughly. Add eggs, pumpkin and water. Blend in dry ingredients except nuts and raisins. Stir in nuts and raisins. Bake in prepared pans 65-75 minutes or until wooden toothpick comes out clean.

Rebecca Facemyer
Facemyer Farms
Wilkesville, OH

Cheddar Cheese Pepper Bread

2¹/₂ cups flour
2 teaspoons baking powder
³/₄ teaspoon baking soda
³/₄ teaspoon salt
1¹/₂-2¹/₂ teaspoons black pepper
8 ounces shredded sharp
   Cheddar cheese

2 large eggs
1 (8 ounce) container plain
   low-fat yogurt
¹/₂ cup butter, melted

Mix first 6 ingredients. Stir eggs, yogurt, and butter. Add to flour mixture. Bake at 375 degrees for 45 minutes.

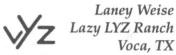

Laney Weise
Lazy LYZ Ranch
Voca, TX

Homestead Biscuits

5 cups flour
5 teaspoons baking powder
1 teaspoon salt
3 tablespoon sugar

¹/₂ teaspoon baking soda
1 package dry yeast
1 cup shortening
2¹/₄ cup buttermilk

Sifted together all ingredients except shortening and buttermilk. Cut in shortening and add very warm buttermilk. Knead lightly. Roll out ¹/₂″ thick and cut with biscuit cutter. (May be refrigerated and used as needed or cut and frozen for later use. If frozen, take out and let rise before baking.)

Variation: Use 2 cups whole wheat flour and 3 cups white four.

Glenda Riddle
The Homestead at GT Ranch
Red Rock, OK

Easy Raisin Bread

2	cups whole wheat flour	1/2	cup molasses
1	cup unbleached flour	2	cups skim milk
2	teaspoons baking soda	2	tablespoons vinegar
1/4	teaspoon salt	1	cup raisins
1	teaspoon cinnamon		

Combine flours, baking soda, salt and cinnamon. Add molasses, milk and vinegar. Mix until well blended. Fold in raisins. Pour into 2 (8"×4"×2") loaf pans sprayed with cooking spray and lightly floured. Let stand for 45 minutes. Bake 30-35 minutes or until done. Makes 20 slices.

Evelyn S. Rasmussen
Rolling Hills Ranch
Houston, TX

Homemade Bread

4	tablespoons shortening	14-14 1/2	cups flour, divided
1	cup very hot water	6	tablespoons sugar
2	tablespoons instant dry yeast	2	tablespoons salt
		4 1/2	cups water

Mix shortening with 1 cup very hot water so shortening will melt. Mix yeast with 4-5 cup flour, sugar and salt. Add 3 1/2 cups very warm water and mix well, then add the melted shortening and water. Continue adding flour and stir with wooden spoon until stiff. Turn dough out on floured counter, add flour and knead dough until smooth and elastic. Let rise until double, punch down. Let rise, shape loaves and let rise until double. Bake at 400 degrees for 45 minutes. Makes 4 large loaves.

Georgia M. Cook
Cook Longhorn Ranch
Ree Heights, SD

Honey Zucchini Bread

3	cups sifted flour	3	eggs
2	teaspoons ground cinnamon	1	cup honey
		1/2	cup vegetable oil
1	teaspoon baking soda	2	teaspoon vanilla
1	teaspoon salt	3	cups shredded zucchini
1/4	teaspoon baking powder		

Into large bowl, sift together first 5 ingredients; set aside. In medium bowl, using wire whisk, beat eggs until foamy. Beat in honey, oil, and vanilla until well blended. Stir in zucchini. Add zucchini mixture to flour mixture; stir just until moistened. Pour batter into greased 9"×5"×3" loaf pan. Bake in 350 degree oven for 1 hour and 15 minutes, or until loaf is golden brown and toothpick inserted in center comes out clean. Cool in pan 10 minutes. Makes 1 loaf.

For variety add 1 cup chopped nuts to the batter.

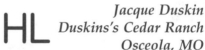

Jacque Duskin
Duskins's Cedar Ranch
Osceola, MO

Zucchini Bread

1	cup vegetable oil	1	teaspoon baking soda
2 1/4	cups sugar	1/2	teaspoon baking powder
3	eggs	1/4	teaspoon salt
3	teaspoons vanilla	2	cups grated zucchini
3	cups flour	1	cup nuts

Combine oil and sugar and beat in eggs one at a time. Add vanilla. Mix flour, baking soda, baking powder and salt and add to batter. Fold in zucchini and nuts. Pour into 2 greased and floured bread pans. Bake at 325 degrees for 1 hour.

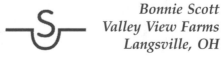

Bonnie Scott
Valley View Farms
Langsville, OH

Honey Oatmeal Bread

This recipe is for West Bend Bread and Dough Makers

TO MAKE 1 LB LOAF:

2/3 cup water	1 tablespoon dry milk
2 tablespoons honey	3/4 teaspoon salt
1 1/2 cups flour	1 tablespoon butter
2/3 cup quick oats	1 1/2 teaspoon dry yeast

TO MAKE 1 1/2 LB LOAF:

7 1/2 ounces water	1 1/2 tablespoons dry milk
3 tablespoons honey	1 1/4 teaspoons salt
2 cups flour	2 teaspoons dry yeast
1 cup quick oats	1 1/2 tablespoons butter

Add liquid ingredients to pan. Add dry ingredients, except yeast, to pan. Tap pan to settle dry ingredients, then level ingredients, pushing some of the mixture into the corners. Place butter into corners of pan. Make a well in center of dry ingredients, and add yeast. Lock pan into bread maker.

Program for Basic/Specialty and desired bread color. Program timer if being used. Start bread maker. If making a 1 lb loaf, use light bread color setting to prevent over browning of the smaller loaf.

HL
Jacque Duskin
Duskin's Cedar Ranch
Osceola, MO

Texas Fritters

2 eggs	1 1/2 cups flour
1 cup buttermilk	4 tablespoons cornmeal
1 teaspoon salt	1 medium eggplant, peeled
1/2 teaspoon baking soda	and cubed
2 teaspoon baking powder	

Blend all ingredients except eggplant to form batter. Fold eggplant into batter, drop into frying pan in pancake-sized portions. Turn once, and drain onto paper towels.

CR
Jackie Craver
Cedar Rose Ranch
Timmonsville, SC

Corn Bread Dressing

3	fryers or 1 fat hen
2	large onions, chopped
1	stalk celery, chopped
1	stick margarine
2	recipes corn bread made in a 12"×9"×2" cake pan

1/2	lb crackers
8	eggs, hard cooked, peeled and chopped
	chicken broth
	salt and pepper

Boil chicken (should have plenty of broth). Reserve broth. Sauté onions and celery in margarine. Crumble up your corn bread and crackers in a large bowl or in a dishpan (the dishpan works better as this makes a lot of dressing). Add eggs and broth from your chicken. Season with salt and pepper. Mix all of these ingredients together and pour into a large roaster pan. Bake at 450 degrees until golden brown.

Serve cranberry sauce with dressing.

Eula Bates

Crockpot Dressing

	cornbread
	bread or bread crumbs
2	eggs, beaten
2	eggs, hard cooked, peeled and chopped
1/2	cup chopped celery
1 1/2	tablespoons sage or as much as you like
	salt and pepper

1/2	cup chopped onion
2	(10 3/4 ounce each) cans cream of chicken soup
5	tablespoons butter
2	(14 1/2 ounce each) cans chicken broth, divided

Crumble enough cornbread and bread to fill crockpot. Add all other ingredients, except the second can of chicken broth. Use enough of the second can to make sure mixture is moist. Cover and cook 2 1/2 hours. (I sometimes boil a chicken or turkey legs and use the broth, instead of canned.)

This makes great dressing. Instead of bread I use bread crumbs.

Kyle Roop
Roop Ranch
Keatchie, LA

Oven Dressing

1	lb ground beef	1	cup raw rice
1	lb ground pork	1	(10³/4 ounce) can cream of
1	onion, chopped		mushroom soup
1	rib celery, chopped	1	(10³/4 ounce) can cream of
1	bell pepper, chopped		onion soup
2	garlic cloves, chopped	1	envelope dry onion
1	cup green onion tops,		soup mix
	chopped	1	cup hot water

Brown meats and drain off excess grease. Add onion, celery, bell pepper, garlic and green onions and cook until vegetables are wilted. Add rice and canned soups. Mix dry soup mix with hot water and add to meat mixture. Bake at 350 degrees for about 45 minutes. Cover and bake 15 minutes longer.

B
C *Bubbles and Brenda Choate*
Judsonia, AR

Calvin's Oyster Dressing

2	ribs celery, finely chopped	4	pieces of stale bread,
1	yellow onion, finely		toasted
	chopped	3	small cans of oysters,
1	stick butter		drained and mashed
4	chicken bouillon cubes	2	(14¹/2 ounce each) cans of
	pinch of sage or as much		chicken broth, divided
	as you like		salt and pepper
5	packages of cooked	2	cups warm water
	Cornkits		

Sauté celery and onion in butter. Dissolve bouillon and sage in hot water. Combine all of the ingredients. Bake in large pan at 350 degrees for 1 hour or until brown on top.

Optional: Add ¹/2 cup chopped green onions, 3 hard cooked, peeled and chopped eggs (folded in at the last), and 1 tablespoon parsley.

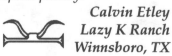

Calvin Etley
Lazy K Ranch
Winnsboro, TX

Across the Rio Grande

In 1966, Texas Longhorns again crossed the Red River at Doan's Crossing following the Western Trail to Dodge City, Kansas. (From the archives of the Texas Longhorn Breeders Association of America.)

Chuck Wagon Dictionary

The men on cattle drives and round-ups had a unique vocabulary. Some of it can be printed!

Beans — Pecos strawberries, Mexican strawberries, whistle berries, frijoles

Beef — Wohaw, slow elk, big antelope

Biscuits — Sourdough bread, soda sinkers, dough gods, or hot rocks, shotgun waddin'

Campfire fuel — prairie coal (cow manure), mesquite

Coffee — Arbuckle's, brown gargle

Dinner is Served — Grub pile, come and git it, or grab a plate and growl

Fried Bacon or salt pork — sow-bosom, sow-belly

Gravy — Cheap-and-easy, Texas butter

Molasses — Lick or larrup

Onions — Skunk Eggs

Pancakes — Splatter dabs or wheelers

Beef Burritos

1	lb lean sirloin steak, diced (or use ground sirloin)	2	tablespoons Worcestershire sauce
1	tablespoon vegetable oil	2	cups chopped green chilies (canned is fine)
1	(16 ounce) can pinto beans	6	burrito size flour tortillas
3	cups peeled, chopped tomatoes, divided	2	cups shredded white Cheddar or Monterey Jack cheese
1½	cups chopped onion, divided	1½	cups shredded lettuce

Brown steak in oil in large saucepan. Stir in beans, 1 cup tomatoes, 1 cup onion and Worcestershire sauce. Cook, stirring occasionally for 10 minutes. Meanwhile, bring chilies, 1 cup tomatoes, and remaining onion to a boil in small saucepan. Reduce heat and simmer 5 minutes. Divide meat mixture evenly on tortillas, fold envelope-style, and place in a lightly greased baking dish. Top with cooked chili mixture and cheese. Bake in preheated 400 degree oven until browned, about 8-10 minutes. Divide lettuce and remaining tomatoes on 6 large plates. Put burritos on top. Serve with chili and red and green salsa on the side. Serves 6.

A fun and popular dish of the Southwest!

6+6 *Myrna Carpenter*
Stephenville, TX

Chicken Enchiladas

Boil chicken or chicken pieces until tender. When cool, bone and cut into bite-size pieces. Set aside. In large bowl combine 1 large can cream of mushroom soup, 1 large can cream of chicken soup, 1 small can chopped green chilies, 1 small can chopped ripe olives and 1 large carton of sour cream. Season to taste with seasoned salt, garlic salt or any other seasoning you prefer. Mix well. Line the bottom of a large casserole dish with coarsely broken Dorito chips, then a layer of chicken, a layer of shredded Cheddar cheese, a layer of the soup mixture. Repeat this with layers until all your ingredients are used. Top with finely broken Doritos and cheese. Bake in 350 degree oven until bubbly.

This is the way I like it, but you may add or take away according to your taste.

 *Beth Kropp*
Lockney, TX

Mom's Nachos—
Way North of the Border

1	(16 ounce) can refried beans	1	bottle taco sauce
1	onion, chopped	1	pint sour cream
3	lbs hamburger	1	(2 ounce) can chopped olives
3	(4 ounce) cans green chilies, chopped		chopped fresh tomatoes
1	lb mild Cheddar cheese, grated		chopped avocado
1/2	lb Monterey Jack cheese, grated		tortilla chips

Preheat oven to 350 degrees and grease 13"×9"×2" pan. Spread refried beans in bottom pan. Sauté onions and hamburger (season with salt and pepper). Spread meat mixture on top of beans. Layer chilies on top of meat. Cover with grated cheese and cover with taco sauce. Bake about 1/2 hour. Cover with sour cream and garnish with olives, tomatoes and avocado. Serve on top of tortilla or as a dip.

Warning! Go lightly. You can fill up on this so fast that you won't be able to eat anything else.

Cream Tacos

2	lbs Texas Longhorn lean beef	1	large can evaporated milk
20	corn tortillas	1	large onion, diced
	oil	1	(7 ounce) can green chilies, chopped
1	8 ounce) can tomato sauce	1	lb Velveeta, grated

Brown meat. Dip tortillas in hot oil, then put meat into tortillas while hot and roll up. Place in large baking dish. Heat other ingredients in sauce pan until cheese melts. Pour over tortillas. Heat in oven at 400 degrees until cheese bubbles.

Carla Jo Payne
CP Longhorns and Quarter Horses
Katy, TX

Quick and Easy Tostadas

corn tortillas
oil
1   lb hamburger meat
    taco seasoning mix
1   (16 ounce) can refried
    beans
garlic powder
oregano

cumin
Monterry Jack or Cheddar
    cheese, grated
lettuce, shredded
onion, chopped
tomato, chopped
jalapeño peppers, seeded,
    deveined and chopped

Deep fry your tortillas. Leave flat until crisp. Remove and drain on paper towels. Brown hamburger and season with taco mix. Spread refried beans on tortillas. Sprinkle garlic powder, oregano and cumin on each. Put spoonful of meat mixture on each tortilla and spread. Top with cheese. Put 3 tostadas on a plate and microwave until cheese starts to melt. Remove and top each with lettuce, onion, tomato and pepper. This makes 12. Serve with chips and picante sauce.

S *David and Patricia Smith*
The Running S Ranch
Frost, TX

Chiles Rellenos Casserole

2   (7 ounce) cans whole green
      chilies, rinsed and seeded
1¹/₂ lbs Monterey Jack Cheese,
      grated
4   eggs, slightly beaten

¹/₂   cup milk
1   teaspoon salt
¹/₂   teaspoon dry mustard
¹/₄   teaspoon pepper

Line the bottom of lightly greased 11"×7"×2" baking dish or casserole with half the chilies. Sprinkle half the grated cheese over chilies; top with remaining chilies and sprinkle with remaining cheese. Combine eggs with milk and seasonings. Pour over chilies and cheese in casserole. Bake at 350 degrees for 30-35 minutes or until lightly browned and set. Let cool 5 minutes before cutting into squares.

W *Joyce Wood*
PayDay Ranch
Wynnewood, OK

Skillet Enchiladas

1	lb lean ground beef	8-12	corn tortillas
1/2	cup onion, chopped		cooking oil
1	(10³/4 ounce) can cream of mushroom soup	1/2	cup chopped ripe olives
1	(10 ounce) can mild enchilada sauce	3	cups shredded sharp American cheese
1/3	cup milk	2-3	teaspoons chopped green chilies

In large skillet, cook beef and onion. Reduce heat and simmer 20 minutes. Stir occasionally. Mix soup, enchilada sauce and milk in a skillet and heat until warm. In small skillet, dip tortillas in hot oil, just until limp, about 5 seconds on each side. Drain on paper towels. Place 1/4 cup meat mixture on each tortilla and sprinkle with olives. Roll up each tortilla. Place in sauce in skillet. Cover and cook 5 minutes. Sprinkle with cheese and green chilies. Cover and cook until cheese melts. Serves 4.

S/K
Karen King
S K Ranch
Granbury, TX

Chicken Enchiladas

1	(10³/4 ounce) can cream of mushroom soup	3/4	cup chopped onion
1	chicken (cooked and deboned) or use canned chunk chicken, chicken breasts	1	(4 ounce) can chopped green chilies
		2	cups grated cheese
		12	flour tortillas
8	ounces sour cream		additional grated cheese if desired

In a large sauce pan mix first 6 ingredients. Warm. Put a couple of tablespoons of mixture into tortilla and roll up. I use a long loaf dish and place the seam down. Pour remaining mixture over top of filled tortillas and top with more grated cheese. Bake covered for about 30 minutes at 350 degrees. You can use as much onion, cheese and chilies as you want, but please be sure you use green chilies and not jalapeño peppers.

W
Joyce Wood
PayDay Ranch
Wynnewood, OK

Manicotti Enchiladas

14	pieces manicotti	1/2	teaspoon salt
1	lb extra lean ground beef	1	jar (16 ounce) mild picante
1	medium onion, chopped		sauce, heated, divided
1	green bell pepper, diced	1/2	cup shredded low fat
1	(4 ounce) can chopped		Cheddar cheese
	green chilies, drained	1/4	cup sliced green onions or
3/4	cup nonfat sour cream,		red onion
	divided		

Prepare pasta according to package directions. While pasta is cooking, sauté beef, onion and green pepper in a large skillet until browned; drain well. Stir in chilies, 1/2 cup sour cream, and salt. When pasta is done, drain well. Fill manicotti with beef mixture. Preheat oven to 375 degrees. Spread 2 cup picante sauce over bottom of glass 13"x9"x2" baking dish that has been coated with cooking spray. Place filled manicotti side by side on top of sauce. Pour remaining sauce evenly over manicotti. Sprinkle with cheese. Cover with aluminum foil and bake for 20-25 minutes or until thoroughly heated. Garnish with remaining sour cream and sprinkle with green onions. Serve immediately with the rest of the remaining picante sauce on the side. Serves 7.

Patty Dudley
Denton, TX

❖

The trail herds of the 1860s and 70s probably averaged 2,000 to 2,500 head. They were driven by about 12 men or boys, a "boss" drover and a cook. The cowboys received an average of one dollar per day and with the traveling rate of 10 to 12 miles per day, were on the trail for a minimum of two months.

❖

Chicken Rotel

1 whole chicken	2 bay leaves
lemon pepper	1 (10 ounce) can Rotel
garlic powder	tomatoes, chopped
cumin	1/4 cup dried onion flakes
oregano	

Sprinkle chicken with lemon pepper, garlic powder, cumin and oregano. Inside chicken place 2 bay leaves. Place in microwave dish sprayed with cooking spray. Pour Rotel over chicken, then sprinkle dried onion flakes around chicken. Do not use any water; this will make its own juice. Cook on High in microwave for 35-40 minutes or until tender.

This is such a great dish when in a hurry. Serve with rice and green salsa.

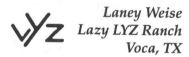

Laney Weise
Lazy LYZ Ranch
Voca, TX

Longhorn Skillet Fajitas

1 packet Ranch Dressing mix	1 medium bell pepper,
2 tablespoons olive oil	cut into strips
1 tablespoon water	1 medium onion, cut
1 1/2 lbs Texas Longhorn round	into strips
steak, cut into strips	flour tortillas, warmed

Combine dressing mix, oil and water. Sauté round steak strips in dressing mixture. Add peppers and onions. Cook until tender-crisp. Place mixture in tortillas along with desired fillings.

OPTIONAL FILLINGS:

guacamole, salsa, sour cream, grated cheese. Serves 4.

Ed Durr, Jr.
Heaven View Farm
Amite, LA

Sour Cream Enchilada Casserole

12	flour tortillas	1	(2 ounce) can sliced black olives
1	lb Longhorn lean ground beef	1	cup sour cream
1/2	cup chopped onion	1	(10³/4 ounce) can cream of mushroom soup
	garlic powder	1	can green enchilada sauce
	salt and pepper	1	cup grated Cheddar cheese
	cumin		

Preheat oven to 375 degrees. Toast tortillas on oven rack for a few minutes until crisp; remove and cool. Cut tortillas into several pieces; arrange 1/3 of the pieces in the bottom of a greased 13"×9"×2" casserole dish. Next, brown ground beef in a skillet with onion, garlic powder, salt, pepper and cumin. Add olives. Put 1/2 of meat mixture on top of tortillas in casserole dish. In a bowl, mix sour cream, mushroom soup and enchilada sauce. Pour 1/2 of this mixture over meat in dish. Repeat layers, ending with a layer of tortillas. Top with cheese. Bake for 30 minutes.

Lani Fairchild
Fairchild Ranch
Stephenville, TX

Tamale Pie

1	lb ground beef	1	(6 ounce) can chopped black olives
1	onion, chopped	1	cup cooked rice
	salt and pepper	1	(16 ounce) can corn
1	teaspoon chili powder	3/4	cup cornmeal
1	teaspoon garlic salt		longhorn cheese, grated
2	(7 ounce) cans tomato sauce		
1	(16 ounce) can tomatoes		

Brown hamburger with onion, salt, pepper, chili powder and garlic salt. Drain, add remaining ingredients. Stir well to mix ingredients and bake 350 degrees for 45 minutes-1 hour. Grate cheese and sprinkle on top during last few minutes.

Loretta Miller
Tim Miller Ranch
Great Bend, KS

Cornbread Fajitas

SAUCE:

¼ cup Liquid Smoke	¼ cup soy sauce
¼ cup Worcestershire sauce	12 ounces beer or red wine

Marinate 2 full-length fajitas in sauce for at least 12 hours.

VEGETABLES:

1 cup diced green onions	1 cup diced bell pepper
1 cup diced celery	3 tablespoons cooking oil

Sauté vegetables in oil. Reserve.

2 envelopes jalapeño cornbread mix	Mozzarella cheese slices

Prepare 1 envelope of the mix and pour in bottom of 13"×9"×2" cake pan. Broil fajitas for 10 minutes on each side. Cut fajitas into strips and arrange on top of cornbread mix. Cover fajitas with sautéed vegetables; then cover with slices of cheese. Mix second envelope of cornbread mix, and put on top. Bake according to directions on cornbread mix.

Dolores Pinn
Pinn Longhorn Ranch
Georgetown, TX
South Texas and Heart of Texas Longhorn Associations

Breath of Fire Hot Sauce

1 small onion, chopped	2-3 green chilies
3 cloves garlic	1 (8 ounce) can tomato sauce
5-6 tomatoes	salt
2-3 yellow hot peppers	pepper
jalapeños	cayenne
(10 makes it fire-y)	curry powder

Blend all ingredients in blender and serve with chips or as a condiment. Keeps in the refrigerator for a week.

Kim Richey
Triple R Ranch
San Angelo, TX

Hot Sauce

2 small tomatoes, peeled	1/2 teaspoon liquid from canned pickled jalapeños
1/4 cup chopped onion	
1 clove garlic	1 teaspoon vegetable oil
1/2-1 whole can pickled jalapeños	1/4 teaspoon dried oregano, crushed
1/4 teaspoon salt	

Put tomatoes, onion, garlic and jalapeños and jalapeño liquid in food processor. Blend until pureed. Heat oil in small saucepan. Add tomato mixture, oregano and salt. Bring to boil and cook for 10 minutes. Remove from heat. Let sauce stand for 2 hours to allow flavors to merge. Makes 3/4 cup.

S *David and Patricia Smith*
The Running S Ranch
Frost, TX

Iron Skillet Salsa

6 ripe tomatoes, peeled	4 cloves garlic, chopped
2 tablespoons olive oil	1/2 cup chopped cilantro
1 cup sliced onions	1/2 cup fresh lime juice
6 jalapeños, seeded and diced	2 teaspoons salt

Place large cast iron skillet over high heat for 3 minutes until smoking. Place tomatoes in skillet and char both sides until black and kind of soft. Remove skillet, lower heat to medium. After 2 minutes, pour oil into skillet, add onions, jalapeños and garlic. Cook 3 minutes, stirring, until soft. Place tomatoes, onions, and pepper mix into food processor. Process until well blended. Pour into bowl, add cilantro, lime juice and salt. You can serve hot or chilled.

CR *Jackie Craver*
Cedar Rose Ranch
Timmonsville, SC

My Own Salsa Recipe

1	lemon	1	small onion, chopped
1	lime	1	teaspoon salt
1	teaspoon vinegar	2	serrano peppers, sliced
4	cloves garlic, chopped fine	2	medium tomatoes, seeded and diced
1	small green bell pepper, chopped	6-10	springs cilantro, chopped

Juice lemon and lime. Pour into ceramic bowl with vinegar and add lighly mashed garlic. Add bell pepper, onions, salt, serranos, tomatoes and cilantro. For full flavor, allow to stand 4-24 hours. Requires refrigeration. Makes 2 cups.

Mary Elizabeth Scott
Copa de Vino Ranch
Goliad, TX

NOTES:

This type of salsa is called a "Salsa Cruda" meaning the ingredients are uncooked. It needs refrigeration and keeps several days. Use with tortilla chips, tacos, fajitas, or scrambled eggs.

For hotter salsa, add another serrano; for milder, remove seeds from peppers. Take care in handling the serranos, as oils can cause burning sensation to skin and especially the eyes, if touched. You can successfully dice serranos by holding firmly with a fork and dicing with a knife.

Cilantro is also called "Chinese Parsley". If unavailable in your area, try growing your own. Coriander is the name of the seed and it can be found at nurseries or by mail order.

Putting up for the Winter

Earl Drummond of the Wichita Mountains National Wildlife Refuge.

Typical "Old-Time" Texas Longhorn? "The cow was long-headed with small elliptical ears. Her horns were not particularly widespread, coming straight out from the skull about 6-8 inches from the head and then they turned up with the points straight back. A few of the old types, their horns came straight out and up, and the horn tips twisted out. The twisty-horned cows had a pretty good spread, though. They were long-legged with a little rise above the hip in the tail head. They had a long, slender tail with a big bush. They came in any color imaginable, and 900 lbs. was a pretty big cow at that time. There was also an old Spanish strain type, described by J. Frank Dobie in his book, **The Longhorns.** *Their foreheads had a slight bulge in them, and their horns came out a little towards the back and then they twisted. The bull's horns had a big base and were not as long as many are today. They curved slightly to the side and to the front just a little bit. Some came out and turned back like the old cows, but would be bigger and more massive at the head. The old Texas Longhorn also had a feisty nature. Many of the breed are now kept in small groups and fed and have lost some of that inherent fighting quality that they had to have in the old days. When I went to sales, any cow that fought in the ring, I bought her. People said I wanted all those old outlaw kind of cattle."*

—**Jack Phillips**
Battle Island Ranch
West Columbia, Texas (1992)

Instant Pickles

7	cups sliced cucumbers	1	cup chopped or sliced
1	cup chopped or sliced		green pepper
	onions	2	tablespoons canning salt

Put cucumbers, onions and green pepper in plastic bowl with cover. Add 2 tablespoons of canning salt. Let stand overnight in refrigerator. Drain, but do not rinse. Pour syrup over pickles and put in any container to store.

SYRUP:

1	cup vinegar, heated to	2	cups sugar
	dissolve sugar	1	tablespoon celery seed

Mix sugar in heated vinegar and add celery seed. Will keep forever in the refrigerator.

Norma Holmes
H and H Longhorns
Robstown, TX

Sweet-Tart Dill Pickles

1	gallon jar Vlasic	4 or 5	garlic cloves
	Dill Pickles	1/4	teaspoon alum
4-5	pickled jalapenos	4	lb bag of sugar
2	tablespoons pickling	1	cup vinegar
	spices		

Drain juice from pickles and slice pickles into 1/2" pieces. Pack back in jar. Add jalapenos, pickling spice, alum, garlic and sugar. Lastly, pour vinegar over contents of jar. Put lid on jar tightly. Turn jar over, then back until sugar is dissolved. Keep in bottom of refrigerator 10 days.

Eat up! Have you wondered why people who know the least, know it the loudest?

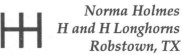

Norma Holmes
H and H Longhorns
Robstown, TX

Kosher Dill Pickles

cucumbers	2	quarts water
fresh dill	1	cup non-iodized salt
fresh garlic cloves	1	quart cider or distilled
small red or green hot peppers, optional		vinegar

Select fresh firm cucumbers, wash and pack in jars with 1 head fresh dill. **To each quart jar add:** 2-3 cloves fresh garlic (depending on size) and 1 small red or green hot pepper (optional). Boil water, salt and vinegar. Pour hot solution over cucumbers and seal jars. Pickles will be ready in 3-4 weeks, depending on size of cucumbers. For plain dill pickles, omit garlic.

Hot Dill Pickles

Drain 1 gallon jar dill pickles spears very well. Add 4 lbs. sugar and 1 small bottle of Louisiana Hot Sauce. Turn jar every day for 2 weeks.

Loretta Miller
Tim Miller Ranch
Great Bend, KS

Santa Rosa Plum Jam

24	cups pitted, chopped Santa Rosa plums	4	package powdered fruit pectin
3	cups water	28	cups sugar
4	tablespoons lemon juice		

Combine plums, water, lemon juice and pectin in a large pot. Bring to a rolling boil over high heat, stirring frequently. Add sugar and return to a rolling boil. Boil hard for 1 minute, stirring constantly. Put hot into hot jars, leaving 1/4" head space. Adjust caps. Process 10 minutes in boiling water. Yield: 16 pints.

Jackie Craver
Cedar Rose Ranch
Timmonsville, SC

Yellow Squash Pickles

20	lbs yellow squash, thin sliced	2¹/₃	cups canning salt
			ice cubes
10	lbs onions, thin sliced	15	cups vinegar
6	yellow bell peppers, cored, seeded and chopped	10	cups sugar
		10	tablespoons mustard seed
6	red bell peppers, cored, seeded and chopped	10	teaspoons turmeric
		10	teaspoons celery seed
6	green bell peppers, cored, seeded and chopped	5	teaspoons ginger
		5	teaspoons peppercorns

Combine squash, onions and chopped peppers in large enamel pan. Layer with salt and cover with ice cubes. Let stand 1¹/₂ hours, drain and rinse. Place remaining ingredients in a large sauce pot and bring to a boil. Add drained squash, onions, and peppers and return to boil. Pack hot into hot jars, leaving 1/4" head space. Remove air bubbles. Adjust caps. Process 10 minutes in boiling water. Let age 4 weeks before eating for best flavor.

Jackie Craver
Cedar Rose Ranch
Timmonsville, SC

Canned Tomatoes

fresh tomatoes
salt
sugar

Scald tomatoes in boiling water about 5 minutes. Peel and cut out green centers. Pack tomatoes in pt jars. Push down into jar until juice comes to neck of jar. Add 1/2 teaspoon salt and 1/2 teaspoon sugar to each jar. Seal tight and place in hot water bath up to neck of jars. Bring to a boil; put lid on and boil for 5 minutes. Remove jars and let cool.

Tomato Jelly

4	cups tomato juice	1	box pectin
1/4	cup lemon juice	5¹/₂	cups sugar

Boil tomato juice, lemon juice and pectin for 1 minute. Add sugar. Boil for 3 minutes. Put in jars and seal.

Agarita Jelly

Agarita is a very small red berry that grows on a very thorny bush all around the Hill Country and South Texas. This makes wonderful jelly, but it's so hard to do. Berries have to be ripe, and do not have a lot of juice or pulp. You will need at least 3/4-1 gallon berries.

First get a long stick and a sheet. Go find the agarita bush. Next poke the stick around the base of the bush to run out any snakes. Place the sheet in a circle around underneath the bush. Take the long stick and whack the hell out of that bush until all the berries fall off onto the sheet. If there is a brisk breeze, winnow the berries in the pasture. If not, use an electric fan to winnow berries when you get home.

Wash the berries and fill your pot with berries. Add water level with the berries. Cook them for 45 minutes to an hour, adding water as it steams away. Put the berries into a cone-shaped colander and smash the berries with the wooden pestle. To six cups of juice, use 8 cups sugar and 1 box of Sure-Jel. Follow directions on the Sure-Jel box.

Maudeen Marks
LH7 Ranch
Barker and Bandera, TX

Dill Green Tomatoes

5	lbs small green hard tomatoes	1/4	cup canning salt
3 1/2	cups vinegar	6-7	cloves garlic
3 1/2	cups distilled water		fresh dill or dill seeds
		6-7	bay leaves

Wash and core tomatoes, and cut into halves or quarters. Combine vinegar, water and salt in a large saucepan. Bring to a boil. Pack tomatoes into hot jars, leaving 1/4" head space. Add 1 clove garlic, 1 head of dill or 2 teaspoon dill seeds, and 1 bay leaf to each jar. Pour hot liquid over tomatoes, leaving 1/4" space. Adjust caps and process 15 minutes in boiling water bath. Makes 6 pints.

Jackie Craver
Cedar Rose Ranch
Timmonsville, SC

Pickled Green Tomatoes

3	cups white vinegar	4	large cloves garlic, peeled and thinly sliced
2/3	cup kosher salt		
1	cup water	4	large sprigs fresh tarragon
2¼	lbs green tomatoes, washed, stems removed and quartered or sliced	½	teaspoon white peppercorns
		½	teaspoon black peppercorns

Use a 2 quart jar with a screw-top with a two-piece screw-band lid for pickles.

Wash jar and both parts of lid well in hot, soapy water. Place a small metal cake rack in a large stock pot and fill the pot with water. Lay open jar on its side on rack. Make sure water covers jar by 2" and bring to a boil. Boil jar for 15 minutes. Using metal tongs or a jar lifter, carefully remove jar from water, letting water pour out. Place jar upside down on a clean rack to dry. Sterilize lid and screw band according to manufacturer's instructions.

Combine vinegar, salt and water in a large pot and bring just to boiling point. Meanwhile, tightly pack sterilized jar with tomatoes, garlic, and tarragon. Sprinkle peppercorns over tomatoes. Pour hot vinegar/salt solution over tomatoes, leaving ¼" of room at the top of the jar. Discard extra liquid. Slide a long, clean knife along inside of jar to release any air bubbles. Seal jar with lid and screw band.

Fill stock pot fitted with cake rack with fresh water. Bring to a boil and lower jar of tomatoes into water, covering it by 2" of water. Boil for 10 minutes. Using tongs, remove jar from water and let cool to room temperature. Store in a cool, dark place. Let tomatoes mellow for 3 weeks before serving. Refrigerate after opening.

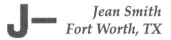

Jean Smith
Fort Worth, TX

Three "N" Six

The Three "N" Six brand took on a lot of controversy in the very beginning. It all started with myself and my two sons, Brandon and Chancy, under the supervision of the more well educated one, Brandon. It was November of '86, as I recall, when we all set down around the wood heater. We put on our thinking caps in order to come up with our own original brand for branding our herd of Texas Longhorns. We debated on the "Three NNN", the "NNN", "Triple NNN", the "Box N" (already being used) as well as the "Diamond N", the Flying N, and so on for about a week. We didn't get anywhere with our figuring and then out of the blue, I got the opportunity to purchase six acres from a fellow I knew in Kirbyville, Texas, just south of Jasper where I reside now. We cleared land, put a well down, and burnt brush until I thought I would drop over dead from smoke, dirt and diesel fumes. About three weeks into clearing a spot to build a house, I was sitting on a stump, cooling a bit with ice tea and a smoke. Chancy, my youngest, started drawing in the dirt with a stick. He looked up at me, just a grinning and said, "Hey, dad, we're three Northerns on six acres." All I could do is look kinda dumbfounded and nod my noggin'. Then he picked up the stick and drew in the sand in front of me 3N6 and explained how and what it meant. The more I looked at it, the better I liked it. It was at this time that I called for the brains of this outfit, my oldest son Brandon. He took one look at the "stick in the dirt art", smoothed it out with his Nocona boot, then said, "Needs to be closed up". Well, me and ole' Chancy looked at each other. We didn't know what closed up meant. So being two of the bloodline and not wanting Chancy to feel he's not all there, I spoke up, with dumbness and asked, "What are you talkin' about. . . closed up?" Brandon said, "It's too long. . . close it up." Well, sir, there were a couple of more dumb looks. You got it. . . me and Chancy, so Brandon picks up the stick and draws XXXX and looks at brother Chancy and his old man and says "Now that was really hard to figure out, now wasn't it?" He turns and walks off like some lawyer in a million dollar deal. He was 14 years old at the time. Chancy, well, he was 11 years old. And me. . . well, let's just say that I was then and still am now "OFC". . . an "Old Fat Cowboy". *

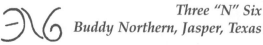

Three "N" Six
Buddy Northern, Jasper, Texas

Index

INDEX

Index

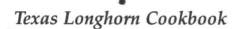

BREEDERS
ASSOCIATION of AMERICA

P.O.Box 4430   Fort Worth, Texas 76164
(817) 625-6241 Fax (817) 625-1388

Order Form
Texas Longhorn Cookbook

Please send _____ copies of cookbook $19.95 each _____

Paper Back _____ copies of cookbook $16.95 each _____

Postage and Handling $3.50 each _____

Texas residents add sales tax $1.85 each _____

TOTAL FOR ALL BOOKS ORDERED _____

Total enclosed _____

Name _____

Address _____

City _____ State _____ Zip _____

Enclosed is my check: _____

Charge my: ❑ Visa   ❑ Master Card   Exp. Date: _____

Credit Card Number: _____

Signature of Cardholder: _____

Interested in joining the Texas Longhorn Breeders Association of America?
See our membership application at the back of the book.

TLBAA Membership Application

Texas Longhorn Breeders Association of America
P.O. Box 4430 • Fort Worth, TX 76164
817/625-6241 • Fax 817/625-1388
www.tlbaa.org

MEMBERSHIP NUMBER _____ _____ _____

Name: _____

Name which will appear on certificates and listing in TLBAA Directory.

Other Name: _____

Address _____

City, State, Zip: _____

Home Telephone:( ) _____ OfficeTelephone:( ) _____

RanchTelephone:( ) _____ Fax Number:( ) _____

PAYMENT OPTIONS: ☐VISA ☐MC ☐ Check or Money Ord.

(Make payable to TLBAA)

Card No:_____ Expires:_____

_____ _____
Print Authorized Person's Name for TLBAA Bus.   Signature of Authorized Person

_____ _____
Print Authorized Person's Name for TLBAA Bus.   Signature of Authorized Person

Referred by: _____

Please draw your brand inside the box exactly as you wish to be recorded.
Reading of Brand

New Active Member*	85.00/yr
Renewal Active Member	60.00/yr
LATE ACTIVE MEMBER RENEWAL (After Aug. 31)	70.00
Lifetime Member	1000.00
New Junior Member (18 yr. & Under) **	25.00
Renewal Junior Member **	25.00
New Outrider (Associate Member) (pays Non-Member rates for animal work)	75.00
Renewal Outrider Associate Member	75.00
Charter Lifetime Outrider	1000.00

Junior Member Birthday ___ / ___ / ___
** Junior membership does not include subscription to the *Texas Longhorn Trails*

Included in your membership is a subscription to the Texas Longhorn Trails. Subscription rate is $36 US address/$50 (US) Foreign address. TLBAA membership dues may be deducted as an ordinary and necessary business expense; however they are not deductible as a charitable contribution.

*New Active Membership includes $25 start-up kit.

OUTRIDER
Texas Longhorn Breeders Association of America

The Outriders serve as the preservation arm of the Texas Longhorn Breed; in order to protect
the unique heritage of the Texas
Longhorn and its link with the
history of America; to produce
more public awareness of Texas
Longhorn cattle; to encourage
others to preserve and protect the
historic breed; to aid in the ad-
vancement of the breed through
scientific research and promo-
tion; to remain ever vigilant of
topics pertaining to the cattle industry such as the environment,
land and water rights, and any
issue deemed important to the
preservation and protection of
the Texas Longhorn.

*"Every man has wanted to be a cowboy. Why
play Wall Street and die young when you can
play cowboy and never die?"*

— Will Rogers

LIFETIME CHARTER MEMBER

A once-in-a-lifetime opportunity to become a leading outrider. Receive a beautiful "Outrider" bronze (shown above) that will merit a
special place in your home or office. This exclusive 12" x 7" x 8"
bronze is signed and numbered by Jack Wilson, talented western
sculptor from Fort Worth, Texas. You will also receive a quality certifi-
cate of membership, a colorful "wild rag," a membership decal, and a
lifetime subscription to the monthly *Texas Longhorn Trails* magazine.
$1,000.

ANNUAL MEMBER

Get a taste of the "Outrider" experience. Help us to perpetuate the
cowboy life and the Texas Longhorns. Coming your way will be a
membership card, "wild rag," a membership decal, and the *Texas
Longhorn Trails*. *$75.*